D1376576

Why Good People Do Bad
Environmental Things

Why Good People Do Bad Environmental Things

Elizabeth R. DeSombre

OXFORD
UNIVERSITY PRESS

Oxford University Press is a department of the University of Oxford. It furthers
the University's objective of excellence in research, scholarship, and education
by publishing worldwide. Oxford is a registered trade mark of Oxford University
Press in the UK and certain other countries.

Published in the United States of America by Oxford University Press
198 Madison Avenue, New York, NY 10016, United States of America.

© Oxford University Press 2018

CIP data is on file at the Library of Congress
ISBN 978-0-19-063627-2

For Lynda.
See? It really is your book.

CONTENTS

ACKNOWLEDGMENTS

I arrived at this project by many paths, and completed it with the assistance of many people.

I am lucky enough to teach environmental studies at Wellesley College. About a decade ago when we reimagined our environmental studies curriculum, we decided that we should have a core course that looked at what social science tells us about why we get environmental problems and how to address them. The course I created to fill that niche (with the unwieldy name of Social Causes and Consequences of Environmental Problems) quickly became one of my favorite courses to teach. It forced me to move beyond my home discipline of political science to look across economics, psychology, sociology, and other approaches, to conceptualize the "social" causes of our individual and collective behavior. I have learned as much from my students as I have taught them; their research projects in the course illuminate the concepts we've worked with, and their questions prod me to a deeper understanding of the mechanisms we study.

Another of the paths toward this book was my service on the Sustainable Energy Committee in the town of Wellesley. At the beginning of my second year on the committee I was asked, as the academic in the group, to give a presentation on what scholarship tells us about how to change environmental behavior. I have never presented to a more receptive audience. For the remainder of the year at nearly every meeting someone would refer back to some insight they had taken from my presentation, and we used it to guide the policies we created to decrease the environmental impact of our town.

So many people have helped bring this book into existence. Many colleagues, friends, and students read (multiple!) drafts of the manuscript, helping me refine the arguments and improve the clarity of my writing. In particular, I am grateful to Thomas Heberlein, Craig Murphy, Ken Conca, Peter Jacques, Lynda Warwick, Angelina Li, Ali Saueressig, Jacqueline Floyd, and two anonymous reviewers for excellent feedback. Other students who did research that contributed to this project include Randelle Boots, Kate Corcoran, Alysha Cross, Meredith Wade, and Janna Zimmerman. Anani Galindo and Jess Hunter provided last-minute help with logistics, and Caroline George and Frances Dingivan helped with the index. Sammy Barkin read this book more times than anyone should have to, and offered useful suggestions throughout the process of writing and revising it. Zoë, and her predecessor Sophie, reminded me to make long walks outside into a habitual part of my day.

I began the writing of this book while on a fellowship at the Newhouse Center for the Humanities at Wellesley College, a glorious place and community for academic thought. I am grateful to then-director Carol Dougherty, who took a chance inviting a social scientist into this community of humanists, and to my fellow Newhouse Center scholars who helped me figure out how to communicate these ideas to people without a social science background. And I have benefited throughout this process from support from Camilla Chandler Frost, Wellesley Class of 1947, who gave the donation to help create the Environmental Studies program at Wellesley and endow the chair I hold.

Why Good People Do Bad Environmental Things

Understanding
Environmental Behavior

Are you worried about the changing global climate? There's good reason to be: the atmospheric concentration of greenhouse gases has nearly doubled since the beginning of the Industrial Revolution, and almost every recent month has set new temperature records for the modern era. The predicted effects of this increase in global average temperature—including sea-level rise, shifting disease vectors, increased drought in some places and storms and floods in others—are already happening.[1]

Maybe you're concerned about toxic pollution, like heavy metals and other hazardous materials from our increasing global use of electronics. At least forty million tons of electronics waste is discarded every year, and these wastes are often disposed of in the most vulnerable communities, contaminating soil and water and causing harm to human health.[2] Possibly deforestation has gained your attention: every year forest cover globally is reduced by eighteen million acres, an area the size of Panama,[3] leading to soil erosion, land degradation, and the loss of irreplaceable biodiversity.

Why haven't we taken serious action to prevent these problems? Perhaps people don't know how serious they are, or don't understand what they do in their daily lives that contribute to them. In my job as a college professor, and as a scholar of environmental issues, I frequently run into sincere people persuaded that all we need to do to fix environmental problems is to let people know that environmental problems are severe and that their behavior is causing ecological harm. Surely, the logic goes, if we educate people about the role their behavior plays in causing these problems, they will change what they are doing.

This framing runs into several problems. Many people know that they are doing things that cause environmental problems, and they do them anyway. Think about how you felt when you took a disposable bag at the grocery store or took a solo drive to get to that store rather than walking or taking public transportation. If you stopped to think about it, you knew not only that plastic waste and climate change were problems, but also what the better environmental choice would have been. And yet you frequently don't choose it.

There is little evidence (as my students frequently discover in the course of their efforts) that letting people know about environmental problems and their contributions to them changes behavior in meaningful ways. When you got into your car to drive to work this morning, would someone telling you that you were contributing to climate change have altered your decision? Many factors contributed to your commuting choice, including the time and cost to get where you were going, the existing transit routes and schedules, and the other things you had to do on your way to or from work. If your contribution to climate change even registered, it was one of many factors you were balancing in making your commuting decision.

Information about the dangers of environmental problems, and your contribution to creating them, may even backfire. People come to see themselves as powerless to address huge global problems, or don't want to think of themselves as the sort of people who would fail to act to prevent such problems. They may respond by pushing these issues out of their minds.

Or maybe the problem is that people just don't care enough. If you or your child grew up in the United States, you almost certainly encountered this environmental wisdom delivered by Dr. Seuss: "Unless someone like you cares a whole awful lot, nothing is going to get better, it's not."[4] Awareness campaigns frequently show environmental harm and its effects on people or ecosystems in an effort to get us to care more about the environment. But levels of environmental concern are quite high worldwide, with people even expressing a willingness to sacrifice for the environment. If you're reading this, you must be concerned enough about the environment to have picked up a book on the topic; has that prevented you from making problematic environmental choices?

Those who attribute behavior with bad environmental consequences to lack of information or inadequate concern about the environment may nevertheless not be entirely wrong. Increasing our knowledge about the consequences of our behavior, and about alternative options, may entice some people to behave differently, although not that many people and not that often. Similarly, coming to prioritize the well-being of the environment, natural resources, or species, may in some cases drive people to prioritize environmental protection over cost or simplicity in their own decisions, especially if their identity is focused on acting in an environmentally responsible way. But lack of information or concern is rarely the underlying cause that connects behavior to harm. For that we need to understand the structure of environmental problems and the incentives created by those structures.

More surprisingly, knowing and caring about environmental problems may not even be necessary for solving them. If the cheapest or most convenient option in purchasing or commuting happens to be the most environmentally friendly one, even people who aren't taking the environment into consideration may make that choice. To be sure, we may need some people to understand and care about environmental problems to create the broader social structures that make better environmental behavior possible, or more likely. But saving the planet does not necessarily rest on persuading everyone to care about the environment.

No one sets out to create environmental problems. There is unlikely to be an "air pollution" lobby arguing for increasing emissions of sulfur dioxide, or an organization advocating that we wipe out elephants or cod. All else equal, we're happy to protect environmental resources; in fact, we tend to prefer our air cleaner and our species protected. Environmental problems do not happen because people are bad or have bad intentions. Good people, simply going about their daily lives, cause or contribute to environmental problems. This book is about understanding why that happens and what to do about it.

Because of inherent characteristics of environmental issues, it is often easy and inexpensive to behave in ways with bad environmental consequences, while acting in an environmentally friendly manner can be more difficult and more costly. The incentives we face, some created by the nature of environmental resources, and some by social and political structures put in place for other reasons, often do not make environmentally beneficial behavior the most likely choice. Even when we want to do the right thing environmentally, we may not have the relevant information to let us know that it's necessary or possible. And our behavior and the context in which it takes place are also conditioned by habit and social norms, which were likely created for purposes other than environmental protection.

It is essential to understand why bad environmental behavior makes sense, especially from an individual perspective, in order to figure out how to change that behavior. The fact that causing environmental problems is never anyone's primary goal means that people are happy to stop causing them if acting differently still accomplishes their primary goals. If we can figure out why those problems are caused, when no one intends to cause them, we can develop strategies that work to shift behavior in a positive direction. Some of those strategies may involve restructuring incentives to reward good behavior and penalize action that causes environmental harm, some may involve changing social norms or providing certain types of information, and some may require working to rearrange habits; many will involve reorienting the social political and economic structures we live in.

WHY INDIVIDUAL BEHAVIOR?

This book focuses on the behavior of individuals in the creation—or prevention—of global environmental problems. That might seem an odd focus; after all, in most cases, an individual makes an unimaginably small contribution to any given environmental problem. No matter how much I drive, my use of fossil fuels is an insignificant contributor to global climate change. Likewise, I could for the rest of my life refuse to take a plastic bag with a consumer purchase, and yet my behavior would be inconsequential in the overall problem of plastic pollution.

But individual behavior aggregates, and collectively these individual behaviors have enormous global effect. Those plastic bags we might unthinkingly use individually add up to at least four trillion per year in North America and Western Europe.[5] Any one household's furnace or lighting is part of the (nonindustrial) electricity use and heating that account for one-quarter of the world's greenhouse gas emissions.[6] Municipal (nonindustrial) solid waste in industrialized countries averages 2.2 kg per person per day, which aggregates quickly: 1.56 million tons of waste per day from people just in urban areas of the most developed countries.[7]

My focus on individual behavior does not suggest that changes by individuals are the solution to environmental problems. To the contrary, I examine the causes of individual behavior to illuminate the systemic constraints to behaving in environmentally positive ways, and the collective and institutional solutions that might influence individual behavior. We will not save the environment by persuading people of the ten, or even fifty, "simple things" they can individually do to save the environment.[8]

Michael Maniates, a social scientist at Yale University-NUS, is among those who caution against the "individualization" of environmental problems.[9] He argues that focusing on individual behavior as a primary solution to environmental problems misunderstands their structural and institutional causes, and misplaces the responsibility for fixing environmental issues onto a set of individual choices that, alone, are inadequate to the task. Even the most committed environmentalists face individual choices constrained by the economic and social institutions we are all situated in. You might not be able to buy a car fueled by non-carbon-emitting energy even if you wanted to, and plenty of people who would take public transportation if it existed in their area or traveled to where they needed to go do not even have that option.

So why focus on individual behavior when the underlying causes of environmental problems are at a structural level? There are several reasons. First, and most important, is that at some level all activity with environmental consequences is undertaken by individuals. That behavior aggregates to create collective environmental harm. Problem characteristics, social structures, and institutions are essential answers to the question of why people behave the way they do and how best to change that behavior. But these institutions, structures, and characteristics themselves are incapable of action.

Even if the primary cause of a problematic behavior is systemic, and the most effective solution is institutional, these systems and institutions are mediated through actual individual behavior. An institutional solution is only as good as the individual behavior it influences. Government-mandated increases in vehicle fuel efficiency standards that lead people to drive their more fuel-efficient vehicles greater distances—for example, a long commute to work is now feasible because it doesn't cost as much for gas—are not a successful intervention in the environmental problem. Businesses that offer greener products will fail if individuals do not buy them. If we do not understand what is motivating individual behavior, an institutional solution may fail to change it in an effective way.

Understanding the relationship between problem characteristics and incentives, on the one hand, and individual behavior, on the other, is particularly important. The causes for environmentally unfriendly behavior and the solutions to increase environmental responsibility may operate independently. It is entirely possible for a systemic problem to have an individual solution. Individuals with sufficient ethical concern for the environment or attentiveness to community norms may be willing to avoid environmentally damaging behavior even if the characteristics of an environmental problem or the related social institutions make it hard or expensive to make good environmental choices. Moreover, it is often groups of motivated individuals who propose the social or political actions that make bigger social changes in how the world is structured.[10]

Conversely, it is possible—and likely—for individual factors contributing to behavior to be influenced by institutional solutions. Someone who is not personally concerned about environmental problems (especially those distant in time or space from the behavior that contributes to them) may nevertheless change behavior if a tax on carbon dioxide emissions raises fuel prices or the local grocery store makes the decision to sell only sustainably harvested fish. If you change the context, you can change behavior without having to individually persuade people to behave differently.

Individual behavior, collectively, is what creates environmental problems. But that behavior is sandwiched on both sides by problem characteristics and institutions. These create the context in which individual behavior happens, and a change in these social structures or institutions may be the most efficient way to collectively change a lot of individual behavior. To turn an old chestnut on its head, most of the time the solution to environmental problems is to "think individually, act institutionally."

WHAT *SHOULD* PEOPLE DO TO PROTECT THE ENVIRONMENT?

Even though this book is about individual environmental behavior, it is not a guide to what people should do to protect the environment. It will not tell you whether to choose cloth or disposable diapers or whether your method of diapering a baby is more or less important than how you commute to work or how high you set your thermostat.

Even though it is clear that not all environmental choices we could make individually or collectively matter equally, this book does not endeavor to weigh in on the relative merits of addressing behaviors that contribute to climate change or to plastic pollution, nor prioritize which individual actions are most relevant in contributing to either environmental problem. It does not pass judgment on what behaviors, precisely, we should be focusing on to protect the environment most effectively.

Individual behavior, taken alone, matters little. Maniates points out that individual agonizing over "the 'paper or plastic' choices at the checkout counter" is rarely useful.[11] Individually, most of what we do hardly matters, and doggedly bringing your reusable mug to the corporate coffee shop, though a praiseworthy effort, is not enough for you to be satisfied that you have done your environmental part.

It's an odd line on which to balance. On the one hand, yes, I make the choice individually to recycle wherever possible, use reusable dishware, walk or use public transportation when it is not too much of a hardship, and when I do drive it is in a small, fuel-efficient vehicle. I believe that those are the right choices to make, an ethical way to navigate the daily decisions I face. I think it is generally better for you to also do those sorts of things than not to do them. But I don't think that persuading individuals that these are the right things to do is the most useful approach to addressing environmental problems.

Take an individual behavior like recycling. We can agree that it is often better environmentally for a given individual to recycle than not to recycle,[12] and that to achieve the socially preferable outcome of a better environment it is necessary for most people to engage in the individual behavior of recycling. The question is how to travel from point A (any given individual choosing to recycle) to point B (most people recycling). The standard approach of many environmental activists is to attempt to get to point B by persuading people, individually, to recycle.

I think that is a misguided approach, for several reasons. First, it is extremely inefficient. If you think about the number of people one would have to individually persuade to change behavior (and how many behaviors each would have to change), in a country of millions or a world of billions, it's easy to see how a solution that focuses on changing individual behavior has no hope of creating change as quickly as ecological conditions require. Second, broad-scale information campaigns (of the sort that would need to be undertaken to have any hope of reaching many individuals simultaneously) about the importance of changing behavior rarely work and frequently backfire, yielding counterinformation from those whose businesses are affected by behavior change or persuading consumers to tune out information they would rather not hear.

The behavior of many individuals can be changed through institutional approaches. Instead of persuading people to care enough or undertake the personal effort to recycle, institutions and incentives can make that choice make sense for many people simultaneously.

The other reason that institutional, collective, and structural approaches are far superior to individual approaches is that to move past the outcome we can get by simply aggregating individual behavior it is necessary to change the framework in which we're operating. Better than recycling is not to need to recycle; individual actions alone do not aggregate to a change in which businesses are required to take back used packaging or create products that can be reused instead of discarded. Using electricity more efficiently will not, on its own, bring about alternatives to fossil fuels for the generation of electricity.

Much more than individual agency is necessary to address environmental problems, whichever ones we choose to focus on. But people play an important role in moving beyond individual solutions. Highly committed individuals are likely the ones willing to work to create the type of broader institutional action that would help change the collective behavior of individuals. The world needs dedicated individual environmental activists, even if turning everyone into an environmentalist is an inefficient way to protect the environment.

My goal is to understand what causes people to behave in ways that have bad environmental consequences. The central argument here is that it makes sense for people to behave the way they do. If there are undesirable consequences of their actions and we think it would therefore be better for that behavior to change, we need to understand what makes it happen in the first place in order to figure out how to make it happen differently. Whatever the behavior is, and whatever the reason we have for wanting it shifted, we need to understand why it happens. This understanding will then provide tools for those who want to create beneficial environmental change.

THE PLAN OF THE BOOK

What can social science tell us about the causes of individual environmental behavior? What do we know about what succeeds—or doesn't—in getting people to change that behavior for better environmental effect? I focus here on the effect that problem characteristics, incentives, information, habit, and norms have on behavior. I draw on social science theory, research, and experimentation from political science, economics, sociology, psychology, business, and other disciplines, bringing these fields into conversation with each other. In the chapters that follow, I examine both how these factors lead to environmentally problematic behavior, and how understanding their effects on behavior may suggest ways to change not only individual behavior, but also the behavior of large numbers of people collectively.

The *problem characteristics* of environmental issues, addressed in chapter 2, involve the framework within which environmental behavior is situated. Environmental problems are externalities—unintended consequences of other goals and activities people pursue. Because of these (usually naturally occurring) characteristics, people create environmental harm without intending to do so. But because they don't individually experience much, if any, of the harm they create (which is likely to affect others distant in time and space), it is difficult and costly for them to prioritize avoiding it. The behavior of individuals, moreover, is a small contributor to the collective environmental damage done. Any one person is unable to make a sufficient difference, and concern about the willingness of others to undertake collective action increases the difficulty of action. These failures of collective action are worse in situations where those who persist in behavior that harms the environment diminish resources even for those of us who are trying to protect them.

These characteristics of environmental issues themselves are embedded in broader social structures we do not directly or immediately control. It is impossible to choose to take public transportation in a location where it doesn't exist, or to recycle where there are no facilities to do so. The infrastructure that already exists, and the regulatory structure that requires or disallows certain actions, create the framework in which our decisions take place. The market capitalism within which most countries operate frames what purchasing choices we have and makes it easy for us to acquire things made in unsustainable ways.

These problem characteristics and social structures give us some ideas about strategies for addressing environmental problems. The unintended nature of externalities means that people do not intend to cause environmental harm and are equally happy to accomplish their goals in a way that does not harm the environment if it can be made convenient for them to do so. There may be solutions that those who create, and those who are harmed by, an externality can reach in which all are better off by taking the externality into account; in some cases these solutions may not require political intervention. Failures of collective action leave open opportunities for those who are genuinely invested in addressing an environmental problem to help create the conditions for people or organizations to work collectively. In some cases aspects of an issue's characteristics can be changed as well—physically or legally closing access to what had been a resource open to all may prevent overuse or create incentives for management, for instance. And although some of the broader social structures like property rights or equal access to the political system can be difficult to change, addressing them not only provides benefits in their own right, but can also improve environmental behavior.

These characteristics also mean that *incentives*, the topic of chapter 3, are skewed from the beginning: making a good environmental choice is often more costly, or more difficult, than engaging in environment-harming behavior, simply because of the inherent characteristics of environmental issues. Incentives against environmental behavior are also created as a side effect of other policy choices: subsidies to support farmers or energy producers, created with reasonable goals in mind, often tilt the playing field even more against environmentally friendly behavior, by decreasing the cost of behavior (like fossil fuel use) that has environmentally problematic consequences.

Changing incentive structures such that the environmentally preferred outcome is less expensive or more convenient than the alternative can make a major difference in behavior. This change is frequently, although not exclusively, undertaken through policy intervention. When incentive structures change, behavior is likely to change, even without a widespread adjustment in values, attitudes, or even knowledge. A good first step to changing environmental behavior, therefore, is to get the incentives right. Incentives can have perverse effects, however: they can discourage intrinsic motivation for a good act and thus decrease the odds that a behavioral change will persist if the incentive diminishes. In some circumstances, they can cause a rebound effect: if appliances become more energy efficient, for example, we may use them more, decreasing the advantages gained from the increased efficiency. Neither of these difficulties with incentives should be overstated: in many cases intrinsic motivation is unnecessary, and rebound effects rarely eliminate the environmental advantage entirely. But it is also the case that changing incentive structures should not be the only tool employed for addressing environmentally problematic behavior.

Information, discussed in chapter 4, is less useful as a way to change behavior than many activists or educators assume. A lack of information about the environmental harm of an activity may initially account for certain types of activities. During the Industrial Revolution, for example, we had no idea that burning fossil fuels could change the global climate, so we didn't factor that possible effect into our fuel choices. But by the point we realize that behavior should change, information is rarely the most effective tool to change it. It is now clear that our industrial activity causes climate change, but simply pointing that out does little against large-scale industrial and energy production. Externalities create the starting point: environmental problems are caused incidentally when people are focused on doing something else. When doing the right environmental thing makes what you are trying to accomplish more costly or more difficult, it is not surprising that information alone is insufficient to prioritize environmental benefit.

In some cases information can even backfire: people faced with graphic information on intractable environmental problems may come to feel that their actions are insignificant or the problem is hopeless and, therefore, stop making choices to minimize environmental harm. In the worst case, dire warnings about environmental harm have been shown in some instances to actually lead people to outright deny the environmental harm or risk, perhaps as a psychological defense mechanism. These types of reactions suggest that there are downsides to motivating behavior change through information alone.

Information can nevertheless play a useful role in behavior change, especially for people who are already motivated to avoid environmental harm. Information that helps people compare the energy efficiency of appliances or the water footprint of food products can, if seen as authoritative, help consumers decrease their environmental impact. Procedural knowledge—on what day should I put out the recycling, and what materials can go in the bin?—can make it more likely that people already inclined to recycle will do so. Providing feedback to people about their own behavior (energy use relative to previous months, for instance) or prompts to remind people to do things they would like to do (such as reminders to turn off lights when leaving a room) can also motivate action. The effect of information in motivating environmentally friendly behavior is, nevertheless, modest.

Most analysis of behavior, including that which is presented in the initial chapters of this book, begins with the assumption that people are rational and choose their actions intentionally. But, as chapter 5 points out, much of what we do is not the result of carefully planned action. We instead follow simplified decision rules, or routines, adopted—consciously or not—to allow us to engage in daily activities without too much mental effort. *Habits* are persistent. When those habits have environmentally problematic implications (our choice of transportation options, or throwing out things that could be recycled, for instance), then even when people intend to make environmentally beneficial choices, their habits may override their intentions. Businesses, likewise, create standard operating procedures that allow systematic and efficient operations. These routines make sense for what they are designed for, but if they cause environmental harm, the fact that they are systematized in business operations may make them more resistant to change than nonroutinized behavior, and they can affect the choices of people who rely on the businesses.

Recognizing the power of habit allows for the possibility of using habit to change behavior efficiently. Although forming a new habit can be difficult, once one exists, it requires no effort to follow. Some things can be done to help create new routines: adding them to existing habits or implementing them at a moment of major life change can make it more likely that people will adopt a new habit; creating habits about what you will do is more successful than focusing on what you will not do. We can also structure institutional processes to make it easier for people to form good environmental habits: setting up environmental options so that they are easy to remember and involve regularized action makes it more likely that people will take actions habitually.

Relatedly, people frequently accept the default option (the action that will happen if they don't choose to do something different) presented to them. Simply making the environmentally preferable option, such as renewable electricity from a utility, the default makes it more likely to be chosen. For the vast majority of people who simply don't indicate a preference, their inaction means that they will contribute to protecting the environment, but those who prefer not to accept that option have the choice not to. The broader lesson is that working to create automaticity in positive behaviors (and avoid it in problematic ones) can be an important tool for environmental protection.

Chapter 6 examines the extent to which attitudes and *norms* (as well as values and identity) influence our behavior. Many people care about the environment and are in favor of protecting it. But these concerns are imperfect determinants of behavior. Social psychologists have long assumed that intentions to behave in a particular way, underpinned by attitudes, account for behavior, but this framing often does not match reality.

There are good reasons for this "value-action gap": incentives are frequently aligned against environmentally preferable action, and we each face so many daily environmentally relevant decisions that efforts to do the right thing consistently are daunting. Attitudinal factors are also imprecise and inefficient tools for changing behavior. These approaches can even backfire, as people dislike feeling judged, may tire of constant efforts to behave, and may backslide on good intentions.

A more promising option for explaining or encouraging environmental behavior is invoking social norms. People show surprising interest in modifying their behavior to fit social expectations, so norms that prioritize goals other than environmental protection—for example, big cars or manicured lawns—may create harmful environmental effects unintentionally.

Conversely, framing information in a way that demonstrates the environmentally beneficial choices of neighbors or group members increases willingness to make environmentally positive choices, as we choose to fit in with our community. Social norms can even affect people you would expect to be especially unlikely to care about the environment, but who care about the perceptions of others. Calling attention to the greenness of choices already undertaken by relevant groups and publicizing positive environmental decisions will help persuade some people to choose better environmental options.

Finally, chapter 7 gives a broad overview of the implications of these findings for designing environmental policy and for other efforts to influence individual behavior in a collective way. This final chapter distills the advice that comes from the book's analysis into a set of clear and specific lessons that should shape our approach to addressing environmental problems—how to get good people (and maybe some who aren't so good) to do good environmental things. These rules of thumb will help guide activists, planners, and policymakers to more effective ways to influence behavior.

Environmental problems are serious, and we need to change our collective behavior to prevent or address them. Because this action is important, it is worthwhile to figure out what works, and what doesn't work, to change behavior. To do that, we have to understand why even good people do bad environmental things.

Problem Characteristics

On a rainy Sunday afternoon I drove to my favorite coffee shop to work on this book. In making that decision, I contributed to global climate change by putting carbon dioxide into the atmosphere. I also, indirectly, contributed to the ecological destruction that came from the extraction, processing, and transportation of the oil that powered my car and the materials that the car is made of.

I did not intend to create those environmental problems, nor, in the moment of decision, did I even consider them. Even though I can walk to this coffee shop, I made the choice to drive because of the pouring rain. The fact that this shop has a parking lot with free parking also influenced my decision.

There are good reasons that people make environmentally problematic choices, both individually and collectively. The things you and others do that cause environmental problems take place in the context of problem characteristics and social structures that predispose us all to make environmentally problematic choices. Certain characteristics of environmental problems—things that for the most part are inherent in the issue rather than created by human design—make environmentally damaging behavior the easier choice. Understanding what those characteristics are is key to either addressing them or figuring out how to work around them to improve environmental behavior.

I wanted to stay dry while heading to a good working environment; I had no desire to contribute to climate change. The fact that environmental problems happen unintentionally when we are pursuing other goals is the starting point for their creation. My decision in the moment to drive to the coffee shop contributed to environmental problems that will be felt a generation from now, most acutely in places like Bangladesh, where sea-level rise will inundate low-lying coastal areas. That our actions here and now create environmental problems elsewhere and in the future makes those faraway consequences hard to imagine or consider. Those characteristics intersect poorly with the political decision-making process, in which politicians care most about what happens in the short term to their direct constituents.

The difficulties include collective action problems. My climate-changing effects from this drive are only consequential in combination with similar actions by others. But that also means that my ability to address the problem by walking instead of driving has little effect on the overall problem, and this limit to my ability may make me even more unlikely to take it into account in my decision. Social science scholarship has both theorized and demonstrated the difficulties that face groups of people trying to work together for the common good. These difficulties are made worse by characteristics specific to environmental issues. Because environmental problems can be made worse by anyone who does not participate in preventing or addressing them, and because it can be difficult to keep people from accessing resources or creating pollution, these collective action problems are worse for environmental issues than for most other social or political problems.

In addition to inherent characteristics of environmental problems, we need to consider characteristics of society—the economic, social, and political structures within which we all operate. Our daily decisions take place in a context we didn't create or choose, in terms of who has political power, who has access to resources, and, in a more direct sense, what broader infrastructure and technological options (could I have taken the train to the coffee shop?) are available and why.

The starting point for understanding and preventing environmental problems is thus their inherent characteristics. These create the initial incentive structures that predispose people to ignore environmental harms in their decisions, and lead to environmental harms no one intends or wants. Recognizing those characteristics is essential for considering how to translate knowledge or norms into action to prevent environmental harm.

EXTERNALITIES

Environmental problems are externalities. They are unintended, unpriced, consequences of doing something intended. My goal is to be able to see in a dark room, which I accomplish by turning on a light. But because of how electricity is generated, my action causes acid rain, particulate pollution, and climate change, none of which were my intention. The costs of these effects are not factored into the price I pay for electricity.

Even environmental problems that are created as inevitable parts of intended activities—like ecological devastation from mountaintop-removal coal mining—can be usefully understood as externalities. Coal-mining companies simply want to access coal in the safest and most cost-effective manner; their goal isn't to destroy ecosystems, even if that is the effect. Understanding that the environmental harm isn't the intention of the activity helps explain why it happens. If there's no immediate economic price to be paid for harming the environment, then activities that do so but are otherwise cheaper or safer are the obvious choice.

Economists refer to externalities as "market failures,"[1] because the market cannot fully (and automatically) take account of the costs (or benefits) of the activity in question. Markets are actually quite efficient at balancing costs and benefits without external intervention as long as all relevant factors have a price. If the full range of costs of making a T-shirt (the materials, the labor, etc.) allow it to be made at a price that someone is willing to buy it for, in a market economy no one needs to direct that the T-shirt be made; someone will step up to do it, to take advantage of the market opportunity. The consumer's interest in obtaining a T-shirt will be met. But if some of the effects of making that T-shirt (like acid rain or climate change from coal burned for electricity used in the factory, or the water use from growing cotton or water contamination from dyeing it) do not produce costs for the T-shirt manufacturer, the true cost of making the T-shirt will not be factored into its price.

Externalities can be positive as well as negative. The flowers planted by the avid gardener on my street may be tended for her own enjoyment, but make the neighborhood look and smell nice for the rest of the inhabitants. Whether an externality is positive or negative depends on your perspective, however; the same flowers I appreciate for their beauty and scent may cause allergies for another resident, an equally unintended consequence. When addressing environmental problems, the focus is on externalities that are causing difficulties for others, be they people or species or ecosystems, so the externalities discussed here are primarily those that cause unintended problems rather than benefits for others.

Externalities can vary in how "external" they are. For many environmental problems there's no relationship between the intentions of the activity and the externality that results—air conditioning (when it used chlorofluorocarbons [CFCs]) and the depletion of the ozone layer, or electricity generation and forest death from acid rain, for instance. In other cases the activity is intended but the consequence is not. Those who catch fish intend to remove fish from the ecosystem for their own use. But they do not generally intend to cause fisheries depletion; in fact, those who fish and would like to do so for the foreseeable future have an interest in maintaining a nondepleted fishery. But their fishing nevertheless contributes to the possible depletion of the fishery.

A key feature of externalities is that they are reciprocal: there are at least two parties (and perhaps many more) to a given externality. There is no harm (or benefit) from an externality if there isn't someone who experiences it. But there is also benefit to someone from the activity that is creating the externality. The reciprocal nature of an externality is key to consideration of what to do about it; it reminds us that there are benefits or costs to all the parties who are connected by the externality, whose interests need to be considered.

Think of a factory making ventilators for hospitals. The manufacturing process emits particulate air pollution that can create smog and haze and cause human health problems like asthma. Demands that the manufacturer stop its polluting activity overlook the benefits of the manufacturing in the first place—would we really prefer that the factory stop its production processes altogether? Ventilators that keep people alive would no longer be made, and the people who worked at the factory would no longer have jobs. This insight is key to thinking about how much of an externality society might collectively want.

That comment may seem surprising; after all, if the externality is negative, shouldn't we be collectively best off if it is not produced at all? Perhaps. There are cases where the collectively best outcome is for an externality to be eliminated altogether. But because the externality is generated in the course of undertaking some activity that has value to at least some people, it may be not be desirable to simply cease that activity. Some balance should be reached between the conducting of that (desired) activity and the production of the undesired externality.[2]

There are a few important things to take from the consideration of externalities. They are unintended, and they happen because the producer of the externality does not bear a cost in producing them. The obvious solution, therefore, is to "internalize" them, by making that cost apparent.

In the short run, at least, internalizing externalities has a cost; that's the centerpiece of what it means to be unpriced in the first place. An externality is a negative effect that someone other than the person or business creating it experiences, and that creating entity does not bear a cost of that effect. For that reason, changing behavior to prevent the creation of the externality will almost certainly cost more than behaving in the way that produced the externality, at least initially. The negative effect ("cost") was experienced by someone else—it wasn't absent. But internalizing an externality means that the cost is now borne by its creator.

The implication of this observation should not be overstated: there are many circumstances in which changing behavior to act in a more environmentally friendly manner can, eventually, cost no more than the original polluting behavior did.[3] And if one considers the costs of the externality to those experiencing it, and thus the overall costs and benefits to the system, the collective benefits will almost always outweigh the collective costs of internalizing the externality; that's the most persuasive argument for decreasing environmental externalities.

But the implication should not be ignored either. At the moment that an externality is internalized, doing so will—by definition—almost always cost someone more. That person or business will likely fight against policies intended to internalize the cost. For reasons discussed below, actors with concentrated interests—small in number, with a strong interest in avoiding action—tend to have more political power than large numbers of people whose preference for a cleaner environment is just one of many preferences they have. The most problematic externalities often have those characteristics. So to internalize externalities, though useful, may not be easy.

SCALE: DISTANCE AND TIME

The basic insight from observing that environmental problems are externalities is that their costs accrue not to the person engaging in an activity that causes them, but to a broader range of other people and ecosystems. If I do not experience the negative effects of an action, and especially if I am not even aware of them, I will be unlikely to consider them when deciding whether to take that action. But where and when those externalities are experienced can increase the likelihood that I will be unconcerned about them.

The greater the spatial distance between the producer of an externality and the context in which it is experienced, the less likely it is that the externality will be considered by the one producing it. If I can see the particulates coming out of my factory, chances are I'm bearing some of the disadvantages, even if it is simply as someone who needs to breathe on the way to work. Even if the costs of the full impacts of my factory's emissions are not internalized, the fact that I experience some of them gives me at least a small stake in trying to decrease pollution. It is also difficult to deny that the emissions are happening, and the uncertainty about cause and effect relationships is small. On the other hand, if the effects produced happen far away, I may be unaware that they are happening.

Of course, one of the standard reactions to pollution produced locally enough to feel its effects is to instead send it elsewhere. Toxic waste is frequently sent to other countries for disposal.[4] Facilities that emit particulates and sulfur dioxide from coal burning have, over time, been built with taller and taller smokestacks, to send those emissions farther away.[5] The externalities become easier to ignore.

Distance becomes even more problematic when the activity causing the externality and the locations that experience it are in different political jurisdictions. In a local community where those who generate an externality and those who experience it share a government that bears responsibility for both sets of people, the government might balance the collective costs and benefits by managing the externality, perhaps by regulation. After all, both the creator and sufferer from the externality are the responsibility of the same political system, and increasing the collective well-being is part of the charge of governing.

But where the producer of the externality and the person who experiences it are in different political jurisdictions, the externality is less likely to be resolved politically: why would a government impose the costs of internalizing the externality on its own citizens or businesses, when the costs of experiencing the externality (and thus the benefits of internalizing it) accrue to people in a different jurisdiction? The farther away in space an externality travels, the more likely it is to encounter this difficulty.

How environmental problems are experienced in time can cause similar difficulties. The greater the length of time between when an externality is experienced and when the activity that causes it took place, the less of a role the effects of that externality are likely to play in consideration of whether to undertake (or modify) the activity. If I know that the effects of my action are going to be felt by me (or others) within a day or so of when I undertake that action, I may consider those effects. If they will not be felt for years, or generations, it is much easier to ignore them.

Just as in distance, a long time between cause and effect can also contribute to uncertainty that the action is causing the effect. That frequently happens at the initial generation of the problem, when there is no sign that what is being done is creating a problem at all. CFCs were seen as an environmentally safe alternative in the 1930s to the toxic refrigerants that were previously used; they were nontoxic and extremely stable. But it turns out that the stability allows them to remain in the atmosphere and travel to the stratosphere, where, in the presence of sunlight, they cause a chain reaction that destroys ozone. It took many decades before this relationship was even hypothesized and still more time before it was observed. The long time between cause and observation of effect meant that people had used these substances for nearly fifty years before anyone even suspected there was a problem.

The time disjuncture can also work in the context of addressing environmental problems. These CFC molecules, which took a long time to manifest their damage, also last for centuries or longer (and some ozone-depleting substances last even longer than that).[6] Most of the world has ended use of most of these substances completely, but the effects will continue to be felt for another century. If the atmospheric lifetime of these substances were not fully understood, the slow progress toward healing the ozone layer now that emissions have mostly stopped could be puzzling. From a political perspective, the fact that most of the benefit of addressing the problem will occur decades or centuries from now can make it a difficult to argue in favor of sacrificing now for a benefit that will be felt by people not yet born. (The fact that the world has worked to end the use of most ozone-depleting substances does, however, suggest that long time horizons may not always cause insurmountable difficulties.)

Time horizons are especially important—and are short—in politics. People in elected office are concerned about the next election; if they don't win, they no longer have any reason to be concerned about an issue, because they are no longer legislating solutions to it. We may wish that we were electing politicians to work for the common good, but they know that in order to do that, they need to get re-elected. So environmental issues in which the benefit of undertaking an activity is felt immediately but the harmful externality does not appear until many years later present a difficult situation for political action.[7] If you open a new factory, it immediately employs people, while the environmental effects (like climate change or acid rain) from operating the factory may not be obvious until a decade or more in the future. It may be difficult to make the case that you should forgo the present employment advantages to avoid the potential future environmental harms.

The longer the time disjuncture, the greater the difficulty in internalizing the externality. As individuals, or as a society, we might be willing to accept a short-term cost for a long-term benefit (I am writing this chapter in an afternoon when I'd rather be playing guitar, because I know I'll be happy when I've finished writing the book and glad I stuck with writing this chapter) if the payoff is in sight. But if the benefit emerges so far away in time that the people who experience it are not the same people who must deal with the cost of changing behavior, that benefit can be extremely politically challenging to accomplish.[8]

Economists have ways to calculate what action is reasonable now when a benefit is experienced in the future, using what is called the discount rate. The concept is a simple one, and is based on the idea of what you could do with your money rather than putting it toward addressing the environmental problem in question. If you deposited $100 in the bank with an interest rate of 5 percent, in a year you'd have $105. So if you're thinking of spending $100 to address an environmental problem now for a resolution that will be experienced in a year, you'd have to get least $105 worth of benefit for that decision to be worthwhile. (Otherwise you could have just banked the $100, withdrawn it next year and have $105 to put toward resolving or coping with the problem.)

There's a logic to that approach, but it starts to be problematic the longer the time horizons are. Because interest compounds, it adds up quickly. Even with a low discount rate (in other words, placing a high value on conditions in the future), a dollar saved in the present will quickly compound to large amounts of money available in the future to spend on addressing or adapting to whatever environmental problem we face, especially as we look several generations ahead. A dollar put in the bank today at a 5 percent interest rate would be worth $1.63 in ten years, $4.32 in thirty years, and $131.50 in one hundred years. That means that unless whatever you're doing with your investment now will yield you that kind of return in the future, in a purely economic calculation you'd be better off waiting to act. Spending that dollar now means you are forgoing the $131.50 it would be worth in the future if you had saved it instead. How certain are you that your intervention is worth that lost revenue? Project long enough into the future and it will never make economic sense to take action now—at least in part because when you get to that point in the future you can still argue that you'd be better off banking the money and waiting before dealing with the problem.[9]

Another important observation about discounting the future is that, in practice, people don't behave the way economic theory predicts that they should. First, not everyone is, functionally, valuing the future to the same degree (or, to put it in economic terms, using the same discount rate). Poverty, in particular, can decrease economic choices available, leading to a prioritization of the short term.[10] If your need in the short term is sufficiently great that you can't afford to wait until the long term, you are going to have an extremely high discount rate—in other words, you will make decisions that prioritize benefits in the short term over those in the long term.

There may be good reasons for prioritizing the short term. For instance, it may be that there is an environmental action—say switching out a facility's energy-inefficient light bulbs for longer-lasting and more efficient bulbs—that unambiguously makes economic sense. But the short-term cost of buying expensive bulbs is more than can be accommodated within the annual budget cycle, so something that makes economic sense may nonetheless not be undertaken.

If you fish for a living, you would obviously benefit from successful conservation measures that allow continued fishing for the long term. It might be economically worthwhile for you to reduce your fishing intensity in the short term as part of collective action to allow the fishery to recover and thus enable you to do much more fishing in the future. However, even assuming successful collective action,[11] it may simply not be possible you to prioritize the long term. Decreased income from fishing in the present may make it impossible to pay the bank loan that enabled you to purchase your fishing boat, which you would lose if you are not able to meet loan payments. At that point it would no longer matter that long-term fishing has been preserved, for you can no longer take advantage of it. In this context, your discount rate is too high for something that would be beneficial over the long term to make economic sense for you.

In practice the discount rate that people are using (as demonstrated by their actual choices) is often far greater than economic theory (based on the interest rate) would predict. Recall that a 5 percent discount rate implies that if you invested, instead of spent, $100 now, you would have $105 a year from now. A study of energy-using durables (like air conditioners) suggested that the actual discount rates people use in their purchasing decisions vary between 8.9 percent and 39 percent, depending on income level.[12] That means that people would only spend $100 on energy-saving technologies now if doing so would net them somewhere between $109 and $139 within a year's time. A similar study found an even higher observed discount rate (which the author called "unbelievably high") for refrigerators, of between 45 and 300 percent[13]—at the extreme end, you would require $400 in savings to be willing to invest $100. In other words, in both cases people were not willing to buy a more expensive model that would save them money (over the longer term, in reduced energy costs), unless that payback time was extremely brief. While there are certainly factors other than pure economic calculations that play a role, the important lesson is that people discount the future far more than economic theory suggests.

Even economic theory predicts that it will be difficult to undertake a short -term cost for a long-term benefit, which is usually necessary when choosing environmentally preferable actions. In practice, people value the present much more than the future (and even more so than economic theory would predict), which makes it even harder to make short-term cost sacrifices for long-term environmental (and economic) gain. The distance in time of environmental externalities makes it difficult to prioritize environmentally positive action.

And if your externality is distant in both time and space? It's easy to understand how it might be easy to overlook. It might be nearly impossible to make the case that present action here should be undertaken to prevent future harm in a distant location. (Time and distance can also increase issues of uncertainty, as discussed in chapter 4.) Climate change is the quintessential problem in which effects are felt at a distance in both time and space from their causes; it is no wonder that climate has been such a difficult problem to tackle politically and behaviorally.

COLLECTIVE ACTION PROBLEMS

Environmental problems often come from the collective behavior of large numbers of people. Because of that, many people need to change the way they act in order to address or prevent these problems. Collective action can come either from many individuals deciding on their own to behave differently, or from working collectively to impose a policy that requires, or incentivizes, everyone to act differently.

It can be hard to persuade people that their individual behavior matters collectively, and even harder to persuade people to work together, even if they would all be better off from collectively preventing or addressing a problem. Economist Mancur Olson goes so far as to argue that "rational self-interested individuals will not act to achieve their common or group interests."[14] Although Olson overstates the problem for rhetorical effect, the underlying observation is important: even when it would benefit us to work together to achieve a goal that we all would benefit from, it will happen less often than we would like.

The intersection of individual and group interests is responsible for this difficulty. Each person's contribution to an environmental problem is extremely small. Even if I know that my taking a disposable cup at the coffee shop contributes to deforestation or waste, the one cup I'm using is such a tiny contribution to the problem that it's hard to think of myself as bearing a major responsibility for the creation of these problems, especially given all the people doing exactly the same thing.

The same is true of any one person's contribution to a policy-related solution to the problem of paper cups. If a number of town residents or coffee shop customers decide to work for a rule that prohibits the use of disposable cups, requires recycling them, or incentivizes the use of non-disposable cups, sufficient pressure by a large enough group of people will almost certainly succeed.

At the same time, whatever policy-related success we might have will accrue to everyone, not just those who participated in creating the solution. If a policy on disposable cups helps prevent the town from increasing property taxes because it no longer needs to open a new landfill, everyone who pays property taxes will benefit, not just the people who participated in the action to create the policy. Other benefits—reduced deforestation and reduced waste—will also be felt broadly, regardless of who participated in creating the solution (in fact, in this example, they will primarily go to people outside of the coffee shop or town). If I did not attend the town meeting or the protest outside the local coffee shop, I will share in any benefits nevertheless.

This nonparticipating approach can seem like the wisest choice: I can refrain from investing my time and energy in political action but still benefit from the political action that everyone else undertook. But if everyone makes that individual calculation, no one will show up to create political pressure, and the outcome we prefer is less likely to happen. This is what is called the free-rider problem: people who do not contribute to addressing or preventing a collective problem benefit from its resolution nevertheless.

Collective action problems show up in any kind of collective endeavor, not just environmental issues. Let's assume, for example, that the residents of my dead-end street would like to make a playground for kids at the end of the cul-de-sac. If all the adults on the street chip in the funding and the labor, it will be easy for us to create the playground, and all the kids in the neighborhood (and, by extension, their parents) will benefit.

Each person's contribution is small, and that may be part of the prob-lem. If I decide, on the day we're supposed to gather to assemble the play-ground, that it's more important to me to get my article revisions in before an impending deadline (or to take my kid to her soccer practice), I won't worry too much about not showing up; after all, there is still a neighbor-hood of people available to help build the playground. And how much will the couple hours of effort I would have contributed actually matter?

Believing that you don't make a big difference is precisely one of under-lying causes of collective action problems, and thus of both the creation of environmental problems and the inability to take action to address them. Although I know my airplane flight contributes to the creation of climate change, I also know that it is an infinitesimal portion of the overall green-house gas emissions of the world, of the United States, or even of air travel collectively. If I were to choose not to take that airline flight, in order to reduce my climate impact, the atmosphere would not even notice. At the same time, I would bear all the costs of my decision to not fly and bear no noticeable individual benefit from my action alone. All the while, other people, even those who care about the global climate, continue to take airplane flights.

The possibility for others to free ride is also a disincentive to cooperate in addressing a collective problem. If I show up to build the neighbor-hood playground and no one else does, I've contributed my time and yet the playground will not be built. If I refrain from taking a flight and most other people do nothing to prevent climate change, I will have missed an opportunity to travel and failed to decrease the magnitude of climate change appreciably. If I show up at a political protest and few others do, we will fail to change policy, and I will have wasted my time. In game theory, those who sacrifice for the collective good in a circumstance in which enough others free ride to prevent the solution from succeeding are said to have received the "sucker's payoff."[15] They bear the cost but do not reap any benefit from their action.

In fact, if you fear that others will free ride, that may increase the odds that you'll decide to do so yourself, as a form of self-protection. As a Rhode Island fisher pointed out, "My only incentive is to go out and kill as many fish as I can. I have no incentive to conserve the fishery, because any fish I leave is just going to be picked by the next guy."[16] In a context in which lack of full participation can prevent success at addressing the problem and in which I have reason to be concerned that others might not contribute, it can be rational to make that same decision.

Seeing how collective action problems work helps us understand in what circumstances they are most likely to show up. First, the greater the number of actors involved,[17] and the smaller their contribution (to the creation of the problem or to its solution),[18] the harder collective action is likely to be. It might seem that it would be easier to change a small behavior than a large one, but if your contribution to the problem seems tiny, it can be hard to believe that changing it can matter; in fact, if you alone change, it doesn't. My neighborhood might have a greater chance of overcoming its collective action problem: my couple hours of labor might in fact be a noticeable percentage of the overall activity, so it may feel to me that my participation matters. And because the potential group of playground builders is small and we know each other, my absence on the playground-building day would be noticed, unlike my choices about airplane travel.

Others argue that it is not a desire to free ride, but rather a lack of belief that collective action will succeed, that prevents people from fully committing to it.[19] In other words, it is not that I intend to let others do the work because I know I can share in the benefit even without contributing; it is that I don't believe my time contributing will be well spent because the group is unlikely to succeed in its collective efforts. The result is similar: individuals decide not to contribute to a collective outcome that they would benefit from if everyone contributed and it thereby succeeded. But there are different implications of this perspective: the smaller the group of people engaging in collective action (especially relative to the behavior that needs to be changed), the less confidence its members will have in their ability to collectively succeed.

A related problem is the issue of concentrated versus diffuse interests.[20] Because large groups experience the biggest problems engaging in successful collective action, problems that are caused by a small number of actors (say, pollution from coal burning for manufacturing) but experienced by a large number of people (those of us whose breathing is affected by the particulate pollution) are the most susceptible to collective action problems. The interests of factory owners are "concentrated," in two different ways. First, there are not that many of them, so coordinating their actions is easier. Second, their livelihoods depend on keeping costs low: of all the issues they might care about, this one is surely at the top of the agenda. Cooperating to resist having to take costly action is thus something they prioritize.

The rest of us are numerous. If one were to do a strict utilitarian calculus, the benefit the sufferers from particulate air pollution would gain from preventing it would likely outweigh the cost to the factories in having to prevent it. But our interests are diffuse: there are so many of us, and we are (likely) geographically so spread out, so it is extremely difficult for us to coordinate our behavior.

The other way our interests are diffuse is that each of us suffering from particulate air pollution has many other priorities: getting our kids educated, feeding our families, addressing other environmental pollutants, and so on. Someone might not show up at the lobbying day to change particulate pollution policy because his kids are sick, and taking care of them is a perfectly reasonable priority; a college student might not participate because she has an important exam the next day. In other words, free riders don't free ride because they are bad people or don't care about the outcome; they free ride, at least in part, because they have other valid priorities. (The fact that they would benefit from the collective outcome, if it happens, can also make the decision to free ride easier, whether or not they are acting strategically to gain benefits without contributing.)

The broader point is that externalities are more likely to be created, and more resistant to being addressed, when those who suffer because of them are more numerous and more spread out (and those who cause them smaller in number and more able to coordinate their actions).

There are ways to overcome collective action problems. Persuading people that their participation matters is key. If they think that the collective action can succeed without them, they are more likely to free ride (or, conversely, if they think their participation is necessary, they're more likely to contribute).[21] On the other hand, you also need to persuade them that there's already enough collective action underway that the endeavor has a chance of success.[22] There is thus a sweet spot that those encouraging collective action need to hit, persuading people that their participation is essential, but also that the collective action in progress is sufficiently robust that it is likely to succeed.

Another way is to offer what are called "selective benefits" or side payments. Public interest organizations that send out calendars or other rewards available to members that cannot otherwise be accessed may help encourage membership (a form of collective action) in a way that can overcome the temptation to free ride. People may become members of the Sierra Club not simply to contribute to the collective action of the group, but because membership comes along with access to the group's outdoor recreational activities, something that cannot be accessed without joining the organization (and hence contributing to its collective action).[23]

Those benefits can even be "psychic"—things that simply make you feel better about the action you've taken. Although you might be tempted to avoid joining your town's river cleanup event, the fact that the cleanup is a social event, with like-minded individuals who might become your friends, might increase the chances you will contribute. These psychic benefits can play a role in identity creation (see chapter 6). It's not accidental that public radio contributions often come with a tote bag or bumper sticker that identifies you publicly as someone who contributes to the provision of a collective good. Markers of an identity that people want to embrace or embody can be appealing as selective benefits for collective action.

There are social processes that can increase the likelihood of collective action as well. Nobel Prize winner Elinor Ostrom's body of work provides many examples of communities of various sizes succeeding in collective action without external coercion.[24] Her work suggests, among other things, that social or familial ties can help collective action succeed.[25]

Similarly, the emergence of social norms—expectations about what is appropriate in a given social setting (discussed further in chapter 6) can support collective action.[26] Especially in circumstances where a subset of relevant actors can succeed in providing collective goods even if some continue to free ride, having actors with different preferences or capabilities can make collective action possible.[27]

Perhaps the type of individually selfish behavior that underlies collective action problems is learned rather than inherent. Studies have demonstrated, for instance, that economics majors are less likely to contribute to collective action in game theory experiments than are college students with other majors;[28] in other words, learning about the incentives to free ride contributes to that behavior.[29] In fact, even in experiments demonstrating collective action problems, most participants contribute more to addressing collective problems than would be expected if they acted as selfishly as theory predicts. The likelihood that people decide to cooperate increases when they expect that others will also cooperate, suggesting that they're not strategically trying to get away with free riding when they think others will contribute to a collective good.[30]

Collective action can be difficult. Concern about free riding of others can diminish collective action in important ways. But acting collectively is nevertheless possible. Understanding, and remedying, the reasons we have difficulty acting collectively can help.

A different approach, though, is to change aspects of the situation. Not all collective behavior needs to be managed collectively. Policy intervention can impose rules about what people must or must not do, or create incentives for behavior. People may then act for the collective benefit because they are required or incentivized to do so, rather than because of an individual decision to cooperate. The environment may not care about the reason for collective action, only that the action happens.

EXCLUDABILITY AND SUBTRACTABILITY

Other characteristics of environmental resources themselves contribute to the likelihood that problems will be created, or the difficulty of preventing or addressing them. Two important characteristics of an issue are the

Table 2.1 ISSUE CHARACTERISTICS

		Excludability	
		Yes	No
Subtractability	**No**	Private goods	Common pool resources
	Yes	Club goods	Public goods

extent to which it is excludable and subtractable (see table 2.1). Most environmental problems come from resources that are not excludable and are, at the same time, subtractable. Issues with those two characteristics are called common pool resources (CPRs).

Excludability is about whether people can be kept from accessing the benefits of a system or resource. An ocean fishery is not excludable legally outside territorial waters; the high seas are "unowned" areas. It's also not practically excludable; it can be extremely difficult to prevent anyone from accessing resources of the oceans. But a local lake, especially if it is fully contained on land someone owns, can be excludable; the landowner both legally and practically has the ability to keep others from accessing the lake.

Many environmental problems pertain to resources that are not excludable. This lack of excludability is key to the collective action problems discussed above. If you are free to access a resource regardless of whether you contribute to its protection, it is easier to free ride, and tempting to do so. If a resource is not excludable—I can't keep you from accessing the lake—its resources (like the fish within it) will likely be less well protected.

The public playground discussed in the section on collective action may be difficult to construct if its use is nonexcludable. We all have demands on our time and resources, and if I'll be able to access the playground regardless of whether I contributed to building it, I might be tempted to free ride.

Subtractability (also called rivalness) describes the extent to which one person's use of a resource affects the usability of that resource for others. Fisheries are subtractable because when someone takes a fish from the ocean that fish is no longer available for others or for reproducing, or even just to continue to function as part of the ecosystem. The same is true with putting pollution into a system. If a factory dumps its waste into the river, the quality of the river is diminished for others.

Subtractability causes major problems that can augment problems of nonexcludability. For the most part, the playground created in my neighborhood is not subtractable—its use by one child does not noticeably decrease its usability by others. The same is not true with a resource that is subtractable. If fishers agree to collaborate (engage in collective action) to ensure that the fishery is not depleted, but one or more fishers don't agree to join the collective action, they can singlehandedly destroy the ability of others to protect the resource.

Common pool resources, which are both subtractable and nonexcludable, are particularly difficult to protect. In the first place, you are likely to get free riders, because you cannot exclude actors from the access to the resource, whether it be a fishery or the atmosphere, even if they don't participate in providing or protecting that resource. And free riders are particularly problematic because of the subtractability of the issue. It can be literally impossible to provide the collective good of environmental protection the face of free riders.

To understand why, consider a public good, which is a resource that (like a CPR) is nonexcludable but is also not subtractable. Public radio is a good example of a public good. Weather forecasts are another example, or even my neighborhood park. My local public radio station is always fundraising—there are a lot of free riders (people who listen to the radio broadcasts without contributing to help pay for the radio shows). What that means is that there is less public radio provided than people would like—less funding (and more fundraising)—because some people who listen don't contribute to making the broadcast happen.

But a public radio broadcast is not subtractable. Once the broadcast is on the air, its quality is not diminished by the number of people who listen to it; my listening to the radio does not make it harder for you to listen. It can't be used up. In the case of a radio station, part of the reason public radio is provided despite the large numbers of free riders is that its use is nonsubtractable. That means that a small group of devoted public radio listeners can, through enough funding, make public radio available generally, even if others listen without contributing. And those of us who don't contribute don't undermine the ability of those devoted funders to create it if they choose to pay more than their fair share to make it possible.

The same is not true of environmental amenities. Take, for example, nitrogen pollution of rivers. Nitrogen used in fertilizers for agriculture can run off (especially when it is used in great quantity) into rivers—the Mississippi has a particular problem with nitrogen pollution. The excess nitrogen is responsible in this case for the dead zone in the Gulf of Mexico, because the nitrogen from the river collects in the gulf, providing excess nutrients for algae that multiply and then die, decreasing the oxygen supply and killing all life in the area.[31]

Those concerned about nitrogen pollution can change their behavior so that they no longer create nitrogen runoff, perhaps through using less fertilizer. But if not everyone along the river participates in the solution—if some farmers continue to use high levels of nitrogen fertilizer, all the changes made by the other farmers can fail to protect the resource. The nonexcludability of the issue means that, at least practically, farmers can't be prevented from accessing the river as a pollution sink. Their input of pollution can prevent the rest of us from ensuring a clean river.

The same is true with the use of resources. Those of us who catch fish in a body of water will benefit if we moderate our fishing so as to leave enough fish to reproduce, allowing us to continue to catch fish indefinitely. However, if most of us agree to fish responsibly (and thereby bear the costs of reduced income or food in the short run) but a few don't, those few might be able to catch enough fish to prevent the stock from recovering. If we can't exclude fishers from accessing the fishery, the subtractable nature of fish means that the behavior of those who do not participate in addressing the problem can make it more difficult—or even impossible—for the rest of us to address it on our own.

We think of these characteristics as binary conditions (something is either excludable or subtractable), but really the differences fall along a spectrum. The extent to which an issue is excludable, or can be made to be, can indicate how difficult it will be to manage. Likewise, the less subtractable a resource is, the greater the extent to which free riders can be tolerated in the system. The subtractability of an issue also helps identify which actors might be the most problematic or are the most essential to involve in a solution.

To some extent, excludability and subtractability are inherent characteristics of an issue, but in some cases they may be changeable, and doing so can be one way to prevent or address environmental problems. Excludability is more amenable to being imposed; you can often take a resource that is open access and close it. That excludability can be imposed practically; you can put a fence around an area of land, for example. Or it can be done legally, by making a set of rules about who is allowed to access it. The same is true even for something like the public radio broadcast discussed above: turn public radio into subscription-based satellite or Internet radio, and you can be excluded from access to it if you don't support it. Put a locked gate around the neighborhood playground, and only those with keys can access it.

These resources that are excludable but still not subtractable then become what are known as "club goods" (also known as "toll goods"). Those who don't participate in creating or protecting them can be kept from accessing them. I might be more willing to contribute to building my neighborhood playground—less likely to be a free rider—if I can be kept from accessing it if I haven't contributed to creating it.

Because of the subtractability of environmental resources, excludability becomes more important for a common pool resource than it might in the case of a public good. If each person's access to the resource diminishes its quality for others, being able to limit the number who can access it can be one way to prevent the problem. The common cow pasture that stood as an analogy in Garrett Hardin's influential work on the commons[32] could be fenced in to restrict access. It would then become what is called a "private good."

Full privatization (in which, rather than sharing a collective cow pasture on which all cows graze, we each have an individual plot) does not reduce the subtractability of the issue, but it changes each person's individual calculus when accessing it, having the effect of internalizing the externality. The grass my cows eat is now on my property, and if they over-graze, I'm the one who feels the negative effects. (Because it is excludable, I can at least keep the cows of others from eating the grass on my property, which makes it possible for me to make my own decisions about what is best to do.)

The extent to which a resource can be made excludable is an important consideration in figuring out how to prevent a tragedy of the commons. We can fence a cow pasture, but not the atmosphere. We can prevent people's access to a local fishery where someone has the jurisdiction to make and the ability to enforce the rules, but not on the oceans when governments have the legal authority to decide not to participate in rules, and even those they agree to may be difficult to enforce.

There may also be contexts in which you do not want to create excludability even if you are able to. A shared cow pasture, if managed well, can probably allow for more cattle grazing than one that is divided up into individual plots. In other contexts the argument against excludability may be about morality rather than about efficiency: is it ethically justifiable to keep people from accessing resources that they need, or to fence off some of the natural spaces on the planet for the benefit only of those who can afford to purchase the rights to access them?

Although subtractability is a characteristic that is much less easy to modify, how subtractable a resource is, and how many actors have the ability to, individually, overuse or pollute that resource, can influence how difficult it will be to protect. And the subtractability of a resource can be made less problematic if you are able to exclude others from accessing it, because you may be able to prevent its overuse.[33]

CHARACTERISTICS OF SOCIAL STRUCTURES

The characteristics discussed so far in this chapter pertain to aspects of environmental issues themselves. They make it likely that we will, unintentionally, contribute to creating environmental problems or fail to successfully act to address them. In addition to these aspects of issues themselves, larger-scale political and economic characteristics structure the available choices we have. These political and economic structures were generally created in contexts that had little to do with environmental consideration, but they now frame—and often limit—the options available to us in ways that make it more likely that we will behave in environmentally problematic ways.

Regulatory Structures

Governments at all levels regulate to accomplish a variety of goals. They want to ensure full employment, safe neighborhoods, and easy transportation, among many other laudable intentions. But any regulation has a set of unanticipated or unintended effects—externalities—that structure the decisions we face. Many of these regulatory decisions were made in a context not set up to consider environmental implications. Many policies that underlie our daily decisions were created before environmental issues were regularly considered, or were developed to address other policy priorities without stopping to consider what broader environmental implications would follow. The fact that those environmental implications are externalities, and therefore don't bear a cost, makes it even more likely that they have not played a role in creating these regulatory structures.

Zoning rules are one example of how policies created for one purpose affect environmental behavior. Zoning in my area does not allow businesses to operate near residential areas, perhaps out of concern for residential property values or to avoid noise complaints. That zoning influences how far I need to travel for daily activities. If I could do my grocery shopping or find restaurants or hardware stores within walking distance, I wouldn't need to drive to shop or dine out, but if residential areas are separated from businesses, I have to travel farther and am likely to do it by car. In the United States it is common for building permits to specify the number of parking spaces that must be constructed per housing unit or business. A policy of this type may stem from concern for avoiding on-street congestion, but it decreases the overall cost of parking (and thus encourages driving). It also limits urban density by taking space that could be used for building and allocating it to asphalt parking areas. Since density generally is beneficial for decreasing environmental impact, these policies unintentionally contribute to environmental harm.

Further effects are likely from decreased density and increased incentives for car use. If there's not enough density to justify a transit line or station, the lack of transit options may prevent people who would like to commute via public transportation from living in the area, and prevent those who do live there from accessing commuting options other than automobiles.

Subsidies are another type of policy that can have unintended environmental effects. Subsidies encourage certain behavior (industrial agriculture or oil exploration and extraction, for example) by making that activity cheaper. They are created to meet policy objectives, like supporting farmers or increasing domestic energy production. But if the activity they support has negative environmental consequences, making it cheaper prioritizes it relative to other choices people might make. Subsidies are discussed at greater length in chapter 3, because they operate by changing incentives.

There are too many examples of public policies with incidental environmental implications to discuss in detail in this book. But it is worth paying attention to the broader regulatory context as one level of explanation for the types of options that are available to us as we go about our daily activities or when looking for underlying explanations for the environmentally relevant decisions we make. Often those decisions are not fully in our hands because of how policy has shaped the context.

Infrastructure

Our choices are constrained by the context that infrastructure creates. If my town does not have public transportation, I do not have that option when considering how to commute. If roads are prevalent (and, likely, subsidized), driving will be easier and safer than biking, especially in the absence of separated bike lanes. If electricity appears in my house via wires that were strung up long before I moved in, and produced by a centralized power plant that uses fossil fuels, that arrangement strongly influences my energy choices. Although the infrastructure that exists in a given location is part of a broader, longer-term set of decisions, at any given moment it shapes the options we have available to us. Again, because environmental issues were not on the collective radar when many infrastructure decisions were made, the existing infrastructure rarely enables beneficial environmental action.

Infrastructure effects can be felt on a smaller scale as well. I live in a three-unit building in which some of the utilities (including the outdoor water) are commonly shared by the building. The water infrastructure of the building, which was there when I moved in, sets up the possibility for a collective action problem in water use. Even if I decide to conserve water, out of either environmental concern or an effort to save money on the collective water bill, my neighbors might still use water abundantly. That practice, or even possibility, undermines my ability or willingness to conserve. Apartment buildings have similar problems: if I pay the utilities but my landlord controls how the building was built or is maintained, I may not be able to insulate, even if it would save me money on heating bills or if I care about preventing climate change.

Sometimes infrastructure issues create what might be seen as a "chicken and egg" problem. Without the relevant infrastructure, it can be difficult to make a desired change, even if the people in favor of that change are a large enough group to warrant new infrastructure. Consider the problem of electric vehicles. It's only realistic to get widespread adoption of electric cars if there are charging stations at regular intervals in the areas where people drive. If you're considering buying an electric car, you may decide not to get one if there aren't enough charging stations. At the same time, someone considering opening a charging station might decide not to because there aren't enough people who drive electric cars to make a charging station profitable. Even if both groups of people are large enough to make widespread adoption of electric vehicles possible, the lack of existing infrastructure may prevent it from happening, or make it take longer than necessary for a desired technology to catch on.

It is thus worth examining the broader infrastructure in which our decisions take place; much of what we do is framed by how the physical structures of the economy have been created, long before any individual decision we are making was considered. Likewise, a change in that infrastructure may render any action easier or harder without the need to persuade anyone to prioritize environmental concerns. I take the commuter rail into Boston because there is a station close to my house and it heads to a part of the city I want to go to. No one needs to sell me on the environmental advantages of rail travel. And at the same time, one of the other places I frequently go in the area is difficult to reach on public transportation, and no amount of environmental concern can get me to take the train to travel there. Infrastructure can influence the behavior of many people simultaneously, with good or bad environmental effects.

Market Characteristics

Most of us in the world live in a system of market capitalism. Much of what we buy, and many other decisions we make, are dependent on decisions of businesses attempting to make money by the choices they offer us. No one mandates what they sell or for what price; instead experimentation with offering goods or services of various types at different prices is a society-level action in which some businesses succeed and others fail based on how well they predict and respond to (or develop) consumer demand. A full examination of the deep implications of capitalism, for environmental good or bad, is beyond the scope of this book, but there are several ways this economic framework structures the options we face as we make environmentally relevant decisions.

One implication of this system is that many people make their living by trying to convince us to buy things. They have every reason to try to persuade us that we need more stuff than we already have, or the newest or fanciest thing, or to replace the thing we own that they previously made.

It may be why that latest piece of technology breaks down, or costs less to replace than to fix, or becomes undesirable when a newer model is made. That's no accident; people make their money when we have a reason to buy things. Because environmental problems created are unpriced externalities, the more of these things we buy, the more externalities are created. Because the cheaper it is to produce something, the greater the profit that can be made in selling it, finding the cheapest ways to produce often involves lack of attention to these externalities created, precisely because there's no cost to creating them. All those things we come to own, and replace or discard, also add up to a major waste problem. So the economic structure we live in depends on an effort to make us buy far more things than we actually need.

Another implication of this system is that despite all these efforts to sell us things, the range of available options might not be the ones we would prefer to choose among. As Paul Stern points out, "Sometimes producers do not supply what environmentally oriented consumers would buy if available."[34] You might prefer organic produce but be unable to find it, and I would choose to buy toys or tools with far less packaging than they currently have. There may be good market reasons for our preferences not being reflected in the choices we face: if few people share our preferences, it isn't cost effective for producers to make our preferred product available to us.

But the same kind of chicken-and-egg problem discussed as a problem of infrastructure emerges in this context as well, and can account for a lack of availability of products that *would* be widely purchased if only they existed, particularly because of the market structure of our economy.

To take one example, for a long time in the United States you could buy a fuel-efficient car or you could buy a luxury car, but you had few options if you wanted to buy a luxury fuel-efficient car. Although there were plenty of people who wanted such a vehicle, auto companies had little incentive to provide it, because they would have made less money selling it than from selling a luxury car with a powerful (less fuel-efficient) engine.

Granted, if there is a potential market for something that isn't being made, it will theoretically be to someone's interest to step in to meet that unmet demand. But if something isn't available, there may be no mechanism for finding out that enough people would be willing to buy it if it were available. So the chicken-and-egg problem appears again: if the product existed, people would buy it. Because it doesn't exist, people can't buy it (to show that there is a demand).

Market capitalism at its deepest levels thus accounts for the externalities that were the starting point of this chapter; without a system in which most of our activities bear a price, the unpriced nature of environmental impacts would not be so significant. But in some ways this market structure is such a central aspect of our global political economy that it is unlikely to change; waiting for, or even advocating, the dismantling of capitalism is not a near-term solution to the structural factors that influence our behavior. Nevertheless, recognizing the role they play in shaping what behavior options we have is key to understanding how, even when we might prefer to make better environmental decisions, we are constrained by the range of choices we are offered by the structures around us.

PROBLEM CHARACTERISTICS IN ENVIRONMENTAL DECISION-MAKING

The environmental consequences of many of our daily decisions can be directly traced to characteristics inherent to environmental issues and the social structures that are so central to our daily lives that we rarely notice them. The nature of these inherent characteristics and social structures may leave us few easy options for changing them. Even so, understanding how structures predispose us toward making problematic environmental choices, even when we mean well, will help us understand what the approaches discussed in other chapters can—or can't—contribute to getting us to change behavior when structures are stacked against us. Diagnosing problems that come from inherent characteristics of problems or widespread social structures that can't be easily changed may draw us toward tools of incentives, information, habit, or norms, presented in other chapters. These other approaches can lead us to better environmental behavior despite problematic underlying structures.

Incentives

An incentive is a condition or policy that encourages a particular type of behavior. The main lesson to take from the discussion of problem characteristics in chapter 2 is that inherent aspects of environmental resources and of broader social structures influence the choices we make about how to behave. The underlying issue is incentives: because of the characteristics of environmental problems, it is often harder or more costly to make a positive environmental choice than a problematic one.

Problem characteristics are not the only cause of incentives that favor acting in an environmentally harmful way, although they are usually the starting point. Other policy decisions can contribute to the incentive to choose a bad environmental action. Policy decisions can either intentionally or unintentionally disadvantage good environmental behavior. One way they do that is by subsidizing actions that, perhaps indirectly, have environmentally problematic consequences. Nonmonetary incentives are important too. If the easiest action or the default choice is the environmentally harmful one, people may take it without considering the alternatives.

In other words, people will—for understandable reasons—generally choose the cheaper, quicker, and easier option. If incentives are pointing us to environmentally harmful behavior, changing those incentives can change that behavior for the better.

It's not as simple as that, however. There is good evidence that focusing on incentives as a solution to problems of environmental behavior is not sufficient. In some cases, it can even be counterproductive. Rewarding people for engaging in desired behavior may make them consider that behavior instrumentally, leading them to devalue it or perform it only when they get a reward. In other cases incentives can work even better than we might think. They can provide signals that (as discussed further in chapter 6) indicate a socially preferred outcome. In these cases an incentive may be smaller than would seem economically rational and still influence behavior in a useful direction. Determining which types of situations are helped or harmed by these incentive nudges, and what type of nudges work best in which situations, is key.

Social systems are complex. Economic incentives that lead us to use resources more efficiently may have a rebound effect. We may use more of a resource if efficiency makes it less costly. Even when there is a rebound effect, it is unlikely to entirely erase the benefit from the increased efficiency. But that effect does mean that it can be difficult to estimate what effect efficiency will have if it leads to decreased prices.

Although most studies show that reorienting incentives in favor of environmental behavior does indeed change behavior, that change is often far less than might be expected. As Paul Stern puts it, "Monetary incentives cannot be adequately modeled by applying a standard estimate of the price elasticity of demand."[1] In other words, people change their behavior less in response to changes in economic incentives than economists might predict. Incentives are thus important both for understanding and for changing environmental misbehavior, but they are not the only answer.

ECONOMIC INCENTIVES

Incentives can be economic or noneconomic (also referred to as non-monetary). Many economists suggest that functionally all incentives are economic, because you can determine the economic cost of something that isn't currently priced on the market (by, for instance, examining your standard hourly wage to determine the cost of your time to sort material for recycling).[2] But most people don't make calculations that explicitly and experience these different types of incentives differently.

Because environmental problems are externalities, acting in a way that has negative environmental consequences often costs less than acting in an environmentally friendly manner. This added cost of environmentally harmful choices may be inherent to the characteristics of the activity, but it is also likely that some form of subsidy is keeping costs even lower than they would otherwise be. A subsidy is a policy that makes a desired activity less expensive than it would otherwise be, to encourage more of that behavior. For example, governments have frequently subsidized fishing, by offering low-interest loans for purchasing or upgrading fishing boats, exempting fishing vessels from fuel taxes, or guaranteeing a minimum price for fish. All those activities make it cheaper for people to fish than it would otherwise be and therefore encourage people to enter, or stay in, the fishing profession. Likewise, an income tax rebate for people who have purchased a hybrid vehicle (as was used as a subsidy when hybrid cars were first introduced) encourages more people to buy hybrid cars.

These subsidies support some public purpose. They exist because of a policy interest in encouraging behavior that might not happen in an unregulated market. The various types of support for agriculture across the developed world (especially in the United States), which have a long history, influence the type and extent of farming by providing farmers with guaranteed income or stable commodity prices, access to low-interest loans, or decreased cost of agricultural inputs.

Agricultural subsidies are created with the best of intentions. They may be used to help farmers persist despite unpredictable global markets (or local weather conditions), which might otherwise drive them out of business. Countries concerned with food security or cheap domestic food want to ensure enough local food production and may thus increase the incentives for farmers to continue to operate. These subsidies, intended

to support farmers and ensure adequate food production, also unintentionally encourage the creation of environmental problems. For example, price supports that ensure a minimum price for crops no matter the
market price incentivize production on marginal lands and intensity of
pesticide and fertilizer use. All of these activities damage nearby—or
distant—ecosystems and water supplies.[3] Any subsidy that increases
the likelihood of an activity also increases the externalities that activity
creates.

Fossil fuels are similarly subsidized. Companies are permitted to drill
for fossil fuels on public lands without paying the full price of doing so.
The creation and maintenance of pipelines to move oil or gas around or
to the country have been subsidized. The US Navy provides protection
for oil tankers shipping oil globally. Fossil fuel companies receive a variety of other tax breaks for their operations.[4] Government construction
or maintenance of transmission lines for electric power generation provides a similar type of subsidy. These subsidies were all created with the
best of intentions. Fossil fuels allow for economic development. Being able
to provide them domestically rather than buy them internationally is an
important national security priority. And ensuring that people have access
to electricity and heat is central to meeting their basic needs. But these
subsidies increase our use of these fuels, and thus the creation of the environmental problems that result.

One additional problem with subsidies is that they can be extremely
difficult to remove once they are in place. They create a constituency that
will be harmed if they are removed. Those who benefit from them (a concentrated interest, as discussed in chapter 2) work hard in the political
process to resist their removal.[5] The bureaucratic structures created to
oversee these subsidies may fear for their own survival if subsidies were
to be removed.[6] So even if we identify unintended environmental consequences from subsides, it can be extremely difficult to remove those existing subsidies.

Explicit subsidies are reasonably easy to identify, but implicit subsidies
influence environmental behavior as well. These may not be a specific
transfer of funding in the same way that a tax break or a direct payment is,

but implicit subsidies nevertheless tilt the economic playing field. Free—or inexpensive—parking privileges benefit those who drive by making it cheaper than it would otherwise be to commute. That can be considered a subsidy because someone had to pay to create and maintain the available parking. The land where a parking lot is placed could have been used for something else (and thus represents an opportunity cost), and the driver is not charged for that cost. The fact that there is an infrastructure to transport fossil fuels around the country or world, and transmission lines to send centrally generated electricity to my house, implicitly subsidizes fossil fuel-based electricity generation, over the installation of individual solar technology.[7]

Subsidies created for one purpose thus often have the effect of making environmentally problematic behavior even less expensive than it would be. When combined with the discount that comes because people do not bear the cost of the environmental externalities they produce and the extra individual effort that would be required to make environmentally positive choices, these subsidies make it even more likely that the rational individual choice will be to contribute to environmental harm.

The additional cost to environmentally friendly choices isn't entirely due to subsidies, though. It is there simply because externalities are unpriced, so—at least initially—choosing to act in a way that doesn't produce them almost always costs more. Office paper made from recycled materials often costs more than paper made from virgin materials. Flying halfway across the country may be cheaper than driving. In my town I can choose to buy electricity generated with renewable resources, but there is a price premium.

The additional cost to environmental behavior is not universal—it is better environmentally to drink (free) tap water in many locations than to spend money to buy bottled water. Nor is the extra price for environmentally preferable options necessarily forever. The extra cost for internalizing externalities is likely to decrease over time. Economies of scale—producing a lot of something reduces the per-unit cost—decrease costs as these new practices are widely adopted. When regulation requires widespread internalizing of environmental externalities or resource scarcity increases costs, people are more likely to invent easier and cheaper ways to run their businesses, in order to avoid those increased costs.[8] But it is nevertheless true that there is often, at least initially, an economic cost (to individuals, businesses, and even countries as a whole) to making an environmentally beneficial choice.

If the inherent characteristics of environmental problems account for the incentives that drive people to engage in behavior that contributes to these problems, one obvious solution is to change the incentives. Reward people for doing environmentally beneficial things, or at least don't penalize them (in money, time, or effort) for doing so.

If it were possible to change the problem characteristics, that would have the natural effect of better aligning incentives. In some cases that may be possible, such as by making a resource excludable. As chapter 2 discusses, the ability to exclude someone from access to a resource can increase the incentive people have to conserve it.[9] Simply limiting who has access is likely to decrease overuse (or pollution). You can also grant access only to those willing to engage in collective action to protect it, and thus incentivize collective action.

Because the nature of environmental problems as externalities is to a large extent inherent, it may be difficult to change that aspect of an issue. Other incentive structures can be used to achieve the same effects. When people refer to policies that "internalize externalities," they frequently mean the addition of incentives that make those who generate environmental harms more likely to have to bear the cost of those harms. Tools like taxing harmful emissions make environmentally harmful behavior costly, and—even without requiring that anyone change behavior—may cause polluters to decrease problematic emissions if it is less expensive to do so than to pay the (now taxed) costs of polluting.

This kind of approach doesn't truly internalize externalities. It may be impossible to know exactly how much harm an externality causes or its economic value, and thus any charge levied is at best an estimate. And there's no guarantee that any additional charge will actually go to remedy the externality or compensate those who suffer. But these types of policies remove some of the economic advantage from not having to pay the costs of environmental damage created in the course of accomplishing something else.

The broad incentive-based approach to changing environmental behavior is to make the desired activity cheaper or easier to engage in than the environmentally harmful behavior. Doing so does nothing to change the way people feel about their behavior or about the environment; they don't need to care about the damage to the environment in order to stop causing it. And it is not an information strategy—people can continue to be ignorant about environmental problems or the best solution and still change to more beneficial behavior simply because the incentives point them in that direction.

One of the primary advantages of an incentives-based approach, in fact, is that it does not require people to be individually moved to understand or care about the environment. Concern and understanding can account for why people change their behavior, but getting people to care and understand, which often requires reaching them one at a time, is extremely inefficient. People can—and do[10]—disagree about whether it is strategically sound to change behavior without changing hearts or minds, but the ability to do so quickly underlies a focus on incentives.

Using incentives to change environmental behavior involves making the desired activity less economically (or practically) difficult. That may be through directly increasing the cost of engaging in the nondesired activity, such as by imposing a tax or a fee. For example, it has been repeatedly demonstrated that people reduce the amount of trash they discard when required to pay per amount (such as by bag, or by weight), especially when they do not have to pay for recycling.[11]

Alternately, subsidies can be used to encourage environmental behavior. Tax breaks for buying hybrid vehicles in the United States and Canada helped make these cars more affordable in the short term, which helped those who wanted to purchase them. They saved money over the long term because of their decreased gasoline costs, but might not have been able to avoid the upfront cost of the vehicle or might not have calculated the long-term savings. These subsidies also helped make the industry viable when it was new by providing a larger market.[12]

Green subsidies are also used in agriculture, such as a provision in the 2002 US Farm Bill that gave payments to farmers who used practices such as conservation tillage, a practice that reduces the amount of tillage and that leaves crop residue on the land.[13] Subsidies can also be used to encourage research and development that might lead to environmentally beneficial technology.[14]

Subsidies for environmentally desirable behavior can have some of the same problems that other types of subsidies do: they can create a constituency that lobbies for their continuation. Similarly, because they depress the cost of behaving in an environmentally beneficial way, if these subsidies are removed, the price will increase and the positive behavior will likely decrease.

There are ways to design "green" subsidies that are less problematic, for example, by keeping them specific and time limited. Even then, choosing what types of things to subsidize is key. Subsidies for energy-efficient appliances or fuel-efficient automobiles, for instance, have a beneficial effect long beyond the initial purchase, because once you've bought your car or refrigerator, it continues to save energy as you use it, and even if future purchases aren't subsidized, the item you've purchased initially will last a long time. Even better are subsidies for technology or infrastructure from which people are unlikely to return once they have made the change. If subsidies for renewable energy make more people adopt it and thereby helped to create the infrastructure to deliver it to users, that increased adoption might then bring down the long-term cost of renewable energy. If this process makes it cost-competitive over the long run with fossil fuels, renewable energy will likely continue to be used even after subsidies are phased out.

Subsidies that create incentives to internalize externalities are deserving of greater consideration than those for other purposes. But it is for good reasons that economists warn against subsidies as a tool for behavior change.[15] Making the less desired behavior more expensive, such as through taxes, can be a better use of incentives than making the more desired behavior cheaper through subsidies. But it is often more politically palatable (especially in the United States) to change incentives through subsidies than through taxes.

Ultimately the goal of an incentives approach is to encourage the desired behavior by individuals through their own process of cost-benefit analysis; people choose an environmentally preferable behavior because that behavior (with the incentive nudge) makes the most sense for the various priorities they have. It is an explicit way to overcome the inherent structural characteristics that incentivize bad environmental behavior, or any additional policy or subsidy approaches that tilt the balance toward environmentally harmful action, to make the environmentally best option easier or less expensive than it would otherwise be. It also can feel less coercive than other policy approaches because people retain the choice: if they want to pay more to engage in behavior that causes more environmental harm, they are still able to.

NONMONETARY INCENTIVES

Even more frequently, the cost to environmentally conscious behavior is not directly economic, but comes in the form of convenience. It may be better for air pollution and climate change for me to take the train into town than to drive, but it requires adapting to the train schedule and dealing with late trains, and I need to walk to and wait at the train station (even in unpleasant weather). I could simply throw everything I discard into the trash, or I could take the extra effort to separate my recyclables into different categories and take them to the local recycling center.

Studies demonstrate the importance of nonmonetary incentives. For example, programs that give financial incentives for home insulation have lower rates of use when they require a home energy audit beforehand than when they do not.[16] Recycling rates are higher in areas with curbside pickup than in those that require people to make trips to recycling centers.[17] In many workplaces and businesses, parking is provided nearby, whereas public transportation may let people off some distance from their destination, which makes choosing public transportation more difficult.

The characteristics of the problem one is trying to solve can contribute to these types of incentives. If the one who bears the economic cost of an activity is not the one performing the task, it may not matter if the environmentally advantageous action is the least expensive; it may not be the one chosen. Take, for example, my local coffee shop. Most people who visit it get their coffee to go, but some of us want to drink coffee and eat pastries there. It is nearly impossible to persuade the people working the counter to deliver drinks and food in nondisposable dishware, though the shop has it available. Even if disposable dishware costs more, the job of the counter staff is made easier if everyone's consumables are delivered in the same manner, and using disposable dishware also reduces the amount of dish cleaning the workers need to do. As long as they are not receiving strong messages otherwise, the employees are likely to do what makes their lives easiest, regardless of the environmental consequences, which they do not directly experience.

Nonmonetary incentives may interact with more purely economic decisions. As discussed further in chapter 6, incentives can be a way to communicate social norms. Some people will change their behavior for shockingly small incentives (like the five-cent discount given for bringing a reusable mug or grocery bag) to a degree greater than the economic benefit would suggest. In these instances the incentive makes the environmentally beneficial action slightly less costly than it would otherwise be, but also serves as a signal about what the desired action is. Such a small economic incentive would be unlikely to work without the social signal and the recipient's interest in doing the right thing or avoiding social disapproval.[18]

The signaling effect of price incentives has also been found when time-of-use electricity pricing has been implemented. This approach charges consumers less to use electricity during off-peak times, when there is more spare capacity. In one study, higher prices during peak times did persuade users to switch some power use to nonpeak times. How much more expensive peak electricity was made little difference. In one experiment, some customers were charged twice as much during peak times. Other customers were charged eight times as much. Both groups changed their electricity use by about the same amount (the eightfold increase only garnered a 2 percent greater change than a price doubling).[19] Having a price differential mattered in demonstrating the preferred social choice, but its specific details were less important than that there was a differential.

There are also cases where nonmonetary incentives play a more important role than monetary ones. A British effort to encourage home insulation through subsidies found that far fewer people made use of the subsidies than economic logic would have predicted. Hypothesizing that one of the obstacles that stood in the way of choosing to make these improvements was the difficulty (both practical and psychological) of clearing out cluttered attics to make insulation possible, the British government offered access to attic-clearing services. The homeowners paid for this service, so it was more a practical than an economic benefit. The extent to which people agreed to the insulation subsidy increased dramatically.[20]

An incentives approach to changing behavior can focus on changing nonmonetary incentives. It can involve making the desired activity easier than it would otherwise be, and ideally easier than the more problematic choice would be. If a recycling bin is far away from the location in which you are about to discard waste, it requires extra effort to recycle, but if recycling bins are easy to access, that practical hurdle is overcome.[21] (In fact, making trash bins harder to find extends the incentive to recycle.) Although nonmonetary incentives rarely trump economic incentives, an attempt to make environmentally preferable actions easier as well as cheaper than other choices can contribute to the same goal, especially if these approaches can be used to frame a decision that is seen as a social good.

POSITIVE VERSUS NEGATIVE INCENTIVES

When thinking about changing incentives in an effort to make it more likely that people will make environmentally beneficial choices, consider whether the incentive change is a reward or a punishment. Is the environmentally beneficial option made cheaper (or easier), or the environmentally problematic option made more expensive (or harder)? The discussion about the role of subsidies to encourage environmental behavior versus taxes or fees to discourage problematic behavior is a part of this question.

In economic theory these two options are considered to be identical,[22] but in practice people behave differently in response to rewards versus punishments or gains versus losses, although in somewhat contradictory ways.

There is mixed evidence about which framing (rewards or punishments) makes desired behavior more likely. People prefer positive incentives.[23] Because they feel better about being rewarded than being punished, positive incentives (economic or particularly noneconomic) may help contribute to the intrinsic motivation to undertake an action in a way that negative incentives do not (as discussed further in the next section). But the effectiveness of positive incentives, unlike that of negative incentives, has been shown to decrease over time.[24] If people come to expect a reward for good behavior, that reward becomes part of their assumed frame over time; acting positively will then require increasingly large rewards for people to experience them as rewards.[25]

Negative incentives can be more effective. A framing of course grades as negative incentives (students start a course with a perfect score and have points deducted for less-than-perfect assignments along the way) causes more stress than the more common positive incentive approach (in which students start the course with zero and gain positive points for their work), but also increases student motivation.[26]

As demonstrated in chapter 6, charging customers a fee for each disposable bag used at a grocery store has a much more dramatic effect on behavior than does offering them a refund for each reusable bag they bring. That result is consistent with the "loss aversion" observation from prospect theory.[27] If people see their current situation as a default and are more concerned with avoiding losses than securing gains, the additional five cents charged for a disposable bag looms larger in the psyche than the five-cent refund for bringing a reusable bag.

There are dangers, though, when negative incentives are framed as punishments for bad behavior. When a true punishment is applied and communicated as such, it sends a social signal that has power beyond its effect as a straight incentive. In those cases, the person who receives the punishment may cooperate because of the necessity of doing so, but is likely to stop the cooperative behavior if it seems possible to get away with doing so.[28]

Someone punished with a fine for speeding may work out a more elaborate way to avoid getting caught, rather than slowing down more generally. Most negative incentives discussed in the context of environmental behavior, however, are not of this type. When the negative incentive is simply a slightly higher cost or inconvenience for the person engaging in the undesired activity, these psychological dangers may not apply.

When thinking about applying positive or negative incentives, it is also important to consider to whom the incentive will be applied. Positive incentives are given to those who perform the desired activity; if everyone performs it, everyone receives an incentive. Conversely, negative incentives apply to those who do not perform the desired activity; if all people act as intended, the incentive will not be used at all.[29]

On a policy level, that distinction has implications for the costliness of a payout or the likelihood that revenue will be generated from a tax. If a positive incentive (like a subsidy for the purchase of an environmentally preferred appliance or vehicle) must be offered to all who undertake the specified action, even those who would have undertaken the action without the subsidy, it will cost more than would be necessary for the behavior change it creates. It can be difficult to know in advance how many people will take advantage of it, and thus how much the incentive will cost. Where collective (and especially noneconomic) incentives are possible, they may help avoid this problem; a concert for everyone who has recycled a certain amount during the year costs the same amount to provide no matter how many people qualify for it.

Negative incentives are less costly. A negative incentive is less frequently applied the more the people engage in the desired behavior. Depending on how these incentives are designed, negative incentives may even generate revenue (in the case of a tax on undesired behavior). The fact that they can bring in revenue makes them easier to implement, and perhaps even desired by policymakers who can make use of that revenue. But from a policy perspective, negative incentives can lead to other difficulties: those who come to rely on revenue from a tax on undesired behavior may suffer when the behavior becomes less frequent and revenue drops. In the worst cases, such as when governments receive significant revenue from cigarette taxes, this downside of success can lead bureaucracies to work less hard to get people to stop smoking: if they do stop smoking, they stop paying the cigarette tax, and the revenue stream dries up.[30] Similarly, towns that earn a lot of revenue from speeding tickets may not want to decrease speeding.

Positive incentives can thus be particularly useful when selective action by a few people can have an important effect on the outcome. An example is a public good, as when a few wealthy donors contributing to the upkeep of a public park can provide sufficient funding to keep it operational. But when participation of almost everyone is important, negative incentives are likely to be more effective.[31] These conditions are more likely to apply in common pool resource problems, which is what we encounter with most environmental problems. The ability of negative economic incentives to bring in revenue can help their implementation, as long as the revenue does not lead to dependency that encourages the continuation of the behavior in question.

INTRINSIC VERSUS EXTRINSIC MOTIVATION

A focus on incentives as a cause for environmental behavior relies on extrinsic motivation, the impulse to do something based on external rewards or costs. In addition to asking whether these external factors lead to better behavior, an important question to ask is what they do to intrinsic motivation, the internal impulses people have for behavior. What message does changing incentive structures send about the reasons for undertaking action? What effect does that message have on how people act in the long term?

There is some evidence that, as economist Bruno Frey puts it, "the use of extrinsic incentives may crowd out intrinsic" motivation.[32] The argument is that if there are both internal and external reasons for people to do something, the latter is what we think of as the reason for our action.[33] In other words, we forget that we were doing something because of its actual merit, and come to think that we are doing it because of the reward we receive. This effect has generally been observed in the context of work, but can be applied to other behaviors as well. The earliest analysis of this phenomenon came from willingness to donate blood when it was considered an altruistic act versus when people were paid for doing so.[34] The altruistic feelings that might be engaged by doing a good activity get subsumed, or replaced, by the extrinsic motivation.

Another early study showed that university students paid to solve an interesting puzzle were less likely to play with it in their spare time than students who were not paid. In this case the act of puzzle solving was not altruistic, but being paid for it turned it into something instrumental. Once it was experienced as instrumental, it became less appealing. The same thing was true when the external motivation was a punishment or negative feedback for failure, rather than a reward. Verbal rewards (positive encouragement about puzzle solving) increased intrinsic motivation, however.[35] It may be that verbal encouragement is similar to the internal feeling of satisfaction one gets from successfully completing a puzzle and may therefore not crowd out the intrinsic motivation. It may even augment the positive feelings experienced.[36]

A similar phenomenon was observed with preschool children who, on their own, indicated interest in a drawing exercise. Those who learned before they drew that they would be rewarded with certificates for drawing later showed less interest in drawing on their own than did children who received certificates without having been promised them in advance or who were not told about, and received no, certificates.[37] It wasn't the reward itself, but the form of the reward—the fact that it was contingent on participation—that dampened intrinsic motivation. These results have been replicated across a wide variety of populations and tasks.[38]

It may also be that the mere offering of an external incentive changes the way people view an activity: it must be undesirable from an intrinsic perspective, or people would not be offering an incentive to undertake it.[39] A bigger problem is that these "rewards" for the desired behavior may work, but their effectiveness will diminish over time. The incentive simply becomes a part of the background (expected) condition.[40] Not only might it be difficult to phase out the incentive and retain the expected behavior, but the incentive may need to be increased over time to produce the same level of behavior.[41]

This finding rests uneasily with environmental legislation, which is often difficult to pass and is thus hard to modify once it has been created. Consider bottle bills, passed in some US states, that require a deposit for each returnable bottle or can and a refund when it is returned. These bills were dramatic successes when introduced,[42] but the amount of the deposit is static, not adjusted for inflation. It has thus decreased in real terms. The first bottle deposit in the United States was a five-cent deposit introduced in Oregon in 1971. With inflation over time, the value of that nickel has declined by more than 83 percent.[43] The bottle return rate is also much higher in areas with higher deposit levels,[44] suggesting that the decreasing real value of bottle deposits may have a problematic effect on returns.

Negative external incentives—such as fines or punishment for unde-sired behavior—can have a slightly different crowding-out effect. In this case they crowd out the intrinsic motivation for behaving well. One study unexpectedly found this relationship in day-care center pickup times. Staff had to stay after work if parents were late to pick up their children. As part of a study, the center created a policy of fining parents for each late pickup. Instead of the expected decrease in late pickups, they increased. The researchers attributed the change to the economic motive crowding out the natural concern the parents had for the teachers that led them to try not to inconvenience them.[45] It is also possible that the policy trans-lated what had been a noneconomic incentive into an economic one; par-ents felt justified in being late once they were paying for the privilege of doing so.

Introducing incentives can also decrease cooperation. People gener-ally value reciprocity. They are concerned with mutual benefit, especially with others with whom they have a social relationship, rather than being concerned only with their own well-being. That leads people to be will-ing to cooperate, especially conditionally (depending on the coopera-tion of others) to a greater extent than economic theory would predict.[46]

Experiments suggest that cooperation among groups decreases when an explicit incentive (be it positive or negative) is introduced into the cooperation.[47] Cooperation declines even further when the incentives are negative rather than positive. Since solving most environmental problems requires reciprocity and cooperation, this effect is worrisome.

The problems created for intrinsic motivation by external incentives are only a problem if there is intrinsic motivation in the first place.[48] So if the desired behavior was demonstrably not taking place, the addition of incentives for environmental behavior might be less problematic.

When do external incentives create problems for existing internal motivation? Primarily when they are considered to be "controlling." If they instead are seen as simply providing information, like positive feedback, they are not harmful to motivation. Along the same lines, rewards (positive incentives) are less problematic for intrinsic motivation than are commands. But the more the reward is contingent on specific performance, the more problematic it is for intrinsic motivation, and monetary incentives are more problematic than nonmonetary in this context.[49]

Not all incentives are equal. It is not only whether a reward is contingent that matters (and whether it is positive or negative), but also its monetary nature. If a reward isn't money, its problematic effect generally disappears. The findings that external rewards for blood donation decrease intrinsic motivation to donate disappear when there is a nonmonetary incentive that makes it easier to donate blood: an Italian policy that gave people time off work to facilitate blood donation increased willingness to donate.[50] This experience suggests that nonmonetary incentives or processes that make it easier to engage in the desired behavior are helpful rather than problematic.

It may also be that using smaller incentives can avoid these problems. Experiments have demonstrated that when people are paid for performance, they do worse the higher the incentive pay.[51] A small incentive may persuade people to try a new activity or behavior (like bring a reusable bag for groceries or mug for coffee); once they have tried the behavior, they must then "find their own reasons" for continuing, since the incentive isn't strong enough on its own to compel behavior. They may then continue it even after the incentive is withdrawn.[52]

The incentive in this case may serve as a form of procedural information (discussed further in chapter 4), in which people are encouraged to learn how to do something; once they know how to do it, their need for the incentive disappears. A discount—or even free fares—for riding a new bus route might lead people to discover the ease or advantages of taking the bus. Once they've tried it, if it is indeed convenient, they will be more likely to take it even when they have to pay the full fare.

Many of the studies of the influence of external incentives on intrinsic motivation take place in the context of education or work; are they relevant in the context of daily, often routine, environmental behavior? Even if they are, these studies have tended to show that the dampening effect of incentives is less problematic for repeated, formulaic action.[53] If recycling or taking public transportation involves habit rather than innovation, giving people incentives to do them may not dampen their intrinsic motivation.

In fact, the more routine the task, the more likely external incentives are to work.[54] Edward Deci and his coauthors point out that "rewards do not undermine people's intrinsic motivation for dull tasks because there is little or no intrinsic motivation to be undermined."[55] For basic daily environmental routines—turning off lights, putting out recycling—their uninteresting nature makes them suitable candidates for effective incentives.

The effect of external incentives on intrinsic motivation matters for the design and continuation of incentive-based programs. If providing incentives for action creates a situation in which people will only undertake the desired behavior in the presence of these incentives, we should know that when designing policy. One early study of incentives-based recycling programs observed that, in that almost all such programs, recycling decreases or stops once the external incentive is removed.[56] Those who use incentives should be careful to choose those that can be applied over the long term.

At the same time, if external incentives identify socially desirable behavior, it helps us understand why small economic incentives change behavior more than expected. And since there is no downside to intrinsic motivation in making the desired task behavior easier to undertake, non-monetary positive incentives are especially useful.

REBOUND EFFECTS

Inefficient use of natural resources causes environmental problems. The more efficiently we can use resources—the more we accomplish with a smaller input of energy, for instance—the less environmental damage we will cause with any given activity. There are natural incentives to use resources efficiently. If we overuse resources, they become scarcer. Because of the characteristics of markets, scarce resources become more costly. This price signal can lead to innovation in technology, because it will be cost-effective to buy technology that allows us to accomplish something with less resource use. A new car may be able to travel farther on a gallon of gasoline, for instance, and the person who produces one will benefit from those of us who want a car that uses less gasoline.

The concepts of supply and demand, which are central to market capitalism (discussed further in chapter 2) create a natural incentive to find ways to use resources more efficiently. This process can be augmented by policy-based incentives. A fuel tax that causes prices to increase will activate the incentive to innovate ways to achieve more with less gasoline.

You would think that efficiency would be wholly positive when it comes to resource use. But economist William Stanley Jevons noted in the nineteenth century that using energy resources more efficiently could increase their overall use. In what has come to be known as the Jevons paradox, he observed that what he called the more "economical" use of coal in mechanical processes during the Industrial Revolution increased the demand for coal.[57] He illustrated this effect primarily with coal used for iron manufacture. As processes were developed that allowed for greater efficiency, iron could be produced less expensively and thus used in previously unforeseen ways, increasing demand for iron and thus the use of coal overall, even though the coal was used more efficiently than previously. Similarly, because coal can be used more efficiently in some production processes, it can be deployed for new uses.

This paradox works through price signals. As use of a resource becomes more efficient, its cost decreases. As a result, you can use more of that resource because it costs less. We might think that greater efficiency would enable us to use less of the resource overall because we could use less of it to accomplish what we were previously accomplishing. Instead of using less, we come up with additional ways to use that resource. Some scholars refer to this phenomenon as the "rebound effect."[58] The rebound may not be complete; the amount of energy newly used with decreasing cost may not exactly equal the amount saved by increased efficiency. But what is clear is that the amount used will not remain constant as prices change. In other words, there are a number of ways increased energy efficiency can lead to increased use of energy, directly or indirectly.[59]

Direct effects are observed in production: increased efficiency in energy use in a process simply makes it easier (that is, less costly) for us to use more if it. But indirect effects can also make a major difference in overall energy use. The technology that allows for efficiency itself frequently requires energy to produce and transport, which consumes some of the energy savings from direct use. For example, insulation that reduces the amount of energy required for heating requires energy to produce. So using more insulation (to decrease energy use) itself uses energy.

Other effects are at the level of the economy more broadly. If the cost of energy decreases because we use it more efficiently, the economy will produce more goods. They can be made more cheaply, so they can be sold at a lower cost, and consumers will buy more of them. Making more goods will require more energy, so the overall energy use may not decrease, even if each product is made using less energy.

A similar effect can be seen in energy markets. Increased efficiency leads to decreased energy prices, which can lead to increased use of energy used to make things. The decreased cost of energy inputs reduces the cost of goods and services that require a lot of energy to produce. If it now costs less than it used to to buy things that were made in a way that used more energy, we will be more likely to buy them and more of them will be sold, contributing to an increased use of energy.

The way these processes operate at the individual level is through consumer behavior. For consumers, decreased costs lead to savings; that money can then be spent on other consumer goods or services that themselves have energy inputs, eliminating any overall energy savings from increased efficiency. In other words, if you can save money by heating your house more efficiently, you may decide to fly to an exotic location for a vacation, thereby using additional energy.

There are arguments about whether these processes, when added together, completely eliminate the energy savings (referred to as "backfire") or simply decrease the expected extent of savings (referred to as "rebound"). The broader point for the purpose of this analysis is that efficiency may not provide as much environmental benefit as might be expected. It is part of the observation that human agency is an important— and undervalued—component of any estimation.[60]

The price mechanism is central to the operation of this paradox. As Jevons noted, "It is the very economy of its use which leads to its extensive consumption."[61] If how much of something you use depends on its cost (what economists call "price elasticity"), it is a candidate for the Jevons paradox. But there may be other processes that have a similar effect. Might people who drive fuel-efficient cars feel so noble about their behavior that they increase the distances they drive, since they no longer feel that their automobile has a negative environmental effect?

Resources other than coal have been the focus of studies of this paradox, though it most frequently involves energy use of some kind. Imagine, for instance, the increasing efficiency of electric lighting. Over the last couple centuries the efficiency of lighting has increased dramatically—more illumination can be provided per unit of price. As illumination has become more efficient, societies have used more of it, in ways that may have wiped out any benefits from efficiency gains.[62]

Increasing efficiency of electricity use has had Jevons-like effects across a variety of uses. As appliances are made in ways that use less and less energy, it becomes realistic to use more and more of them. Air conditioning in the United States provides an example. The efficiency of residential air conditioning increased by 28 percent between 1993 and 2005; during that period the household consumption of energy used in air conditioning increased by 37 percent.[63]

A similar process can be seen in car use. As a result of a combination of natural price increases and regulatory requirements, automobile engineering has produced vehicles that can do more from a given unit of energy input. A direct result, from a consumer perspective, would be if those who own more fuel-efficient cars respond by driving more. There is some evidence of this phenomenon, although it may be small.[64] Indirect effects are also likely. An automobile owner who does not increase driving distances in response to increased fuel efficiency will have more disposable income. If that income is used to purchase additional consumer goods or take a vacation, the energy savings in automobile fuel are used elsewhere by that person. Even more important are indirect effects at the society level. If cars become more fuel efficient, it becomes relatively less expensive to own or drive one, which may lead to increased car ownership and increased driving overall.

These society-level rebound effects of fuel efficiency can be seen with light trucks in the United States, demonstrating the Jevons argument. In the United States the increasing efficiency of the light-duty truck fleet over a seventeen-year period led to greater fuel use by the fleet.[65] First, as light trucks became more fuel efficient, companies produced—and people bought—trucks that were heavier than those previously used. The size increased at a faster rate than the fuel efficiency; in other words, fuel use increased per truck, even though trucks were on the whole more fuel efficient. Second, light trucks (pushed in part by automobile manufacturers) became a greater proportion of automobile sales.[66] And third, the distance traveled on average by each light truck owner increased.[67]

Might the Jevons paradox appear among nonenergy resources? Paper use in the context of computer technology has also been analyzed as displaying a Jevons-type effect. When computers became more prevalent, many observers imagined that the use of paper would decrease, because it was not necessary to retype a document to fix an error, as it had been in the era of typewriters. (One can consider this a case of substituting one process for another, rather than greater efficiency of production, but with the same effect.) But paper use has generally—and often dramatically—increased within offices.[68] Although electronic communication and information storage are substitutes for paper, the efficiency of printing increased, and it became easier and more cost-effective to use paper than it previously had been.

Another resource to which the concept has been applied is food production. Producing food more efficiently may lead societies to eat differently, consuming more meat and dairy products. These foods are higher on the food chain: they require more inputs and are thus produced less efficiently than grains and vegetables. (You get more energy from the grain that goes into feeding a cow than you get from the cow, for instance.)

This changed diet, possible because these more energy-intensive forms of food are relatively cheaper than before, diminishes the benefits of the efficiency gains. At minimum, increasing levels of wealth (to which decreasing food prices contribute) lead societies to eat higher on the food chain,[69] which is a less efficient way to eat.

There are those who doubt the existence, or relevance, of the Jevons effect for environmental resources today. Some critics argue that these rebound effects are overstated.[70] At the individual level, at least, it is rare for the increased efficiency of a light bulb to increase lighting enough to cancel out the beneficial effect. If I move to high-efficiency LEDs, which use one-tenth the energy of incandescent bulbs, I'm unlikely to light my house by ten times as much. Physicist Amory Lovins agrees that any rebound effects are likely to be much smaller than the efficiency improvements. At the societal level, if people expand their use of energy, it comes from increased wealth rather than energy efficiency per se. Attributing the full extent of rising incomes directly to energy efficiency is misguided.[71] Lee Schipper, another physicist, argues that Jevons was right for the time and resources he was writing about, but is of limited applicability today; the effects he observed will be felt only where energy is a particularly large component of the cost of the product or process.[72]

The broader lesson to draw is that any analysis of the benefits of efficiency gains has to consider the potential rebound effects, which work primarily through price and the incentive it creates. It seems unlikely that a rebound would come close to eliminating the efficiency gains at the individual level. For instance, the rebound effect of the efficiency of a given appliance is likely to be small or nonexistent,[73] except for a few appliances (like freezers), in which case consumers might continue to use older ones in addition to newly bought more efficient ones. But looking only at the individual level misses the environmental point. Many of the effects, if they exist, are likely to be indirect. Decreasing costs of refrigeration or air conditioning or lighting means that much more of both are used at a societal level; it is there where the rebound effects are likely to be greatest.

At the level of society, though, it becomes harder to measure just how much rebound there is, or from what cause. The variety of factors that contribute to collective behavior are numerous enough that the efficiency contribution is likely not the only relevant aspect. Increased overall wealth, which comes from a variety of factors (of which increased efficiency is only one) likely plays a key role. Nevertheless, the relationship of individual-level behavior to aggregate social behavior is important for understanding the effects of increased efficiency on resource use. Individual incentives have effects that reverberate far beyond individuals.

INCENTIVES AND ENVIRONMENTAL CHOICES

Most of the time, doing the right environmental thing is harder, or more costly, than the alternative. Even if we care about the environment, most of us have limited time and resources and have many concerns to keep track of. And plenty of people don't prioritize the environment; for them the extra difficulty or expense virtually guarantees that they will not go out of their way to make environmentally preferable choices. Incentives are thus key for understanding, and addressing, environmental behavior. Most notably, changing incentives so that the environmentally preferably choice is cheaper or easier than other options entices people who might not prioritize the environment to reduce their environmental impact.

4

Information

Environmental activists, with the best of intentions, often begin with the assumption that if only people understood the environmental damage they cause, they would change their behavior. If you have ever encountered a sign on a paper towel dispenser telling you, "These come from trees," or on the office photocopy machine telling you how many trees had to be cut down to produce the paper, you have been the beneficiary of this type of thinking.

This approach is appealing and widespread.[1] For those of us who teach for a living, it is encouraging that so many people think of education as a productive route for changing environmental behavior. The trouble is it almost never works. That is not to say that information can't play a role in influencing environmental behavior, in both a negative and positive direction. But the kind of information that changes behavior is not the kind that raises public or individual awareness of a problem, the individual's contribution to it, or the importance of addressing it, at least not in a universe in which most of us understand the basic nature of environmental problems. As sociologist Thomas Heberlein puts it, "Educating the public doesn't work."[2] Psychologists Gerald Gardner and Paul Stern make the only slightly more modest argument that "even the best educational programs cannot overcome external barriers to action, such as financial expense or serious inconvenience."[3]

In part the ineffectiveness of information comes from the problem characteristics and incentives that create environmental problems, discussed in chapters 2 and 3. When my father was in the intensive care unit in the hospital, I knew about—and even cared about—the environmental problems caused by plastic waste. But at that point my primary concern was his health, and the enormous waste caused by the procedures to ensure sterility was much lower on my agenda than was ensuring that he did not get a life-threatening infection.

Even though I knew enough to be horrified at the plastic waste (and am enough of an activist and an academic to try to figure out how processes could be arranged to decrease it), the last thing I was going to do was interfere with the hospital processes that produced that waste in the course of saving my father's life. It was simply an externality of some other priority both I and the healthcare workers had. The incentives were aligned such that the hospital did not bear the economic cost of its plastic waste and benefited from the added convenience that single-use plastic packaging provided. The healthcare workers and administrators had little incentive to rethink the procedures that contributed to waste or come up with approaches that would ensure sterility (and easy and quick access to medically necessary paraphernalia) while decreasing the amount of plastic waste. Lack of information about the problem of plastic waste had nothing to do with our contribution to creating it, and presenting more information would not have been the way to change anyone's behavior.

Presenting environmentally relevant information is not useless. Some highly motivated people will be willing to prioritize environmental benefits over other values, and information may help them figure out the best course of action. Likewise, in cases where the better environmental choice may not be obvious and choosing it is not a hardship, information may help. While knowledge is not itself a motive for environmental behavior, "lack of knowledge can be a barrier."[4] Information is key in another way: many environmental problems are caused by actions or products that no one initially knew had serious environmental externalities. At the heart of moving to both individually and collectively responsible environmental choices is understanding the processes that create environmental problems.

But information is rarely the panacea that many activists and policy-makers assume it is. One estimate suggests that provision of information can change behavior by no more than 10–20 percent, and that result holds only for simple behaviors that do not require much effort, inconvenience, or expense. Even then, the effect of information is likely to be modest and short-lived.[5]

The behavior that can be changed by information, moreover, is rarely the most environmentally relevant behavior that individuals engage in.

A starting point for the importance of information comes in basic research about the causes and consequences of an environmental problem. Without an understanding of how serious an environmental problem is and what activities contribute to it, it is difficult to consider any useful change of behavior or policy to create that change. This type of information, though it is essential, is not usually what people mean when they talk about education or information as a way to change environmental behavior. And at this moment in time, in most societies, this background level of knowledge already exists.

When considering the effects of this most common approach to environmentally relevant education, what matters is what people are being educated *about*. Education that attempts to change attitudes is unlikely to make a major behavioral difference for two reasons (discussed in greater detail in chapter 6). First, attitudes are generally stable, so changing them is difficult and time-consuming. Second, the relationship between attitudes and behavior is indirect. Many environmental problems are caused by the behavior of people who care about protecting the environment. So contributing to the development of attitudes rarely translates directly into changed behavior.

Beyond attitudes comes education about impacts of behavior. Although I may be concerned about environmental issues and prioritize behavior that won't harm the environment, I may not actually know whether (for instance) natural gas or oil contributes more to climate change, or whether recycling aluminum is more energy intensive than recycling glass. Information of this type may be politicized. Those who would be economically harmed if we acted to protect the environment may try to provide misleading information; they fear that if people know that certain actions harm the environment, they will change how they act or politicians will create policy to prevent environmental harm. That politicization of information about environmental harms, unfortunately, makes it even less likely to lead to the desired behavior change.

One potentially useful form of information contributes to what might be called "procedural knowledge";[6] information about how to do the desired activity, be it recycling (When is it collected? How should it be sorted? What types of things can be included in the recycling?) or energy conservation (How do I program my thermostat? Whom do I call for an energy audit? What is the process for changing from oil to natural gas for home heating?). Education here is practical; it simply seeks to inform people about what they should be doing to correctly implement a choice they have already made. Of the types of information that can be provided, this type has the clearest and most direct relationship to behavior change.

Feedback provided to people about what their actual behavior is, or prompts reminding people about an action, can be useful as well. These responses help people who already want to behave in a certain way to ensure that they are doing so. Eco-labels and mandating the provision of information allow people who seek information about the environmental effect of their choices to find it, although far fewer make use of this information than say that they will. As with other information strategies, these approaches work best when the structures and incentives favoring pro-environmental action are also aligned. All information strategies are also filtered through existing cognitive biases that influence the way people take in and respond to information. Understanding the regularities in these biases may help those who want to frame environmental choices in ways that people are most likely to respond.

Finally, education in a broader sense, focusing on teaching children about environmental issues and values, may have long-term effects. When approached in ways that orient people's attitudes, it can create generational effects in how people approach environmental issues. This kind of approach is unlikely to change immediate behavior, but in the long term it can move society more generally in an environmentally friendly direction.

Information can thus make a difference in behavior, but that difference is both more modest and more specific than those who focus on environmental education foresee. Many of the roles that information does play in changing behavior work in conjunction with other approaches; it may be difficult to determine how much of the effect is actually from education. That is not a knock on information strategies, but a reminder that they must be designed with consideration for the broader causes of environmentally relevant behavior.

WHY INFORMATION IS INSUFFICIENT

When doing the environmentally correct thing is more costly, more difficult, or unlikely (because of collective action problems) to result in an environmental benefit, it is not surprising that information about the problem or desired behavior will not persuade most people to change their behavior.

In industrialized democracies, most people are already aware of, and concerned about, environmental problems.[7] Whatever effect could be achieved by providing basic information has already happened. So the role of information in explaining or changing behavior must be considered in this context.

The two forms of education with which this chapter begins—informing people about the consequences of their actions, and persuading them that they should be concerned about environmental problems—have been demonstrated repeatedly to have little effect on behavior, for reasons that social science can help explain.

People who are not already concerned about environmental issues are unlikely to be motivated by information about their own environmental impact. Even those who are concerned might not change their behavior after a rational calculation of its costs and benefits.

The second approach is an attempt to change attitudes by small-scale intervention. Chapter 6 discusses the formation and role of attitudes in greater detail; they can indeed contribute to environmental behavior (although they do so less than one might imagine). But for the purposes of this chapter, the important observation is that attitudes are extremely difficult to change except in the long run. And however they are developed, environmental attitudes have a tenuous relationship with behavior. So information plays little role in changing attitudes in the short run, and attitudes have a surprisingly small relationship with environmental behavior. We need to rethink what role information can play.

Informing people of the basic cause-and-effect relationship between their actions and environmental problems has been shown not to have a strong effect on attitudes or behavior. But there are still ways that information contributes to the creation, or resolution, of environmental problems. Understanding them is important for figuring out why people behave the way they do.

SCIENTIFIC KNOWLEDGE

The first stage of information is a basic scientific understanding of the relationship between human behavior and environmental damage. Because environmental problems are externalities, they are often created not only without intention, but also without knowledge of the environmental harm. Ozone depletion, from CFCs and halons, is one such example. Acid rain, created in locations that are not where the electricity is generated, is another. Similarly, the health effects of many persistent organic pollutants (especially in remote areas where people were not using them) were entirely unanticipated. When a problem is completely new, disseminating information about it is important. But once a level of basic understanding is widespread, providing more information has little beneficial effect.

Knowing that there is an environmental problem but not knowing the extent to which you are affected by it can also prevent action to address it. This lack of knowledge can be a factor for individuals but is particularly important at the level of political jurisdictions. One of the most useful aspects of the agreement to address acid rain in Europe required that states conduct assessments of their own resources and the extent to which they were being harmed by acid rain. It was only when Germany did forest surveys (including of its iconic Black Forest) that it discovered that it already faced serious forest destruction from acid rain.[8] This information changed Germany's position on binding emissions controls. This information made Germany willing to regulate, changing how electricity was generated. That, in turn, meant that individual users of electricity—whether they cared or even knew about acid rain—became less likely to cause environmental harm by their behavior.

Most scientific information relates to our understanding about the environmental issue at the problem level, rather than relating directly to individual behavior. Individuals' level of information about what specific activities contribute to specific environmental problems might be expected to be useful, but this information can cut both ways.

Uncertainty can be a hindrance to individual environmental action. If people genuinely don't know what the best environmental action to take is, or whether that action will have the desired effect, they are less willing to undertake it, especially if there are other incentives that do not prioritize it. At my college there was a period of time when custodians were, in some cases, simply throwing out the carefully separated paper in the recycling bins. Once people became aware of the possibility that their recycling efforts (which at that time required walking down the hall to find the recycling bins, rather than simply throwing paper in their nearby trash can) were not having the desired effect, it became much harder to persuade people to go through the extra trouble to recycle.

Industry actors have learned to play up—or even manufacture—this type of uncertainty. In the United States the fossil fuel industry has funded think tanks that produce studies of questionable academic quality designed to cast doubt on the processes of climate change or human contributions to it,[9] in an effort to prevent people from pushing for policy action or taking individual steps to prevent climate change.

A less obvious effort to deceive with information is the use of life-cycle assessment to cause confusion over what the best environmental alternative is. Life-cycle assessment (or analysis—LCA) is an important tool for calculating environmental costs over the entire life of a product or process. It looks at the environmental harms cradle to grave, or back to cradle in the case of recycling or reuse. The idea is that environmental problems may be caused at different stages (extraction of resources, manufacturing, transport, use, disposal, etc.) of the life cycle, and that the only way to gain a full understanding of the environmental harms or benefits of an action, or to compare different products or processes, is to look across the entire life cycle.

This logic is sound, but because of the vagaries of calculating LCAs, it is possible to use such analysis to make false arguments or to sow confusion. For instance, it has been demonstrated via LCA that riding a bicycle is more harmful to the environment than driving an SUV: since riding a bicycle is good for your health, you are likely to live longer—and thus cause greater environmental damage over your extended lifespan—if you ride a bicycle rather than drive an SUV.[10] Similarly, the argument has been made that walking is more environmentally harmful than driving, assuming that those who walk will need to consume more food, and assuming that the extra calories consumed will match the environmental harmfulness of the standard American diet.[11]

This type of analysis has been applied in efforts to confuse people about environmental choices. The consulting firm CNW posted an LCA in 2007 arguing that the Toyota Prius had a worse energy impact than a Hummer SUV.[12] The analysis was picked up by a number of right-wing news outlets but then was subject to more transparent analysis by environmental organizations that debunked most of its findings. These new analyses suggested that the original report used selective data and "untenable assumptions."[13] But many people only heard about the original, misleading, LCA.

Similar efforts were undertaken by the plastic industry when jurisdictions around the world began to limit the use of disposable plastic bags. Industry groups sponsored websites claiming that the environmental effects of plastic bags were much less than paper bags, often via unproven or unquestionable assumptions (and through picking and choosing which environmental effects to focus on).[14]

True non-politically motivated LCAs can provide useful information that helps frame decisions about environmentally preferable alternatives and determines where in a life cycle the worst environmental impacts are. They can help determine reasonable alternatives to environmentally damaging products or processes, especially when they do not pick a comparison designed to produce an industry's favored outcome. For example, the best comparison to the environmental harms of a disposable plastic bag is not a disposable paper bag, even if it is less environmentally harmful; it is a nondisposable bag.

But the economically or politically motivated information that is put forward by people seeking to prevent policy or behavior changes that would hurt their economic interests complicates the information landscape. It increases confusion among people who want to avoid environmental harm and wonder what the best option is. Journalists, trained in a tradition of showing "both sides" of an issue, help bring prominence to these industry-promoted studies even when the broad scientific consensus discounts them.[15]

This kind of information increases the uncertainty people feel about environmental issues and actions. The public, it turns out, is extremely sensitive to perceptions of scientific dissent or uncertainty. Political scientists Michaël Aklin and Johannes Urpelainen conducted a survey-based study to determine at what level of purported scientific dissent the public was likely to support action to address an environmental problem. Those who were told about the scientific details of the problem but not given any information on the percentage of scientists who believed in the credibility of that information were reasonably likely to support action on the issue. These people also generally believed that the problem was accurately described. Those who received information about the level of scientific acceptance of the hypothesis about the existence and cause, however, were less likely to support action or to believe that the problem was real. While that might be a reasonable reaction when people were told that only 60 percent of scientists believe the credibility of the results (the first treatment), the same held true when it was reported that 80 percent or even 98 percent, of all scientists accepted the results.[16] These results suggest that efforts to create the impression of dissent, even when there is a high level of consensus, can dramatically decrease the extent to which people believe in, or support remedies for, environmental problems.

PROCEDURAL KNOWLEDGE

The most directly useful role of information in changing behavior comes from providing information about how to act effectively to people who already prefer to act in an environmentally responsible manner. Even in this context, the types of actions that can be influenced through information are primarily simple and easy.

Public health studies illustrate this observation well. In one study, researchers were trying to find out whether scaring people about tetanus would increase the likelihood that they would get tetanus vaccinations. As is further explained later in this chapter, motivation by fear largely failed. But what turned out to be effective was providing information about where to go to get the shot.[17] Similar results were found with smokers, who were not persuaded to stop smoking by efforts to increase their fear of the dangers of smoking, but were much more likely to stop when given instructions on how to stop.[18]

In a metastudy of recycling behavior, the strongest predictor of level of recycling was this type of procedural knowledge about how to recycle.[19] The same has been found across a wide range of behaviors.[20] There are reasons to be skeptical of the causal direction of this relationship, however. It may be true that people with the greatest procedural knowledge are the most likely to engage in a given behavior, but that does not prove that it is the knowledge that leads to the behavior. It's possible that a third factor, such as level of environmental concern, is correlated with both, and it is likely that engaging in the behavior is what imparts the procedural knowledge.

Despite that caveat, helping people understand how to engage in a behavior they are perfectly happy to undertake does increase their likelihood of doing it, at least a little bit and in the short term. This is where labeling and prompts (discussed below) can be useful. An important determinant of recycling behavior is the clarity of the information about what can be recycled and about how and where to recycle; if this kind of procedural information is made available in ways that are easy to understand and notice, people are much more likely to recycle.[21]

My students recently discovered the importance of procedural information. In a study of which information strategies were most successful in increasing recycling rates in college dormitories, they measured how many items were in the "wrong" place, such as recyclable materials in the trash. Most of their information strategies increased the number of items in the recycling bins. But that increase included dramatically more nonrecyclable items in recycling bins, or recyclable items in the wrong bins, such as cans in the paper recycling. The various strategies they used to increase awareness of, and concern for, recycling did so—but residents lacked the knowledge of what was recyclable or not and which bins items should go into. In the absence of clear and accessible information about how to recycle, increasing interest in recycling will not accomplish its intended goal.

Procedural information has been found to be especially useful when a program is new or has undergone a change. In the case of college dormitories the program may not be new, but the students may be. People need to be informed at those moments, and that information can have a big effect on behavior. Additionally, if the procedures to be followed are complex,[22] people can benefit from regular reminders about (for instance) which materials can be recycled or how to use a piece of technology they use only infrequently. My town's recycling center requires us to sort our recycling into an astonishing number of different subcategories, and if it weren't for the signs at the facility reminding me which category egg cartons go into, I would never remember.

The importance of procedural knowledge also suggests the usefulness of keeping environmentally beneficial processes as simple and consistent as possible. If recycling is picked up every week in curbside programs (rather than only some weeks) and on the same day each week, it will be easier for people to remember on which day they should put recycling out. Keeping procedures simple makes procedural information easier to communicate.

FEEDBACK

It is also useful to provide information to people about their own behavior. Letting people know how much energy they are using on a daily (or even hourly) basis, or which activities or appliances are using the most energy, allows them to modify their behavior in useful ways. As with other types of information, however, its effects on behavior are likely to be modest.

It can be surprisingly difficult to know how much energy or water you are using or how efficiently you are driving. Although people should be able to find out this kind of information, it is often difficult to access, at least in usable form. Most standard feedback about utility use comes from a monthly bill, which appears too infrequently for people to connect it to specific actions. Even if people can read their own electricity or water meters, they are unlikely to be able to determine what behaviors contribute most to their energy or water use. And they have to think to go looking for that information, something they are unlikely to do in the midst of a crowded life. Making this feedback easily accessible can be useful.

Providing this kind of feedback can be even more powerful in organizations or businesses that can collect information about behavior of subunits but do not necessarily think to do so. The dining services at my college provided a recent example of the power of information in this context. A group project by students in one of my courses focused on decreasing student use of disposable cups in the dining halls. My students were convinced that they could persuade other students to stop choosing disposable cups if information was presented to them about how problematic these cups are. I was dubious that such a project would succeed, for reasons anyone reading this book is now familiar with.

The students never had the chance to find out, because the information they gathered succeeded in ways they had not intended. As part of their project, they went to all the dining halls to collect baseline information about how many cups were being given out. Each dining hall gathered and provided that information, and the students were shocked to discover that students on campus were using 2.5 disposable cups per student per day. They were not the only ones who were shocked: the dining services management had not previously gathered that information either. When faced with the stark numbers on what was, for the organization, costly waste, dining services removed disposable cups at all meals other than breakfast. Information hadn't been gathered or examined, and once it was, it provided the impetus for change.

There are good psychological reasons that feedback affects behavior. People usually prefer to save energy or water, either for reasons of environmental concern or for the cost savings. Feedback lets people know if they are successfully accomplishing a task they already want to undertake.[23] Dining services undertook a change, in the example above, because of the cost of providing disposable cups. It was a change adminstrators wanted to make once they knew the relevant information.

Feedback also can serve an educational purpose, teaching people about the relationships between their behavior and their environmental effect. With feedback about my water use, I may learn that the toilets in my house are the biggest users of water, and that it is more effective to save water by installing a water-saving toilet or flushing less often than by going through a daily effort to try to shorten my showers. Without some type of learning, user behavior that might have been influenced in the short term by new feedback may revert to old patterns once the feedback is no longer new.[24] This learning may lead to new habits, addressed further in chapter 5, that help to cement longer-term changes in behavior. Or if information leads to a change in infrastructure—like new water-saving toilets—daily decisions to decrease water use are no longer required.

Useful feedback must be "clear, immediate, and user-specific."[25] People need to understand the information being presented, and it should be in a format that is consistent with how they best comprehend it. Users of smart meters in one study found energy information presented in CO_2 emissions meaningless because that was not how they thought about energy, whereas information about costs or savings was more useful.[26] Some kind of comparative framework is also useful for making information easy to interpret, such as a comparison with previous behavior, like energy use compared to the same month in the preceding year. And, as discussed further in chapter 6, comparison to other groups, such as neighbors, can be a motivator to align with collective norms.

The closer in time to the behavior the feedback is given, the more useful it is likely to be.[27] Direct feedback, in which users can determine in real time what the effect of their behavior is, is both most effective in influencing behavior and preferred by users.[28] Although most of the analysis of feedback looks at real-time information, other less-intensive forms of information given to people about their behavior can be useful. The format of electricity bills has been widely studied to examine how to give feedback in a way that will have the greatest effect on behavior. One study in Oslo found that presenting actual usage statistics more frequently, and providing comparative use statistics, resulted in a 10 percent reduction in use of electricity over the study period.[29]

Feedback also needs to be given in a way that will cause people to notice it, both initially, and over time. Information that people have to seek out will get much less attention than information that appears without effort in ways that are easy to interpret. But even easy-to-notice information may become less useful once it is no longer new. Studies of real-time energy or water monitors suggest that after an initial period of intense interest, people stop paying as much attention to the feedback given by these monitors.[30]

As with other information strategies, feedback on its own will have little effect if people are not already motivated for other reasons—incentives or norms—to attempt to tailor their behavior based on the information provided. That observation has led some scholars to argue that feedback is unlikely to make a difference in the absence of a goal.[31] If a person has no interest in reducing energy use, information about how much energy is being used is unlikely to change that person's behavior. Moreover, the goal without the feedback is unlikely to make a difference.[32] Goals can be helpful whether externally given or self-set; which works better depends on how socially oriented individuals are.[33] Contests or challenges act as externally given goals; they increase environmental behavior more than does simply providing informational prompts.[34]

One information approach for energy that makes the underlying incentive especially clear is pay-as-you-go metering. Users pay for a certain amount of electricity in advance on a plastic card. They apply this amount to a smart meter in the home that reflects how much energy is available. This meter gives real-time feedback on how much energy is being used or has been used over time, as well as how much credit is available. Because the electricity is cut off when the credit runs out, people are much more attuned to not only their actual electricity usage, but its implications for the amount they have remaining. Most of these efforts allow for an available emergency supply and an alarm that warns before it cuts off electricity, so that people are not surprised or unduly harmed. This approach has resulted in energy savings between 4 and 12 percent.[35] This system is not entirely unfamiliar: it's akin to how we pay for the fuel used in our cars.

The value of goals also suggests that the underlying incentives must be in place and point in the right direction. A renter who does not pay the water bill is unlikely to be moved toward conservation by use information alone. The renter in this case does not gain any of the benefit of reducing water use, but does have to bear the inconvenience. The incentives are thus tilted against action. Having the incentives aligned such that there is a meaningful advantage to the consumer in reducing water use can help frame or support a goal. In many cases, working to change the underlying incentives or structures before using an information strategy is key.

PROMPTS

One specific form of feedback is a prompt. Remind people to do things they are aware they should be doing and are interested in doing, but that are not yet part of their routine. Prompting them at the right time can easily shift behavior in a useful direction. For instance, reminders in cars to use seat belts increase seat belt use 3 percent.[36] Reminders to residents about newspaper recycling can increase recycling rates by 50 percent.[37] Signs on a store shelf that point to the recycled content of products increase the purchasing of products with recycled content by 27 percent.[38] These prompts work especially well when they signal a behavior about which there is already a social norm or individual attitude.[39]

In order to work successfully as a prompt or reminder, however, the prompt has to be specific—general reminders about environmentalism have been shown to have little effect.[40] It should also be self-explanatory and understandable with a quick glance.

Proximity in both time and space to the relevant behavior is also key for the effectiveness of a prompt. People may be reminded to turn off the lights when they leave the room if the sign reminding them to do so is in the place they look when they exit. The shape of lids on recycling bins, especially if they reflect the type of material to be deposited in them, can serve as a just-in-time reminder to put materials into the correct bin.[41] I recently found myself about to throw out a napkin in a café garbage can, until I saw the sign on the lid saying "Stop! Can that be recycled or composted?" The prompt came at exactly the right moment to change my behavior.

Unless prompts are designed into the process, however—such as a recycling bin that only allows the correct material to fit through the lid—prompts fall prey to the problems of most information strategies: when they simply become part of the background, they are not noticed and less likely to influence behavior.

CREDIBILITY OF INFORMATION

For information to be useful in influencing behavior, it needs to be credible. Consumers and citizens are aware that businesses are attempting to influence their behavior for economic or political gain, and that may make them distrustful of the information they receive. For that reason, the source of information matters. Information from authoritative sources that the individual can validate receives the greatest attention.

People are more likely to change their behavior in response to sources that are seen as not only reliable, but also disinterested. In one experiment, consumers received letters describing ways to reduce their electricity use. One group received letters from the electricity provider, the other group from the public service commission. Both groups reduced their use of electricity in comparison to a no-letter control group, but the group whose letters came from the public service commission reduced it more. They were also much more likely to take the opportunity the letter offered to receive additional information about energy savings. The difference in effectiveness of the letter can be attributed to the credibility that came from the disinterested source.[42] Personal communication is also a much better way to impart information than impersonal approaches like mass mailing.[43] And, as chapter 6 notes, information framed in the context of a social norm (indicating, for instance, that a relevant community is engaging in the desired behavior) is the most persuasive of all.

LABELS AND CERTIFICATION

Even people who are concerned about the environment, and who would act on information about relative merits of actions, may be unwilling to spend the time and energy to research environmental impacts. They may have difficulty interpreting information they do have, especially when environmental harms or benefits differ in type. What amount of carbon dioxide is a lot? Is water pollution more or less of a problem than energy intensity?

This type of information is relevant to purchasing decisions. A majority of consumers in both the developed and developing world indicate an interest in prioritizing green products and services.[44] Businesses attempt to capture that interest by touting the greenness of their products. The efforts that marketers go through to persuade consumers that their products are environmentally friendly suggest that this information affects purchasing decisions, in at least some instances.

Because of the economic advantage to be gained from green-interested consumers, the information presented by businesses may range from truthful to outright deceitful. Even when laws prohibit misinformation, markets may tout true but irrelevant information, advertising that their shampoo "does not deplete the ozone layer" (something it has been prohibited from doing by law for decades). These claims are also encountered in contexts that are not directly environmental, such as when jelly beans are presented as "fat free" or tea labeled as "gluten free." These approaches target low-information consumers—most of us, that is—who may generally support the idea of an intact ozone layer or fat-free food without fully understanding the issues.

Labels that are in some way systematized and officially recognized, whether by a government process or a nongovernmental entity, can serve as a reliable source of information on the environmental contribution of products. These labels allow environmentally aware consumers to choose based on environmental impact. Those sufficiently motivated to make their purchasing decisions based on environmental effects may be willing to pay a price premium if they can be sure that the option they choose is environmentally preferable. Businesses that can produce products in this way find it helpful to identify themselves to these consumers.

Does eco-labeling actually change behavior? First, people have to notice a label and recognize its meaning. Labels in regular use are likely to be recognized.[45] Second, people need to understand the implications of the information. Most consumers' understanding of labeling information is shallow at best.[46] They are frequently unable to distinguish types of certification or labeling and misinterpret the information given. Consumers are also unlikely to understand the difference between governmental and nongovernmental labels[47] and their implications. Since businesses make green claims to increase sales of their products, not just to disseminate information, it is not surprising that consumers are confused about the finer points of the information presented.

This lack of consumer knowledge suggests an important role for official certification that can guarantee the credibility of information. Even claims that are technically true—for instance, that a product is biodegradable or compostable—may not be relevant in the context in which it is likely to be used. A landfilled product may be insufficiently exposed to light to degrade, or composting facilities may be unavailable. Few consumers have the knowledge or experience to evaluate these claims. If people change their purchasing behavior based on irrelevant or false claims, there is no benefit for the environment. And people who find out that they have been taken in by these claims may be more distrustful of environmental information in the future.

Finally, for information to matter, people have to pay attention to it. We all face information overload.[48] People who could be moved by the information conveyed by a label may fail to notice it. As discussed further in chapter 5, people rarely make fully calculated decisions for every action or purchase, relying instead on rules of thumb.[49] They may, therefore, just continue their purchasing habits without paying attention to environmental information presented.

Use of an eco-label increases sales.[50] Consumers indicate a willingness to purchase environmentally friendly goods; numerous surveys have reported that consumers prioritize green purchasing.[51] Actual consumer behavior suggests that this interest translates into greener purchases only some of the time, however. In one study in Britain looking at how much consumers spent on products for which a green-identified alternative was available, only about 10 percent of the purchases were of the green option.[52] Were consumers not as interested in green purchasing as they originally indicated, or were they simply so overwhelmed by information and the demands of the day that they did not follow through on their intentions? It is likely that both considerations play a role.

There are downsides to eco-labeling as a strategy for influencing behavior. If increased consumerism generally has a negative environmental effect, actions that make consumers feel better about the marginal difference between products may encourage them to consume more, which may have a greater aggregate environmental impact,[53] a kind of consumer version of the Jevons paradox described in chapter 3. Green labels may also encourage the use of products that are more processed or disposable, and thus labeled, over those that may be better for the environment but not labeled.[54] A reusable dishcloth or an apple may be better for the environment than recycled content paper towels or eco-friendly snack bars, but the latter may be the ones that are labeled as green. The provision of faulty or irrelevant environmental information can also lead to increased cynicism from consumers and thus backfire in overall effect.

It is difficult to calculate the broader environmental effect from eco-labels. If labels persuade people to make environmentally conscious purchasing decisions, the more important effect may be beyond the individual level as businesses decide to allocate resources toward producing products with a better environmental footprint. So they may have a more systemic effect than individual purchases suggest.

Green purchasing behavior may also have broader effects on individuals. If buying an eco-labeled product helps me see myself as environmentally conscientious, this identity may persuade me to make additional environmental decisions. This effect is most likely when potentially identity-creating actions are undertaken in a public and voluntary way, both of which apply to purchases of eco-labeled products.[55] This phenomenon is discussed further in chapter 6.

Certification takes the labeling step further. A nongovernmental organization or governmental entity certifies that a product or process meets a set of standards. Whatever the standards for certification are, an external entity determines whether a product or a business is meeting those standards. That avoids the problem of businesses making erroneous or irrelevant claims.

Certification can be taken even further when businesses or procurement offices agree to purchase or sell only products that have certification of a particular sort (or meet some other standard). For example, Walmart, the world's largest retailer, announced in 2006 that by 2011 it would sell only fish certified by the Marine Stewardship Council as coming from sustainable fisheries; Canadian supermarket Loblaws vowed to do the same by 2013.[56] In such cases the certification influences even those who don't seek it out. Consumers who purchase wild-caught seafood at either Walmart or Loblaws do not have to make a decision about whether or not their seafood purchases are certified as sustainable, since everything available for purchase is. The US government made purchasing requirements for paper products as early as 1993, mandating that paper with 20 percent postconsumer recycled content be purchased by federal agencies. This rule was made stricter in later years.[57] People using paper in government agencies in the United States thus use paper with recycled content, without ever having made that decision themselves. The institutional adoption of certification and labeling standards thus extends its reach.

MANDATING INFORMATION PROVISION

Most labeling and certification schemes are voluntary. Those who label their products or processes do so because they believe that it will give them a competitive advantage with consumers. But if information can make a difference, it would be useful for that information to be available about all products or processes. The requirement that businesses or industries provide certain type of information, particularly about hazardous substances, has been an important tool in changing environmental behavior. The idea is that there are some kinds of information that the public has a "right to know." This approach has been called "information-based governance."[58] Even though no behavior change is mandated, the primary effect of this required information provision has been through changing the behavior of the businesses themselves, rather than through changing individual behavior.

The best known of these strategies is the Toxics Release Inventory (TRI) in the United States. There are similar policies in Australia, Canada, Mexico, and the European Union. The idea for a TRI was first proposed in a *New York Times* op-ed following major releases of toxic materials in India and West Virginia. The authors argued that information should be gathered to answer basic questions about how much toxic material is used and for what purposes.[59] The actual program was created as part of the

Community Right-to-Know Act of 1986. The legislation required companies that released, recycled, or otherwise disposed of listed toxic materials to disclose that information. The Environmental Protection Agency compiles that information and makes it publicly available.

This regulation makes no rules about how much of a given substance can be released; it is entirely a mandate to provide information. That mechanism of publicly available information was meant both to contribute to general data collection and also to empower local groups or governing bodies. A primary intention was to help communities create contingency plans in case of accidents and to manage risks involving hazardous materials.[60]

People, organizations, and companies have indeed made use of TRI data. Nongovernmental organizations have produced reports, and journalists have written news stories, publicizing the hazards of these toxic emissions. But the reason the legislation is pointed to as a success came from the immediate reduction it created in releases of listed substances. The time lag between when the rule was created and when the release of information was mandated allowed facilities to change their behavior before information about it was made public. Once information was released, firms with lower emissions initially outperformed their competition in stock prices[61] and the price of some stocks declined after information became public about their toxic releases, leading to corporate commitments to reduce emissions.[62]

This program is widely credited with dramatically reducing releases of toxic chemicals. One EPA estimate put the reduction at 40 percent,[63] and others generally agree that its effects have been notable. A General Accounting Office report found that the program led to more than half of the relevant facilities making operational changes.[64] The information presented may not always be accurate, and recent changes to the legislation have weakened the reporting threshold. But it is nevertheless clear that the mere act of making information available has had a dramatic behavior change across industries with toxic emissions.

Other types of governmentally mandated information provision include energy efficiency or consumption information for appliances, and automobile fuel efficiency. These follow a long line of other types of information, such as about nutrition or consumer safety, that governments have required that manufacturers or sellers produce. These mandated provisions of information can have the same systemic effects as the TRI. For example, regulations in the United States requiring calorie information for menu items at chain restaurants were intended primarily to allow consumers to make an informed choice about the foods they order. But new food items introduced in the wake of these regulations mandating information provision represented notable decreases (approximately 12 percent) in calorie content,[65] suggesting that businesses changed how they prepared food simply because they were required to report information.

Similar effects come from public information about pay disparities. A California law requiring that cities publish municipal salaries led to a decrease in the gender gap in wages.[66] British firms that are transparent with wage information also have higher overall wages for similar work and backgrounds of employees.[67] Several countries in Europe require major companies to publish pay information by sex; "even being cognizant of gender pay disparity being an issue can change norms."[68]

Some refer to these mandated provisions of information as market-based incentives.[69] Firms that release information may find themselves the target of action by consumers or others, pushing them to change behavior through the possibility of economic losses if they do not. These approaches differ from standard incentive policy approaches, however, in that there is no necessary economic incentive from the information disclosure.

The most important information provided may be to the firms themselves.[70] Mandating information disclosure requires them to find out what their actual behavior is, and allows comparisons with other businesses. In combination with the implicit public pressure for changes in behavior, it makes voluntary decisions to reduce toxics or calorie-counts or wage-gaps realistic.

WHEN INFORMATION CAN BACKFIRE

Sometimes providing information can actually make it less likely that people will choose environmentally beneficial behavior. This is the "mobilizer's dilemma": pointing out a crisis not only may not help to address it, it may even lead to counterproductive action.[71] Information can backfire in several different ways: by persuading people that that their actions are insignificant compared to the magnitude of change required to address the problem, by engaging fear in a way that makes people close off their rational consideration of the issue, and by challenging—and thus sometimes strengthening—previously held political beliefs.

Information that demonstrates to people how dire a situation is can undermine their belief that they can improve the situation. If people feel they are individually powerless to make a difference, they may be discouraged from taking action either individually or collectively.[72]

This feeling of ineffectiveness is particularly likely for people who are not already engaged environmentalists. One demonstration of this phenomenon has been in studies of ecological footprints, a measure of a person's overall environmental effect. While committed environmentalists may respond to information about a high ecological footprint by taking action to reduce their environmental impact, most people are actually likely to behave in a less environmentally responsible manner *after* being told about the environmental harms they cause. In one experiment, students first were asked to fill out surveys that assessed how much their self-image depended on a commitment to environmental protection. A week later they completed an environmental footprint questionnaire and received a "score" that was randomly chosen to be either good or bad, and told how that score compared to other students at the university. All students were then given an opportunity to engage in an environmentally related behavior.

Being told of a bad ecological footprint marginally increased the extent that environmental-oriented students took the environmental action offered, but it significantly decreased the extent to which the non-environmentally focused students did.[73] These findings are consistent with another study suggesting that people who were told about their environmental footprint experienced "reduced feelings of self-efficacy," and demonstrated "lower intentions to engage in behaviors that reduce global warming."[74]

People who learn about some of the structural difficulties in working to protect common pool resources or provide public goods also become less likely to work cooperatively to address them. Economics students are generally taught the structural benefits to be gained by free riding while others cooperate. Multiple studies have shown that students enrolled in economics courses are less likely than others to cooperate in collective action situations in which freeriding is possible and problematic. (See chapter 2 for more detail on these types of situations, which account for most environmental problems.) Similarly, economics professors are less likely to donate to charity than professors in other fields. While one might attribute that to personal characteristics of people who choose to study economics, there is evidence that at least some of the effect is specifically about learning. Experimental data show that students who have been taught about prisoner's dilemma (a particular type of structural cooperation problem akin to a tragedy of the commons) are less likely to cooperate than those who had not learned about the concept.[75]

One response to this effect of learning could be to hide information about the difficulties of cooperation to address environmental problems, which would argue against writing this book in the first place. But the best way to address this source of information backfire might be to provide information about specific strategies for overcoming collective action problems, or make use of social norms information (discussed further in chapter 6) that demonstrates that others hold similar goals and are behaving in an environmentally beneficial way. Procedural information about how to act environmentally might also reassure you that your contributions can make a difference in addressing an environmental problem.

The broader backfire effect may also be driven by fear. When people face an external threat that they cannot control, such as a global environmental problem, they may instead seek to control their internal fear, by denying it.[76] "Dire warnings" actually decrease the extent to which people believe factual information about environmental problems. This phenomenon has been examined experimentally. Two groups of people were exposed to the same factual article about climate change; for half, the article concluded with two paragraphs about the "possibly apocalyptic" consequences of climate change. For the other half the final two paragraphs instead presented possible solutions. Those who received the dire messages were less likely to believe in the basic factual information about the existence of climate change after this study than reported in their prestudy beliefs.[77] It's worth restating that result: it's not simply that people were less likely to want to do something about the problem when they were scared by information about it; it is that they became less persuaded that it was a problem in the first place.

This effect has been evaluated within the area of public health, where fear is often used as a strategy to persuade people to change behavior. The idea is that presentation of a threat (such as disease effects of smoking or likelihood of dying from HIV) creates "fear arousal" that should motivate people to be willing to pursue change. But as one review of nearly a half-century of these campaigns suggests, there is little evidence that these approaches actually drive people to decrease the problematic behavior, and in some cases the behavior may intensify.[78]

The fear result can happen even without explicit efforts to scare people. One experiment was designed to correct misinformation about the dangers of vaccination for childhood diseases.[79] An increasing number of parents in the United States are opting out of childhood vaccinations for fear of risks, including the possibility (which is not supported by scientific evidence) that vaccines lead to autism. Scholars tested different approaches to providing information.

The two least effective interventions involved frightening descriptions or images of the effects of not vaccinating. In one, parents were given descriptions of the terrible effects of the diseases vaccines were intended to prevent, and in the other, they were shown images of children with the diseases in question. Parents who received these messages actually *increased* their belief in the likelihood of side effects from vaccination and *decreased* their likelihood of vaccinating, the exact opposite of what the campaign intended. It may be that when people are given information that increases their fear about one thing—in this case, the diseases vaccines were intended to prevent—it triggers a fear response more generally, and increases their fear of other effects, like the side effects of vaccines.

In this study another intervention simply presented scientific information demonstrating that vaccines are effective and that any potential link to autism has been disproven. People who were given this information reported a decreased belief in the danger of autism from vaccines, but at the same time—counterintuitively—*also* decreased the likelihood of vaccination. Although this intervention did not intend to use fear as a strategy, it is possible that even introducing the idea of something people feared— side effects of vaccines—created enough fear that people decreased their likelihood of vaccinating even while reporting that they did not believe in the dangers from vaccination.

Another set of public health studies reaffirms that perspective. Scholars provided information about dangerous health conditions to people. When the information was presented in a neutral way, those for whom the information was likely to be relevant (because they were susceptible to the conditions) responded to it to a greater degree than did those for whom the information was not likely to be relevant. That finding makes intuitive sense: the people for whom the information mattered were more likely to pay attention to it. But when the information was presented in a fear-inducing manner, those for whom it was relevant were actually less likely than others to pay attention to it.[80] Those who had reason to be afraid stopped paying attention to relevant information that called attention to that fear.

A similar study focusing on climate change suggested that fearful messages lead people to focus on the extent to which the results of climate change are likely to take place far away in both space and time.[81] Fear leads people to mentally emphasize the characteristics of the problem that make it least likely to apply directly to them.

The best way to overcome the demotivating effect of fear is to include specific information about what can be done. Providing information to people about what they can do to reduce the fear-inducing outcome makes it less likely that they will act contrary to the information provided.

Although dire health warnings initially decrease the extent to which people change their behavior in the desired direction, [82] when fear appeals are
combined with messages about the effectiveness of action, they can have
a motivating effect.[83]

A third reason that information can be counterproductive for environmental behavior is defense mechanisms that affect how people see the
world.[84] People may be unable to take in information about issues they feel
powerless to address. We have an innate tendency to believe that the world
is fair,[85] and when that belief is undermined, we are less trusting of the
information presented on that topic.[86] In the experiment about apocalyptic warnings about climate change described above, increased skepticism
about climate change was greater for those who came into the study with a
belief that the world was just. The scholars conducting this study were able
to create this effect separately in a different experiment by priming different groups of people with articles suggesting either that the world was fair
or that it wasn't and then showing everyone videos that portrayed climate
devastation and its effects on children. Those who were primed to believe
in a just world were 29 percent more skeptical of climate change at the end
of the experiment than those who were not, and 21 percent less likely to be
willing to take action to address the issue.[87] These results suggest potential
downsides to focusing on the inequalities inherent in climate change.

Information may also backfire when given to people who are politically
motivated to hold the (scientifically incorrect) beliefs they hold. In the
United States, healthcare reform under President Barack Obama did not
include what some people referred to as "death panels," that is, payment
to physicians to provide counseling about end-of-life choices and related
issues. A study examining efforts to correct this mislabeling succeeded
in correcting misperceptions among those without strong partisan leanings, and also those with relatively little political knowledge. But those
whose political leanings led them to support right-wing politicians and
oppose healthcare reform became more, rather than less, likely to believe
the incorrect information when given corrective information. That effect
was most pronounced among those with the greatest level of political
knowledge.[88]

Another study found that white men were less concerned with environmental risks than were other segments of the population. The study authors conclude that this minimizing of risks came about because if these men accepted that there were environmental risks, they would "justify restrictions on markets, commerce, and industry—activities important (emotionally and psychically, as well as materially) to the status of white men with those outlooks."[89] In other words, because they weren't willing to accept the actions that would follow from the existence of environmental risks, they responded by denying that those risks existed.

Scholars argue that in some cases it is simply impossible to overcome "motivated reasoning," the situation in which political biases drive informational belief.[90] In these circumstances, people trust information that confirms their preexisting beliefs and resist—sometimes so strongly that their preexisting beliefs become stronger—anything that attempts to correct misinformation.[91] This phenomenon is generally more pronounced with knowledgeable or highly educated people.[92] In these contexts, information has no chance of changing belief or behavior in the desired direction. Other approaches—such as mandating or incentivizing action—are necessary to change behavior without changing beliefs.

There are ways to make it less likely that information will backfire. Information that plays to people's fear can be problematic. The activist strategy of scaring people with information about the dire nature of environmental problems will likely do more harm than good, unless it is accompanied with clear information about what to do and why those actions will be effective.[93] The same thing is true with encouraging collective action. People engaging in it will benefit from information that demonstrates not just why this action collectively is important, but also that collective action is feasible or likely. Showing that cooperation can succeed may persuade those who understand the benefits (and also the long-term risks) of free riding to cooperate.

Finally, in situations in which information is likely to backfire, strategies that go beyond presenting information may be key. In the case of vaccines, for instance, making it more difficult for parents to opt out of vaccinations for their children doesn't require persuading them of anything, which is a good thing, since persuading vaccine skeptics not to be worried has repeatedly failed. But a stiff opt-out requirement does increase the likelihood of vaccination.[94] Requiring that people sign up for healthcare does not necessitate changing their (incorrect) beliefs about what is in legislation. Using incentives or regulation can be especially important when information not only fails but runs the risk of making the situation worse.

COGNITIVE BIASES

One of the reasons information may fail to change behavior has to do with the way people take in and process it. People have cognitive biases that interfere with their abilities to understand or act on information, in ways that are relevant to environmental behavior. Discounting the future more than economic logic suggests (as discussed in chapter 2) is one type of cognitive bias. Similarly, people are more concerned about losses than they are about gains of similar magnitudes (as discussed in chapter 3), and thus the way that an issue is framed can affect behavior.

People also have difficulty accurately understanding uncertainty and risk, two concepts central to environmental problems. There are systematic ways people misperceive risk; these have implications for how they prioritize or value their own actions, or advocate for policy to address environmental problems.[95] People underestimate the effects of most types of risks. There are some types of hazards, however, that they overestimate. When faced with these two types of misperception, information may fail to lead to action, even if there are good reasons for us to change behavior.

The argument for environmental action frequently rests on the idea of risk: that the danger of not taking action outweighs the difficulty of acting. If you don't properly evaluate the need for action, or if you see the benefits as not worth the cost of action, you may behave in ways that cause environmental harm. Psychology and evolutionary biology can help explain why we systematically downplay risk.

It can make psychological sense, in order for us to make it through the day, to ignore the myriad risks we face. Everything we do—driving a car, crossing the street, riding in an elevator, drinking a cup of coffee—carries with it some risk. Even more risky are the societal contexts (the dam on the river, the nuclear power plant providing electricity, and the natural gas burned for heat) that are the background to our lives. If we had to calculate a risk-benefit analysis for every action we undertook, making it through the day would be impossible. Since for most of these activities the risk of harm is quite low, it makes sense to simply ignore the possible dangers.

Car seat belt use was an early subject of this analysis. Lack of seat belt use may be considered, from the perspective of the user, rational. Buckling a seat belt involves undertaking an inconvenient action to prevent the extremely low likelihood of a bad outcome. Information campaigns that attempted to persuade people to use seat belts failed because they did not account for people discounting the likelihood of the risk of needing a seat belt.[96] Campaigns that tried to get people to use seat belts by presenting information on the seriousness of belt-less crashes or on how their friends and family would feel if they died in a car crash was ignored by people who didn't believe they were likely to get into a crash in the first place. People have a broader tendency to undervalue low-probability events, even if these events would have catastrophic consequences.[97]

Two things nevertheless succeeded in increasing seat belt use. The first worked by "elongating people's time frame," presenting information about the advantages of seat belt use that emphasized the lifetime risk, rather than per-trip risk, of death or injury from a car crash.[98] When people were told that their lifetime risk of injury was one in three and of death one in one hundred, those who had not previously indicated willingness to use a seat belt reported that they would do so. This approach has obvious implications for responding to environmental risks, many of which involve long time frames.

The second effective tool in changing seat belt behavior, which was evaluated in the early studies, was habit, as discussed further in chapter 5. In the 1970s when this research was initially undertaken, seat belt use was not common, and buckling a seat belt required an active decision. After decades of safety campaigns and regulations (which provided penalties for failure to use seat belts), seat belt use has become a habit for most people in industrialized democracies. Few calculate the risk-benefit analysis before deciding whether to use a seat belt; it has simply become an automatic part of sitting in a car.[99] One way to deal with people's misapprehension of risk is simply to take the calculation out of their decisions, by making the desired action less voluntary.

In addition to underestimating their likelihood of suffering the negative consequences of a risky event, people also overestimate their ability to address or avoid any potential consequences should the risky event transpire. Most people, for instance, see themselves as better-than-average drivers and thus able to avoid potential car accidents.[100] They also are likely to overestimate their control over a variety of health and other hazards.[101] While that tendency might not seem immediately relevant to environmental issues (especially because even when undervaluing risk, people do seem to conclude that they have little control over environmental problems),[102] it does square with the idea that people are less likely to believe that they will suffer the consequences (such as floods or extreme weather events) from environmental problems, and may therefore be less likely to want to take action to prevent them from happening.

Another way people cope with risks they are unable to control is by denying them. Psychological stress theory argues that people do not act on stressors that they view as uncontrollable.[103] In fact, people are more likely to deny or downplay the risk the greater their likelihood of experiencing it.[104] Devaluing the extent of a threat allows people to put it out of mind instead of worrying about it. This approach might explain why people who live in areas where a disaster has just happened are quick to state that it could never happen again.[105] People may cope with these uncontrollable risks by turning to wishful thinking.[106] By not thinking about the risk or planning to mitigate it, people avoid experiencing the stress that it might cause (until, of course, the feared event materializes). During the 2016 presidential election in the United States I frequently found myself trying to avoid thinking about the worst possible outcomes, to decrease the stress I was feeling from the election. Those who are the most powerless to mitigate or avoid a risk are those who are most likely to seek the reassurance of ignoring it.

That may not be entirely irrational. People with less social power may recognize that risk isn't shared equally across the population. Studies show that white men are less concerned about environmental risks than women and nonwhite men. People in more vulnerable social positions may understand that they are more vulnerable to any environmental risks that exist.[107] Conservative white men are especially likely to engage in climate change denial (and especially in the United States).[108] Those who are unconcerned about environmental risks might be those who are aware that their place in society insulates them from these risks and they can afford to ignore them. The same information about risks has different meanings to different people.

Finally, it is possible that true cognitive biases (as distinct from the coping mechanisms described above) might account for the failure to accurately assess risk. Most people are not able to make complex calculations and so act on the basis of simplified mental models (what some scholars call "bounded rationality")[109] of how the world works. These models are sufficiently accurate to be useful most of the time, and thus using them saves mental energy in general, given the large number of daily decisions people need to make. But for unusual situations they are particularly unlikely to apply. That may be why, for example, people underestimate the risk of low-probability events. Because these events are unlikely to happen, for the most part people are safe considering them impossible rather than improbable. But many environmental problems have their worst effects in low-probability. high-magnitude risks, the ones people are least likely to perceive. Information demonstrating that these risks exist may not be understood or accepted.

On the other hand, there are some contexts in which we tend to overestimate risk, many of which can be explained by the cognitive biases discussed above. First, we overestimate the likelihood of dying from high-visibility, dramatic events (and conversely underestimate the risk of prosaic dangers like tornadoes or asthma).[110] The availability heuristic can account for this overestimation: these dramatic events are more attention-grabbing (and more likely to be taken up by the media). We also tend to be especially concerned about risks to which we are involuntarily exposed, rather than those we have taken on voluntarily, as well as those that involve unfamiliar situations or exotic technology.[111] These biases might help explain public concern or even conspiracy theories about certain kinds of agricultural technology (like genetically modified organisms) or even fluoridated water.

Other cognitive biases may influence how information is received. People tend to be "more confident in their judgments than is warranted by the facts."[112] Some of the studies demonstrating people's inaccurate rankings of risks also asked people to indicate how confident they were in their rankings. Often those with wildly incorrect risk estimates are the most confident in the accuracy of their assessments,[113] one version of what has come to be known as the Dunning-Kruger effect.

People also engage in "anchoring"—a tendency toward sticking with a belief regardless of how accurate it is. Psychology studies have demonstrated that people will anchor to completely ridiculous things. In one study, people spun a number wheel and were asked to estimate the number of African countries in the United Nations. Those who turned up a low number on the spin estimated a lower number of African countries.[114] Although the kind of anchoring produced in psychology studies may not frequently be encountered in real life, the broader observation of the difficulty in changing existing beliefs is more generally relevant.

Anchoring effects are observed even when people are warned about the tendency of anchoring.[115] The more knowledgeable you are about a subject, the less prone you are to anchoring effects.[116] So although superficial presentation of information may not be able to overcome the problem of anchoring, deep education on a topic can.

This bias can be particularly problematic as information changes but people fail to update their beliefs. People may anchor on scientific understandings (such as predictions about the severity of or confidence about climate change) or even behavioral options. Those who learned to recycle during an era in which only white office paper was accepted in many recycling programs may be resistant to taking in information that all paper products can now be recycled; when told of this new situation, they may fail to internalize it.

There may be a relationship between anchoring and overconfidence. At minimum, the combination of the two can be dangerous as people hold tightly, with great confidence, to information that may not be accurate. These factors help explain why simply providing information about an environmental problem or the need for action might not change behavior, if people are anchored and overconfident in existing beliefs.

Finally, in part because of the phenomenon of loss aversion, the way information is framed is likely to have different types of effects. People are much more concerned with avoiding losses of things they already have than they are (or would be) with gaining something of equal value. This effect has been demonstrated across a wide variety of experiences, both through experiments and through observation of everyday behavior. The amount people are willing to pay to buy lottery tickets is far less than the amount of money they would be willing to take to sell them back (without knowing whether they were winning tickets).[117] In one study of attitudes about exposure to disease, the amount people demanded for accepting an increased risk of death of 0.1 percent was typically fifty times higher than the amount people were willing to pay to decrease the risk of death by that amount.[118] In another study, half the students in the room (at random) were given college-branded coffee mugs. Those who had been given mugs were asked how much they would be willing to sell their mugs for, and those without coffee mugs were asked how much they would be willing to buy them for (with knowledge that some of these sales would take place). Students with mugs asked for more money than those without mugs were willing to pay for them.[119] Across a large number of studies, people required greater payment to "accept" a loss than to purchase a gain, with a margin a high as sixteen to one.[120]

This loss aversion (also referred to as the "endowment effect")[121] has important implications for how information pertaining to environ-mental problems is received. Because of the nature of environmental issues as externalities, people are frequently asked to stop engaging in current behavior in return for some potential future environmental pay-off. Without intending to, this approach frames behavior change (for the sake of environmental protection) as a loss, of whatever current activity or practice you are engaged in.

Intentionally changing the way information is framed may have helpful effects on behavior: emphasizing the loss that would be expected from an environmental problem may be more likely to elicit the desired behavior change than would focusing on the benefit of taking action. Similarly, people may be more amenable to environmental goals when they are framed as returning conditions to what previously existed (cleaning up a river, for example, or reducing emissions levels to an earlier amount) rather than as a decrease of present activity.[122] In addition, efforts to persuade people to better insulate their homes or install energy-efficient appliances might be more effective if they emphasize the amount of money people are losing by not making the change,[123] rather than how much they will gain by making it.

ENVIRONMENTAL EDUCATION

Most of this chapter has focused on efforts to educate people by providing specific types of information designed (with varying levels of success, depending on the type of information) to change specific behaviors in the near term. But there is a quite different aspect that some people refer to when they discuss education: a broad introduction, usually in childhood, of basic knowledge of and awareness about environmental issues. This approach is conceptually different from information provided as a specific intervention to directly influence behavior. Instead, this broader education is aimed to create a generally environmentally informed and responsible citizenry.

Although the kind of information provision discussed elsewhere in this chapter is generally ineffective in influencing attitudes and awareness, this broader type of education is one of the only things that has been demonstrated, in certain circumstances, to have a long-term effect on attitudes.

This education can account for the big-picture knowledge people have about environmental issues and their support for environmental protection generally.

When is education is likely to succeed at raising awareness and concern? It really is a long-term proposition. Education creates the context for generational change; people brought up when environmental concern was mainstream and environmental information was regularly presented tend to keep that perspective as they age.[124] One of the ways this educational process can work is through the creation of identity, discussed in greater detail in chapter 6. One study of this type of change, in this case about general political ideology, followed Bennington students from the 1930s for decades afterward. The liberal attitudes and approaches they gained while at Bennington followed them as they grew older.[125]

Direct experience is an essential part of successful environmental education. People are much less likely to remember, or be moved by, things they are told about. They respond to things they experience in one way or another. Programs that take place "in" nature create more, and more lasting, positive attitudes toward the environment than those that take place in a classroom.[126] Dramatic events provide lasting impressions. And factual information is less likely to be remembered than a general interest in and concern for the area of study. For that reason, emotions may be a more productive focus of broad-scale environmental education than information.[127] Looking at the issue from the other direction, between half and 80 percent of environmentalists point to significant experiences in nature as central to developing their environmental attitudes and interest.[128]

Finally, education of any sort is most successful at influencing behavior that is consistent with underlying attitudes and values. These factors, discussed in chapter 6, are not amenable to quick changes themselves, and, if they can be developed though educational programs, this development occurs only over a very long term.[129] Educational programs that build on existing attitudes are likely to have the greatest long-term success. Education can help, but it alone won't reorient people to behave in an environmentally preferably manner.[130] But in the long term, alongside other efforts to create social norms, and accompanied by the right incentives, it may be part of a useful strategy for influencing environmental behavior.

INFORMATION AND ENVIRONMENTAL CHOICES

As the introduction to this chapter suggests, information is rarely as powerful a tool for explaining or changing environmental behavior as activists assume. It may be a necessary background condition, but once most people are aware of environmental problems and the factors that contribute to them, giving them more information is unlikely to make a major difference in their behavior. In that context, information is most often effective at helping people understand how to do things they have already indicated a willingness to do. It may be up to other approaches to ensure that the normal framing or incentives are in place to increase the likelihood that people will choose environmentally preferable options.

Education, or provision of information, can nevertheless have some effect on environmentally relevant behavior, in the absence of other major structural barriers to making good environmental choices. The most important role that education can play is to provide people ways to overcome the barriers between intention and action; in this role it is best deployed in conjunction with incentives (particularly noneconomic ones) that contribute to making the desired action easier.

The kind of general environmental education that might lead to long-term understanding of, and appreciation for, the environment is unlikely to have a direct effect on the types of choices discussed in what follows but can play an important role in creating attitudes and values (chapter 6) that themselves can contribute to broader social changes that can work to prioritize or enable better environmental choices.

Habits and Other Routines

Are people carefully weighing costs and benefits in making decisions about their environmental actions? The standard approach to economics frames individual choices as being about rationally maximizing utility in situations with complete information.[1] While few genuinely believe that behavior perfectly reflects this approach, many efforts to explain environmental behavior implicitly assume that we make conscious choices about how to behave.

Many actions are not the result of carefully planned decisions, however. Economists recognized decades ago that cognitive limitations bound the extent to which we behave in a fully rational manner.[2] Political scientist Herbert Simon coined the term "satisficing" to convey the inability of people to take full account of all the factors required to make an optimal choice. Instead, he argues, we make decisions sufficient to meet current needs without requiring an in-depth analysis of every option to find the one deemed mathematically best. This kind of bounded rationality is a form of rational behavior: the time and effort saved by not having to make a fully calculated decision on every factor can itself be valuable. Psychologists began to create decision-making models that recognize that people seek outcomes that are satisfying, rather than maximizing, expected utility.[3]

We stray from fully rational decisions for good reasons. We save time and mental energy by establishing routines that allow us to go about our daily activities without needing to consider all the ramifications of every action. We benefit from simplified decision rules. Businesses or organizations save effort and money by setting up standard ways of behaving that are likely to accomplish their goals in a systematic manner. These standard operating procedures allow complex organizations to ensure efficient and consistent operations.

Establishing routines can be a powerful way to accomplish goals. My father, a long-time recreational runner, decided one year that he was going to make running habitual by simply doing it every day. He wanted to remove it from the realm of decision and thus ensure that he didn't leave himself open to deciding not to go running—as he pointed out, "You don't get up in the morning and ask yourself whether or not you feel like brushing your teeth today; you just brush your teeth." His habit creation worked, and he went nearly three years without missing a single day of running, because he just got up and went running without wondering whether to do it or not.

Understanding that some behavior is not fully rational has important implications. The idea that some—or even many—of our actions are not intentional calls into question many of the models people have of behavior and of environmental decisions more generally. A core psychological model is the theory of planned behavior, which explains the likelihood of action based on "behavioral intentions."[4] This approach, discussed further in chapter 6, formalizes the common-sense notion that people choose to act by evaluating the likelihood that their behavior will lead to an expected outcome. The theory expects there to be a close link between an intention to engage in a behavior and actually undertaking that behavior. Habit challenges that direct link, and hence our understanding of why people behave the way they do.

The power of habit also calls into question the value of information for changing behavior. If the type of behavior people hope to influence—such as commuting or purchasing—is largely in the realm of habit, information is likely to be ineffective. The power of habit to trump information has been demonstrated in public health campaigns, which frequently fail to educate people to change unhealthy behaviors.[5]

The same difficulty hampers efforts to alter behavior by calling on attitudes or values. People may know what the environmentally preferred choice is, and they may be willing to make that choice. But if their behavior happens in a way that bypasses thought, neither information nor attitudes has an opportunity to make a difference.

From an environmental perspective, habits can be problematic. Because making good environmental choices often requires a decision to behave differently than the standard approach calls for, our default behavior is likely to have bad environmental consequences. Moreover, habits are often formed for efficiency, expedience, or cost savings. If environmental choices are more difficult or expensive, they are unlikely to be the default option, even if they might be chosen when given full consideration. Habits also often evolve for short-term individual benefit; many environmental decisions involve making a harder short-term choice for a long-run or collective advantage.

The same is true at the collective level. Organizations such as firms develop routines and standard operating procedures that help systematize their operations. These processes, which were often developed to address nonenvironmental priorities, can prevent them from locating efficiencies that might create both environmental and economic benefit.

On the other hand, the power of habits suggests that making environmentally beneficial options the default choice or the routine action can be an effective tool for changing behavior of either individuals or organizations. Once a habit is established or a default option chosen, it tends to persist. Creation of a habit avoids the need to repeatedly make a conscious environmental choice. If good environmental behavior can be made routine, people and firms will be more likely to undertake it.

INDIVIDUAL HABITS

Many of our actions are habitual. We set out for work in the morning by the same method we always use, rather than deciding each day whether to walk, take public transportation, or drive. In the grocery story we buy the brand of cereal we most often eat and the type of paper towels we have used in the past, rather than deciding anew which cereal is the tastiest, which towels are most absorbent or least environmentally degrading. We dispose of our waste by whatever method we usually use, rather than considering the implications of different disposal methods and choosing the one that best meets our values. By one estimate, more than 40 percent of our daily actions are habits rather than fully calculated decisions.[6] Another study suggests that up to half of our time is spent engaging in habitual behavior.[7]

Habits are adaptive. Not having to make a decision or pay attention to an action frees up our mental abilities for something else. It can save time and reduce stress. It can prevent us from experiencing emotional reactions about decisions we face.[8] If we had no habits, we would drain our memory and tax our decision-making abilities.[9] Habit allows for the creation of mastery, as parts of an activity become routinized so that they can build to greater skill.[10]

Habits can be problematic in a number of ways, however. Because they represent action without thought, people may not act in an environmentally conscious way even when they intend to, because their action bypasses decision-making processes. For instance, if people are in the habit of driving to the store, they will generally choose that method of transportation even for stores that are within walking distance.[11] People who have not recycled in the past are less likely to recycle, even if they profess an intention to do so.[12] People with incentives or intentions to reduce water use are less likely to do so if they habitually water their garden or are used to taking long showers.[13]

Habits may be formed in one context, for one purpose, but conflict with other goals. A habitual and enjoyable trip to the local coffee shop in the morning may interfere with my effort to cut down on caffeine consumption or to save money. The practice of keeping a porch light on all night for safety may interfere with my desire to cut energy consumption. Habits may meet short-term goals (this cup of coffee and doughnut will keep me awake through my morning meeting) but conflict with longer-term goals (I would prefer to consume healthier foods).

Habits may also persist even as conditions change and the habits become less adaptive. Someone may form a habit of driving to work when driving is initially the most time-efficient way to commute. Once the commuting habit is in place, she may simply habitually drive. Even if she develops a new interest in minimizing environmental impact, the practice of commuting, which is already habitual, may not be re-examined.

When people engage in habitual behavior, they cease to consider alternative approaches and rely less on information in making their decisions,[14] even when such information is available. Our hypothetical commuter may be unaware of a new bus route that would make noncar commuting easier, or of discounted transit passes offered by her employer, because how to get to work is not something she treats as an open question.

When people are acting habitually, they are not fully and rationally considering information in their decision processes. Habits also override intention, including a personal interest in making environmentally friendly choices. As some scholars have observed, "With a strong habit in power, personal norms to protect the environment have hardly any effect on behavior."[15]

In order to address the environmental implications of habitual behavior, we need to understand how and why it comes about. Habits develop in predictable ways, whether they are created intentionally or unintentionally. Practically speaking, they form the same way a new skill does, through repetition and practice. Once you do something often enough, the cognitive processes become automatic, and you can do it quickly and without having to pay attention or to make an active decision.[16]

But why does the habit stick? A useful way to think about it is to see a habit as a kind of feedback loop that involves a cue, a routine, and a reward.[17] When the cue happens (I get into the shower), I engage in an activity that becomes routine (I wash my hair) and experience a small reward (the joy of clean-feeling hair). Eventually a habit bypasses conscious thought.[18]

I have found myself taking a quick shower before bed when I already showered in the morning and find myself halfway through washing my hair—something I wouldn't have intended or needed to do—before I am even aware that I'm doing it. It's just what I habitually do as soon as I step into the shower. How likely a behavior is to be habitual depends on how frequently you engage in it.

The fact that habits involve activity that you have, at some point, chosen does not mean that habits are consciously chosen. Although you voluntarily undertake the action initially, you do not necessarily intend for it to become so habitual that you no longer think about it. The first time you run out of coffee and grab your car keys to go buy more, there might have been a time-sensitive reason you needed to make a trip by car to wherever you buy coffee beans, but once it becomes habitual you don't stop to think that it's a nice day and you could walk to the store.

Habits, routines, and other quasi-automatic actions are important for understanding environmental behavior. Because so much of our behavior is habitual, environmentally problematic behavior can be difficult to change, even when people prefer to take less environmentally harmful action. By the same token, habits can be productive avenues for change. If we can turn a frequently performed action into one that has better environmental consequences, we can create a bigger effect than if we focused on changing each individual action.

Habits represent a short-term advantage that may have negative effects in the long term or in the aggregate. The benefit I get from using a disposable coffee cup is experienced immediately—I can get take-out coffee on the way into work. My repeated disposable coffee cup use, combined with the same behavior by others, creates unnecessary waste in the aggregate. But even in the unlikely event that I experience any negative environmental effects of this behavior, it would be over the very long term.

It is particularly difficult to create a habit when the payoff is long term or diffuse. Because of the cue-routine-reward structure of habits, they form when a reward for a behavior is immediate. Environmental problems, on the other hand, happen when an action taken in the present has a problematic consequence that may be felt in the future. So the benefit of preventing that consequence is not close enough in time to the behavior to serve as the reward in the creation of a habit.

One of the major areas for environmentally relevant habits is commuting. The way we decide to travel, especially to work or to other places we regularly go, has environmental implications. If our travel choices are habitual (as repeated studies have demonstrated), they are not conscious choices and thus are difficult to change. Car use generally happens in a stable context and repeatedly,[19] the background conditions for habit development. People who habitually travel by car do not seek information about other travel methods.[20] Intentions to use public transportation have almost no predictive power for those who regularly commute by car.[21] The best predictor of both the desire and intention to use public transportation is the extent to which people already regularly use public transportation.[22]

One of the implications of travel being habitual is that we tend to use the same mode of transport no matter where we are going.[23] A person who drives to work is likely to drive to run errands, regardless of the distance to the destination or how convenient a subway stop is. In experimental situations it has been demonstrated that habit "reduced the elaborateness of information use" as people were choosing among potential modes of travel,[24] taking action without fully contemplating options.

For that reason, changing the way people commute requires interrupting their habitual behavior, to make it more likely that they can carefully consider the full range of information about travel choices. This interruption of habit is necessary if people intend to reduce their negative environmental impact. Sometimes changing circumstances—such as the appearance of a new bus route—can provide that interruption, though only if people begin with an intention to make use of such an option.[25] This process would also only work if they became aware of the option in the first place, something that might not happen if they were sufficiently engaged in habitual behavior. Making people aware of changes in commuting options can therefore help.

Other forms of more deliberate interruptions can make a difference. Giving people a reduced-fee bus pass for a period of time can make it more likely that they will use the bus[26] and continue doing so even when they have to pay the normal fare.[27] This approach is particularly interesting because it uses an incentive (making the bus cheaper than it would otherwise be) to convey procedural information to people, by giving them the experience of riding the bus. If the behavior persists when the subsidy is removed, it has become sufficiently valued on its own that people will engage in it without the additional incentive. The new behavior may already have become routine.

The ability of an interruption in habit to allow redirection of behavior may depend in part on the values of the person engaging in the habit. People who have a moral conviction about the value of reduced car use are more likely to change their behavior once their car commuting habit is interrupted in some way.[28] That's not a necessary condition, though. People who are opposed to policy measures to reduce car use were also more likely, in a different study, to take advantage of subsidized public transit tickets than were those in favor of restrictions on car use.[29]

DEVELOPING BENEFICIAL HABITS

Ensuring that every individual choice is made with the environmental consequences in mind is an inefficient way to deal with environmental behavior. People make so many decisions in any given day that attention to every choice, even for those who are committed environmentalists, is unrealistic. It can also backfire, as discussed further in chapter 6. The self-discipline required to make a beneficial environmental choice, when it is undertaken for noble reasons and is harder or more costly than the alternative, can use up reserves of willpower people have or can make people feel they have done their part for the moment. Either effect can make it less likely that subsequent actions will be as environmentally aware.

Developing good habits can affect the environment in a more efficient way. A habit can regularize positive environmental behavior. Rather than having to make a conscious decision every time you commute or purchase something, your default action will be one with benign environmental consequences. And in the quasi-automatic way habits work, it does not require self-control and thus is unlikely to suffer from the subsequent backsliding that can otherwise accompany good acts. Habits are also useful for creating regularized behavior. Something that should be done a certain way all the time is more easily accomplished as a habit than through exercising individual choice every time that action is undertaken.

The experience of seat belts is illustrative. As discussed in chapter 4, information about the risks of riding in a car without a seat belt largely failed to influence the behavior of drivers and passengers, despite dramatic reductions in risk from seat belt use. In most countries, public education campaigns had little effect on the use of seat belts. What did account for widespread change in behavior was legislation that required seat belt use, and the enforcement of these policies.[30] What the legal requirement did, in large part, was create a new habit. Most people who currently use seat belts (in parts of the world where their use is legally mandated) no longer decide each time they enter a car whether to put a seat belt on; instead they automatically engage the seat belt.[31] In addition to a legal mandate, most vehicles now also prompt users to fasten seat belts, which is the kind of information provision that actually can work to influence behavior and help to create a habit.

Once seat belt use did become routine, attitudes about using seat belts generally became more positive.[32] Many people believe that attitudes precede behavior, but this experience suggests that the reverse can be true. Those who study habit would not be surprised by that result. There is evidence that we infer intention from behavior rather than the other way around, assuming that if we are engaging in an activity it is because we have chosen to do so. So developing a habit can make you support or value the behavior you habitually engage in.

The seat belt example suggests that habit can be created by legislation, which fits into the underlying contention of this book that incentives and social structures are the most effective ways to make collective changes in individual behavior. What else can be done to change habits, or scripts, on a broader basis?

As chapter 4 suggests, one kind of information useful for inducing environmental action is procedural knowledge—information about what can be recycled, or on which days the recycling should be put out for pickup. Paying attention to habit when designing these types of programs can also help a program become more successful. A town yard waste pickup program with pickup days scattered somewhat randomly through the warm months of the year, for instance, is unlikely to gain a high level of yard waste collection, because people have to make an effort to remember on which day to put out the yard waste. If they forget, they are likely to simply put it in the garbage if the next collection date isn't for another six weeks or so. If, instead, yard waste were collected on a regular and predictable schedule (say, the first Monday of every month other than winter months) the odds that people would be able to access or remember the information increases. The advantage of a regular schedule for habituating people to the activity may be sufficiently useful that it would be worthwhile to have yard waste pickups throughout the year (which might allow for well-scheduled pickup of used Christmas trees too), even in months when there is likely to be little to pick up. In other words, make use of the benefits of habitual behavior and its relationship to information retention when designing a program to encourage or enable environmental behavior.

It is easier for some types of activities to become habitual. Things that are frequently repeated (like disposal of trash) are better candidates for habit than activities that are undertaken much less frequently (like purchasing a new appliance). Similarly, it is easier to create a habit about something you always do (I walk to work, no matter the weather) or never do (I don't use take-out containers) than something you are trying to do sometimes (I will cut down on my consumption of meat). Even so, how you frame the behavior can help make it more or less amenable to habit formation: stopping consumption of meat at home or always choosing chicken over beef at restaurants would have the effect of decreasing meat consumption while still maintaining a habit with categorical consistency.

Most habits are formed around positive action rather than negative (something you do, rather than something you don't do).[33] "I put cardboard in the recycling bin" is a more likely habit than "I don't throw cardboard in the trash," even though they seem conceptually identical. Because habits are generally behavioral responses to cues ("It's time for my first class") the response is usually an action rather than a lack of action. Again, framing can play an important role in developing a habit. If you want to avoid doing something, the most effective approach is to figure out what you are going to do instead and create the habit around doing that. This is an insight animal trainers have figured out; if a dog is engaging in a behavior you want to discourage, the most effective way to change it is to redirect it to a preferred behavior.[34]

CHANGING HABITS

Habits are easier to make than they are to change. The best measurement of the strength of a habit is how often the behavior is performed; things that we do weekly (like our grocery shopping habits), daily (like our commuting habits), or even more frequently (like using lights or appliances) are extremely difficult to change, because we have so adjusted to them that we don't even notice that we're doing them.

The best opportunity for changing habits is therefore at moments of other change, in what scholars call the habit discontinuity hypothesis. Studies of consumer behavior determined that changes in purchasing behavior most frequently happen at times of major life changes, like getting married, moving, or changing jobs.[35] University students were better able to establish new habits when they transferred to another university.[36] People who are environmentally concerned are more likely to change their travel choices to act on that concern when they move to a house in a new location, compared to equally concerned people who have not moved.[37]

Since moving to a new home or getting married is not something you do frequently, it would be useful to figure out how to change habits without necessitating major life changes. Anything that interrupts the automatic nature of a behavior can help that process. Prompts, discussed at greater length in chapter 4, can remind you of a behavior you want to do at a moment in which you might not otherwise be thinking about it but be open to change.

Finding a way to introduce people to the desired behavior can serve this function. The college where I teach held a walking challenge for two months in a recent spring. There were several incentives to participate: those who did were given fitness trackers, and we had additional financial incentives for participating. And, of course, those who walked the greatest number of steps or participated in other ways could win prizes. While the challenge certainly didn't change everyone's behavior, I found myself taking on new routines, like walking instead of driving to the grocery store. More than three years after the contest was over, walking has become my assumed transportation method for getting to the grocery store, and the challenge was what prompted me to try this new behavior. Other faculty and staff members reported similar lasting changes. The approach of giving people free transit passes for a period of time may have this effect as well. Although it's likely not the case that habits form after a set number of days (twenty-one is frequently mentioned),[38] finding ways to induce people to begin an activity and perform it regularly is the best way to make it habitual.

Goals can also be key. Although habits challenge the supremacy of intention, intention nevertheless is an important aspect of changing a habit or creating a new one. When habits are weak, intentions are a strong predictor of behavior. But in the face of strong habits, intentions have much less power.[39] Nevertheless, creating what people call "implementation intentions" (or what some call "scripts") helps create habits or replace old habits. This strategy involves forming a plan of action for how to act in a particular situation. An example might be: "If I have to run an errand, I will first check whether I can walk to where I'm going," or "When I buy vegetables, I will buy organic if there is an option to." Having a plan of action makes your action closer to automatic, because it doesn't require a lot of thought at the moment you invoke it.[40]

In the same way that habits are themselves positive rather than negative, positive implementation intentions are more effective than negative ones.[41] Focusing on what you will not do simply puts the thought of that activity into your mind (it's like dieters saying, "I will not eat chocolate" and then being unable to stop thinking about eating chocolate). So formulating an intention along the lines of "I will walk to the store" is likely to be more effective than "I will not drive to the store."

One of the difficulties, though, is that even prompts and intentions can fade into the background; you stop noticing the note reminding you to walk rather than drive or stop paying attention to the device that tells you how much electricity you are using; when behavior becomes habitual, you will no longer notice reminders. (The good news is that if you've managed to establish the habit you wanted to by that point in time, the behavior might stick.)

And old habits rarely die; they just become dormant. It is easy to reactivate a habit that you have moved past, if the old cue arises.[42] If you have become a vegetarian when you eat out, your first trip to a summer barbeque might find you, unthinkingly, with a burger in your hand. For that reason, creating a new habit that replaces the old one in the same context is key; better yet are interventions to avoid creating the problematic habit in the first place.

RULES OF THUMB

Habits are formed because they liberate us from having to make a complex decision every time we undertake an action. Similar approaches, like developing rules of thumb, can play a similar role in making environmentally beneficial choices. Complex information can go into decisions to prioritize behavior that avoids environmental harm. That information is frequently difficult to access, and too much to consider when making decisions on a reasonable timescale for all the choices we make in any day.

Instead, general practices that we follow, and that guide more specific decisions within these practices, can help. Ideas like "Eat low on the food chain," for instance, can guide decisions about which forms of protein to buy, without having to investigate the sustainability of farming or fishing practices. A rule of thumb may be an imperfect representation of the full environmental impact of protein choices, but its simplicity makes it much more likely to be remembered and followed, and thus more effective over-all. The principle of avoiding disposable products, or always purchasing organic products if they're within a certain price differential, are other examples of environmentally relevant rules of thumb.

These approaches allow simpler navigation of daily practices without having to engage in intense data gathering, and they require less mental processing to remember. It is unproblematic to then adjust individual decisions to fit in with the broader rule of thumb. Such rules of thumb are also generally teachable, which makes them candidates for conveying an approach to others. For example, the Environmental Working Group, an NGO headquartered in Washington, DC, advocates "eating lower—and better—on the food chain," in a post on its website.[43] Michael Pollan's most-quoted food rule—"Eat food, not too much, mostly plants"[44]—also guides the food choices of many people, in part because it is simple and memorable.

DEFAULTS

Defaults—the option you get without making a deliberate choice—structure choices. Because environmental problems are externalities, the default way of behaving may represent a problematic environmental choice, unless it has been deliberately set up for environmental purposes. Like habits or routines, defaults shape behavior without persuasion or conscious thought, and thus are powerful tools for creating either good or bad environmental behavior.

There are many nonenvironmental examples of the power of defaults; the two most commonly discussed are organ donation and retirement savings. Internet privacy policies[45] and insurance selections[46] are other contexts in which defaults are shown to determine behavior. Understanding the role of defaults in these contexts can inform efforts to influence behavior that has environmental implications.

How a decision about organ donation is presented dramatically affects the likelihood that people will choose to become organ donors. The difference between countries that use an opt-out approach (in which you must choose to remove your name from the list of organ donors) and an opt-in approach (in which you must put your name onto a list of organ donors) is stark. For example, Germany and Austria share numerous political and cultural similarities. In Austria people are automatically organ donors unless they opt out, and 99 percent of residents are organ donors. In Germany, with an opt-in system, only 12 percent are.[47] An analysis of European organ donation consent rates shows them to be above 85 percent (and most above 95 percent) for countries with opt-out policies, and ranging from 4.25 percent to 27.5 percent for those with opt-in requirements for donation.[48] Laboratory experiments show organ donation rates twice as high when people have to opt out rather than opt in.[49]

In the United States, where retirement savings plans are often optional, few people participate, even though there are long-term benefits to joining these plans. (This behavior is reminiscent of discussions in chapter 2 about the difficulties of prioritizing the future.) Often employers will match contributions up to a certain amount, and so not enrolling in the programs involves forfeiting this money from employers. Most of these programs require active enrollment; workers must choose to contribute and fill out additional paperwork do to so, and must choose the level of savings. Both natural and laboratory experiments have shown that changing the default to automatic enrollment dramatically increases the number of people who participate, or who save more than the bare minimum.

One study looked at several large companies that switched from requiring workers to choose to participate in a 401(k) program to automatically enrolling them but allowing them to opt out. Before automatic enrollment, the percentage of participants in one company ranged from 26.4 (for those employed for the shortest period of time) to 64 percent (for those employed for the longest period measured). After automatic enrollment, these percentages ranged from 93.4 percent to 98.8 percent. The other two companies followed similar patterns.[50] Even when enrollment was made automatic, a default savings rate had to be chosen. Not surprisingly, the most likely savings amount, by a large margin, was the default rate, even when it was lower than the maximum match rate.[51] These findings have been replicated across a wide variety of studies.[52]

Information about the process and benefits of retirement savings has been found to have little effect on plan enrollment or savings behavior. Most workers seem to know that their current savings are below what they should be, but that has not affected their retirement savings rate,[53] suggesting that attitudes and even preferences are easily trumped by defaults.

Some scholars attribute our overreliance on default options to cognitive biases.[54] But there are good reasons for people to follow the default option, even when changing away from the default might have economic benefits. Doing enough research to determine whether it is better to shift away from a default option takes time and effort. There may be required steps to take—forms to fill out, appointments to make—that make selecting away from the default more difficult.[55]

This difficulty is more pronounced when people are unfamiliar with the choices they are given.[56] But the default effect is strong in laboratory experiments even when there is no additional effort required for the switch,[57] which suggests that it is neither information nor difficulty that fully explains why people stick with the default option.

For environmental issues and other issues with powerful defaults, decision-making can be seen as stressful or unpleasant.[58] A choice is rarely completely one-sided, so switching requires assuming risk—the possibility that the new option you choose will be worse than the original option.[59] Unlike standard assumptions of economic theory, it has been repeatedly shown that people are more concerned about the possibility of losses than the advantage of equally valuable gains.[60] The possibility of making the "wrong" choice engages this loss aversion, because the default is seen as the status quo.[61]

Similarly, the types of choices we face for environmental behavior often involve trading off unrelated benefits (like the value of protecting the environment versus the value of saving money).[62] By not choosing—by accepting the default option—we are able to avoid what might be a complex moral decision.[63]

Finally, there is a social component to defaults. We may, not unreasonably, interpret them as a recommendation from the entity that creates the default. We may interpret a default as the best option for our interests,[64] or the best social choice, given that it is the option put forth most prominently.[65] Terminology used in describing the default option can contribute to this assumption.[66] Practically speaking, the default *is* a form of recommendation; it is the action that will be chosen if no choice is made, and in that sense, whether intended or not, it is the most likely outcome. It should be no surprise that it is the most frequently chosen.

This default bias suggests an easy policy solution for environmental behavior: make the environmentally beneficial outcome the default option. From a policy perspective it is a much easier solution than other options, because it allows people to retain full choice. If they do not want green electricity (and the higher price it often entails), do not want their department's paper purchases to be on 100 percent recycled paper, or do not prefer the use of greener cleaning products by a cleaning service, they have complete autonomy to choose another option. But for those who opt not to choose, greener behavior will result.

But the important insight from marketing is that default is most powerful when those choosing it are not concerned that the entity offering the choice benefits from the default selection. Using the default as an implicit recommendation will be more successful if the entity offering the choice isn't seen to gain commercially or individually if people select the default. Fortunately, in most environmentally relevant circumstances, defaulting to the better environmental option is unlikely to be seen as a gain for the government or organization offering that choice.

There are a few other dangers. People resent having been put into a situation where they need to spend more money. When the default option is more expensive, they may actually become more likely in those instances to select away from the default. A study of taxi services that automatically suggest a tip level suggests that while the average tip is larger when the default tip is higher, a greater number of people opt to leave no tip at all.

Other studies have found that people automatically enrolled in programs that they would not have chosen are more likely to opt out; in one instance of a green energy program, some of those who withdrew from the default option actually increased their energy use after doing so.[67] So defaults are not necessarily a panacea and must be designed carefully.

Even if green behavior cannot be made the default in a setting where there is one, there are ways to decrease the default effect and allow people to choose the greener option. Reduce the difficulty of changing away from the default, by providing information or reducing the paperwork or other effort required to change. When I was on a committee in my town that sought to persuade people to sign up for (more costly) renewable electricity, our biggest success came from bringing the enrollment forms (and a pen) to people who attended a town event; all they had to do was sign the form and they would be switched away from the default of nonrenewable electricity.

If people face consternation about the difficult trade-offs implied by having to choose, emphasizing the advantages of the greener option may help tip the balance. Increased education may be one way to accomplish this goal,[68] although, as chapter 4 suggests, it has its limits. Information can nevertheless reduce people's uncertainty about their own preferences, which can make moral or complex decisions easier to make, or can reduce the implicit deference to the authority that set the default.[69]

BUSINESS ROUTINES

Organizations, as well as individuals, are guided by habit. This tendency may be even stronger at the collective level, because organizations are composed of many people acting together. Most of them are simply performing one part of the action that contributes to whatever the organization or business is trying to accomplish, and do not have much in the way of decision-making authority. The classic text on the subject argues that much of the behavior of firms can be "understood as a reflection of general habits and strategic orientations coming from the firm's past,"[70] rather than as intentional decisions about future action. Others go so far as to argue that "organized social systems *require* at least some routinization of behavior to get work accomplished."[71] Unlike individual habits, which usually emerge without focused attention, business routines are often intentionally created. Those organizational habits, in turn, affect what individual choices are available.

Although firms can make strategic decisions to operate differently, most of what they do, most of the time, is routine. Those in business "do not always 'calculate' before they make decisions and they do not always 'decide' before they act."[72] There are procedures in place for how people are hired or fired, processes for how production is increased or decreased depending on demand, standard ways the inputs are ordered or investments are undertaken, along with nearly every other action a business is likely to encounter in its everyday operations.[73] Firms need routines to manage the complexity of information and choice in a context of the complexity of an organization of individuals.[74]

In addition, because the operations of firms depend on the actions of the people who work there, the habits of individuals are a core part of activity that happens within a firm.[75] The skills that workers have are themselves routines, characterized by "tacit knowing," the ability to perform an operation, even a high-level one, without being able to fully explain all the aspects required to do it.[76] Because behavior of most people who work in a firm is intentionally routine, behavior in a business context is likely even more habitual than in everyday life.

The idea of "rules of thumb" also applies in a business context; this simplified decision-making model can be particularly important for individuals acting in the context of an organization to make quick and consistent choices based on abbreviated levels of information. A firm may, for instance, generally spend 5 percent of its revenue on marketing, or a store may restock when its inventory falls below 20 percent. This approach can be particularly effective when applied by those with limited time or training.[77]

As with individual behavior, these standard approaches can be adaptive. Routines can help groups of people working together avoid coordination problems.[78] In particular, they can decrease transaction costs that would come from having to determine who will carry out which step in a collective task.[79] They can lead to organizational stability and careful evolution,[80] as well as accountability and efficiency.[81] Rules of thumb allow for quick decisions without the need for complex calculation or data gathering, and routines thus make efficient use of time and attention available to people within an organization.[82]

But they can also cause problems for firms. Routines that are ideal when created become less beneficial over time, as external conditions inevitably change. The very presence of a routine, and the efficiency it creates, reduces a firm's ability to adapt to changing circumstances.[83]

And these routine operations can be environmentally problematic. As with individual behavior, routines in businesses and organizations were often set up for nonenvironmental purposes, and those purposes are likely to involve environmentally problematic consequences. A clothing store that wraps all purchases in tissue paper and puts the receipt in a fancy envelope is creating solid waste in the service of its business effort to signal luxury. A coffee shop that routinely puts its coffee in disposable takeout cups even if many of the patrons are consuming their beverages onsite may be able to increase the speed of its operations, with the effect of increased waste. A store that regularly keeps its lights on at night to showcase its wares in the storefront is using more energy and creating more greenhouse gas emissions than if it were turning off the lights.

That is not to say that these business routines are bad business decisions; to the contrary, they were almost certainly created because they were believed to be to the business's advantage. Once they are routines, their other effects are unlikely to be regularly evaluated. Especially if they are chosen for efficient operations—or if operations are efficient precisely because there's a routine to follow—it may be extremely difficult to interrupt the routine, even if you don't want your clothing wrapped in nonrecyclable paper or your coffee in a disposable cup.

Organizations or individuals acting in routine ways are unlikely to make the conscious effort required to avoid environmentally degrading action. That may be even more true for businesses than for individuals, since the logic of a business is to make money, and often environmental choices are more costly, at least initially, than business as usual.

Another way that routines can be problematic for the environment is in the area of innovation. Existing standard operating procedures and rules of thumb dominate not only current operating procedures, but also any efforts to develop alternatives.[84] The more mired in routine your organization is, the less likely it is to come up with new ways of operating. Studies show that groups of people operating in routinized ways are more likely than individuals to continue using these processes even when they prove counterproductive.[85] That can keep a business from being on the cutting edge of whatever industry it is operating in, and can prevent a firm from exploring new ways to minimize its environmental impact.

The efficiency gains created by standard operating procedures contribute to the difficulty of change. Because these procedures ensure compatibility between different parts of an organizational structure, individual processes often can't be changed without coordination with all other parts of the firm. That makes change much less likely than if innovation can be undertaken in isolation.[86]

An important perspective on this issue comes from economist Michael Porter.[87] He posited that environmental regulation, normally understood to bear a cost, could actually be economically advantageous for firms. It would require them to innovate, something that will realistically only happen when forced by some external constraint.[88]

This perspective was initially counterintuitive within the study of business. Because businesses seek to maximize profit, the assumption has been that anything that saves money would be preferred, without the need for external regulation. The parallel to individual habit is clear: decisions by firms, despite a general belief to the contrary, are not made in the context of complete information and rational decision-making. Instead, firms face "highly incomplete information, organizational inertia and control problems reflecting the difficulty of aligning individual, group and corporate incentives."[89]

The Porter hypothesis itself is controversial, and subsequent studies have found varying degrees of empirical support for it.[90] But the broader point stands that firm-level procedures are not the fully profit-maximizing rational behavior that economic models foresee. The assumption by neoclassical environmental economics that "markets are flawed but that firms are perfect" is odd.[91] Instead, there are good reasons to believe that firms are often prevented by their standard operating procedures from investigating new approaches, and that systematic "organizational failures" operate in a similar way to the market failures that produce environmental externalities.[92]

The experiences of routines within organizations suggests the power they can have when harnessed in the service of improving environmental effects. In the same way that making environmental behavior habitual can change individual behavior in a more lasting way than working to influence action on a per-decision basis, integrating environmental consideration into the routines of a business can have a much more dramatic effect than periodically making environmentally beneficial operating decisions. The same resistance to change that prevents operational exploration promotes consistent and widespread adoption of new routines designed to decrease environmental impact. These may be taken on for different reasons: a firm may realize the possibility for decreased costs from efficiency or waste reduction; a CEO may decide to position a company as an environmental leader; or external regulation may require a shift in behavior in order to meet legal obligations.

A classic example can be seen in decisions made by the delivery company UPS in the United States. Beginning in 2004 it changed the way its delivery trucks were routed, in order to avoid the idling inevitable when waiting to make left turns. The company's goals were to increase delivery speed and to reduce gasoline consumption. Building on data it had been able to collect as vehicle-tracking systems became more sophisticated, it determined that both time and fuel could be saved, even if trucks had to drive farther, by avoiding left turns. The company concludes that it saved 10 million gallons of gasoline and reduced 100,000 tons of carbon emissions in the first five years of its change in practice.[93] In 2012 alone the practice is credited with saving 1.5 million gallons of fuel, 13,000 metric tons of carbon emissions forgone, and "206 million minutes" saved.[94]

Walmart has done even more to integrate environmental issues into the routines of its business. It has done so primarily because of the economic advantages it has reaped from increased efficiency and decreased waste.[95] Its actions have garnered good press and reputational benefits as well. Walmart is such a large company, earning more annually than the GDP of Australia,[96] that any systematic change it integrates into its operations will have a huge effect, for reasons of scale alone. Increasing gas mileage in the vehicle fleet by one mpg for the company was estimated to save more than $52 million per year.[97] It met its goal of doubling fleet efficiency by 2015, which it accomplished in part by training drivers in driving techniques and by creating systematic efficiencies in loading and routing.[98] Other changed procedures, enforced throughout its supply chain, concern packaging and energy use. An early decision to reduce the packaging size of a toy truck by several inches allowed the same number of toys to be shipped using 497 fewer shipping containers, saving $5.2 million in shipping costs for these toys alone.[99] Demanding this type of change throughout its supply chain as a matter of routine business practice could make a huge difference because of the size and reach of the company. Whatever one thinks of Walmart or its motivations for tackling sustainability, it has clearly addressed the issue—and done so with dramatic effect—through changing its business routines and those of its suppliers. Small but systematic changes in operating procedures can make a big environmental difference.

HABIT AND ENVIRONMENTAL CHOICES

When our activities are habitual, we aren't making conscious choices to engage in them. Existing problem characteristics and incentives mean that those habitual choices are likely to have problematic environmental consequences. That means that even when our intentions are to make better environmental choices, we may not be able to implement those intentions. Figuring out how to interrupt and change those habits can have a deeper effect than making discrete decisions to do the right environmental thing.

Because of the power of habit, any environmentally relevant decision we can make into a routine that is automatically undertaken or a default option that happens if we don't choose otherwise will have a greater reach than any one-off decision. Systematizing environmental behavior (or creating the context in which actions taken by many people are likely to become routine) can make a greater environmental difference than focusing on single actions by individuals.

Attitudes and Norms

Does it matter whether we care about protecting the environment? Activists frequently try to convince us to be concerned about the fate of endangered species, old-growth forests, or the global climate system. Or they work to raise awareness of problems and our contributions to them, in the hopes that our innate belief in the value of the environment or concern about people harmed will engage our behavior. Can our environmental misdeeds be explained by inadequate concern or fixed through changing our attitudes?

People often do feel morally obligated to protect the environment. Majorities of people in many developed countries express a willingness to "do what is right for the environment, even when it costs more money or takes more time."[1] Although this level of concern in developed countries has declined slightly over the past two decades, it has increased in developing countries.[2] The World Values Survey in 2005 found majorities in twenty-eight of the thirty-seven countries surveyed indicated that "looking after nature" is important to them.[3] Environmentalism has been called a "consensus" movement: supported by the vast majority of people and opposed by only a small minority.[4]

Much of the effort to explain the role of values, attitudes, and similar characteristics in influencing behavior begins with a set of interrelated theories in psychology. The theory of reasoned action (TRA) posits that attitudes lead to an intention about how to behave, which then can lead to action.[5] The stronger the attitude and the stronger the intention, the more likely it is that the action will take place. The theory of planned behavior (TPB) modifies the TRA, by adding the idea of "perceived behavioral control," the ease of performing the action.[6] In this framing, the easier it is to perform the intended action, the more likely it is to happen. Another modification of the theory adds identity into the framework,[7] and values create the framework for attitudes in the first place.

But the link that runs from values and attitudes to action is tenuous in practice. Decades of research attempting to demonstrate that action relating to the environment begins with values or attitudes has failed to show a consistent connection. Even our identity is not a clear guide to our behavior: we each hold many different views of ourselves simultaneously, and they may be in competition with each other for influence.

It shouldn't be surprising that many of our daily activities are not driven by the attitudes or values we have about protecting the environment. Problem characteristics and incentives are often aligned in a way that makes it more difficult or more expensive to protect the environment than to do otherwise. It is easy to dismiss the environmental benefits or harms from our behavior, which are likely to be minimal in an individual calculation. From a purely rational standpoint, making the inconvenient or costly choices we would have to make to diminish our environmental footprint often doesn't make sense. Moreover, the hundreds of choices we make in a given day (many of which, as chapter 5 explains, become sufficiently habitual that we're not even aware that we're making them) overwhelm our capacity to constantly choose the more difficult and costly path. To make a difference, billions of people across the globe would have to prioritize environmental action over other goals. Our values would have to be powerful indeed to regularly overcome those incentives.

That so many of us express environmental concern and then fail to act based on it suggests that our environmentally damaging behavior cannot bye convincingly explained by attitudes. Likewise, focusing on attitudes as a way to change environmental behavior is inadequate at best and misguided at worst.

It's a slow process. Values, attitudes, and identities tend to be quite stable over long periods of time and thus not amenable to quick adaptation for political goals. Addressing many environmental problems requires widespread behavior change on a short time-frame from large numbers of people. Attitudes tend to be formed early in life, with opportunities for change coming primarily at moments of major life changes.

A focus on persuading people to make environmental choices because it is the right thing to do may even be counterproductive. People resist being told what to do and may dig in their heels at the suggestion that they are making the wrong ethical choices. Constantly having to decide to do the right thing can also backfire as people "use up" their reserves of willpower or relax their standards once they've established their moral credentials, and become less likely to choose the "right" option over time.

And yet people do sometimes make moral decisions to act in environmentally responsible ways, even when doing so is inconvenient. More importantly, the people who are the most morally invested in environmental protection may be the ones who put in the political effort to change the rules, incentives, or even norms of a community to increase the odds that others will improve their environmental behavior. So even if, as this book argues, an effort to change collective environmental behavior through values, attitudes, or identity is a hopelessly inefficient path to protecting the planet, these aspects may still play an important role in collective behavior change.

Social norms—the behavioral expectations that we hold collectively as a community, and our individual desires to live up to these standards—hold more promise as ways to change behavior in support of environmental goals. We prefer to fit in with the principles of the groups we are in, especially if these ways of acting are consistent with individual values or attitudes we already hold. Discovering what those community norms are, or moving from one community to another one, can motivate reasonably quick change to fit in with newly discovered expectations. Moreover, those norms can drive attitudes by changing our behavior. Even then, the social pressure to adhere to collective norms works best when these pressures tap into feelings we already have about central values. We are unlikely to make a wholesale adaptation to fit in with a tendency we don't see as important.

While exploring the details of how and when attitudinal factors affect environmental choices—or don't—this chapter argues that values, attitudes, and identity are a less powerful tool for direct and widespread behavioral change for the environment than many activists implicitly believe. These factors nevertheless play an underappreciated role in supporting efforts to change behavior through social norms, and collectively can be important in motivating the individual choices and political action of some of the most committed environmentalists. They underpin and are likely necessary for most widespread structural and political change, which is ultimately central to creating large-scale collective behavior change.

VALUES, ATTITUDES, AND IDENTITY

Environmental behavior is often framed as a moral issue. We are urged to do the right thing for the planet and its inhabitants, as an ethical choice. With that framing, an obvious approach to addressing environmental problems would be to ensure that people have the right values, attitudes, or identities, with the assumption that developing an ethical concern about, or framework toward, the environment would lead to better behavior.

Values are "guiding principles important in a person's life."[8] They are big overarching ethical orientations, like altruism, or abstract ideals, like openness to change. Because values are vague and general, they may not provide clarity on how to approach specific decisions. There are nevertheless some reasons to expect that values should play a role in environmental behavior. For most of us, the majority of environmental issues do not directly and immediately affect us, and new environmental problems are regularly emerging. If we have little direct experience with or knowledge about environmental issues, we may approach these issues by looking at whether the issue will be harmful for things that we value.[9]

Attitudes are evaluative judgments by individuals. They are more specific than values and apply to a broader range of things—you can have an attitude about an object ("I like trees") or an issue ("I'm against fracking"). Several components are likely to comprise an attitude: feelings, beliefs, and behavior. Emotion, or what psychologists call "affect," may be the "real driving force of attitude."[10] The love you feel for a specific landscape, or the anger that surges when the cement truck drives by spewing foul-smelling dark smoke, indicates—or plays a central role in creating—your attitude about environmental protection.

Identity is a kind of shorthand for a person's sense of self. A common way to look at it is "the label used to describe oneself."[11] An identity can be seen as a shorthand approach you take when facing decisions, similar to the way habits or standard operating procedures (discussed further in chapter 5) provide a framework for behavior. Developing an identity as someone who cares about the environment or who engages in environmentally friendly behaviors may lead you to make certain types of choices.

In this explanation, I recycle because I believe myself to be the type of person who recycles.[12] Or perhaps I recycle not so much because of what type of person I actually am, but rather how I see my ideal self; recycling expresses something about who I want to be,[13] and how I want others to perceive me.

My identity as an environmentalist certainly influences my behavior. I walk to work, except in the most punishing weather, and I make sure to bring a reusable mug with me when I walk to our local coffee shop. In fact, when I have walked halfway to the shop and realize I have forgotten my reusable coffee mug, I am likely to walk many blocks home to go pick it up, something that cannot be accounted for by the incentive of the ten-cent discount for bringing my own mug. And it's not even clear that the environmental benefits of the reusable mug (less solid waste) clearly outweigh the environmental downsides (increased water for washing). From an economic standpoint my behavior is irrational; my time is worth far more than the ten cents I'll save. But my identity is wrapped up in being an environmentalist, and using the coffee shop's disposable cup is anathema to that identity.

Although the concepts of values, attitudes, and identities are studied by different research communities, they are interrelated. Values predict environmental attitudes in consistent ways across countries.[14] Identities generally reflect the values and attitudes a person has. Studies regularly show consistency among identity, attitudes, and values relating to the environment.[15] These three concepts also share similar characteristics and affect behavior—or don't—in similar ways.

GENESIS OF VALUES, ATTITUDES, AND IDENTITY

Values, attitudes, and identity are generally formed early in life and tend to be stable over time.[16] That makes them a tricky tool for environmental persuasion. On the one hand, if you can contribute to the formation of these attitudinal frameworks in a person or a population, they are likely to endure. On the other hand, there may be few opportunities to create them because people are not routinely seeking new ones. How are they formed in the first place?

Value orientations are probably first created by socialization processes in childhood; families and early experiences play a strong role. Attitudes are formed from feelings, beliefs, and behavior.[17] People read their attitudes from their feelings. Beliefs (often referred to in the scholarly literature as "cognition") are the nonemotional understandings that underpin attitudes.[18] Education may contribute to values through this belief function. There is evidence that the more people know about the environment, the more they have favorable environmental attitudes.[19]

Past behavior, especially direct experience, contributes to the development of attitudes. More interesting, though, is the role of indirect experience.[20] People who form attitudes from hearing about something they did not themselves experience have attitudes about it that are more polarized, less nuanced, and more extreme than are those attitudes that come from direct experience.[21] It may be that hearing about something rather than experiencing it fails to communicate contextual or mitigating information that would allow a more nuanced understanding of it. If this effect holds for environmental attitudes, about which we rarely have much direct experience, it can help explain the polarization on issues like climate change.

These emotional, cognitive, and behavioral aspects of attitudes may be difficult to disaggregate. Think of attending a rally for an environmental cause. You may enjoy the communal aspect of a rally (the "feelings" component), believe that it will have a positive effect on creating an environmental policy you want implemented (the "belief" component),[22] or remember that you have previously attended rallies and conclude that you support attending rallies. Or, having attended this one and enjoyed it, you will then conclude that you favor rallies.[23]

Identity is related to these concepts. One way to think of identity is as something we adopt to create coherence across our attitudes and behaviors, as well as others' expectations of us.[24] As with attitudes, past behavior plays a role in identity creation: one of the ways we come to understand our own self-identities is through observation of our own behavior. We then rationalize this behavior into a coherent identity.[25] Habit thus can also contribute: behaviors that are undertaken repeatedly are key candidates for identity formation. Someone who does something repeatedly (such as bicycling or binge drinking) comes to self-identify as the sort of person who does those types of things.[26] From an analytical perspective it can be difficult to determine whether it is the habit or the identity that causes the behavior going forward (since the two interrelate in this context). A study of binge drinking, for instance, concluded that identity most directly affects intention, whereas habit most directly affects behavior.[27]

Aspects of individual identities may be formed in adolescence, when people are open to new ideas and coming to define who they are in relation to others.[28] Other aspects of identity are probably continually formed, as people experience and interact with their environment and social context.[29]

DO ATTITUDES AFFECT BEHAVIOR?

Values, attitudes, and identity, however, are only tenuously connected to behavior. Scholars refer to the "value-action gap"[30] and an "attitude-behavior gap"[31] in environmentalism. Whatever we know about values and attitudes gets us only so far in explaining why people behave the way they do environmentally.

People who hold altruistic values are more likely to report that they engage in environmentally friendly behaviors.[32] Some researchers have found that prosocial values relate to environmental intentions, and that a focus on "self" in a social dilemma correlates with less concern for the environment.[33] But that finding is not consistent, and a number of scholars have found no relationship.[34]

The same is true of attitudes. A review of thirty-one studies on attitudes concluded that, rather than being able to draw a close link between attitudes and behavior, "it is considerably more likely that attitudes will be unrelated or only slightly related to behavior."[35] Social psychologists have also pointed to a "low or nonsignificant" relationship between attitudes and behavior.[36] Not everyone believes that attitudinal factors play no role in environmental behavior. Other meta-analyses do find some relationship between the two.[37]

Numerous other studies across environmental issues and geographic areas show little or no effect of attitudes on behavior. One study, conducted when unleaded gasoline (the less polluting option) was just becoming available and cost slightly more than its leaded counterpart, examined attitudes people had about environmental protection. It found that people who expressed support for protecting the environment were no more likely than those who did not to buy unleaded gasoline.[38] A study of poaching endangered antelope in the former Soviet Union found that, when it comes to conservation of endangered species, "positive attitudes towards a resource are not necessarily linked to positive conservation action."[39]

Perhaps identity is the missing element for turning attitudes into action. Attitudes that are expressed with the personal pronoun (and thus more likely to be seen as central to identity) predict behavior better than those expressed without.[40] Having an environmental identity does correlate with environmental behavior in some cases. In one study, people who ranked highest on an environmental identity scale were also most likely to report engaging in sets of environmentally sustainable behaviors.[41] Other questionnaires determined that environmental identity contributes more to (reported) environmental behavior than do values such as ecological worldview.[42]

It is possible that self-reporting about behavior should not be taken at face value, however. People work to project external consistency with the values or identity aspects they want to hold. It would therefore not be surprising for those with an environmental identity to over-report environmental behaviors, though some of the scholars of the identity studies believe that the subjects did not "overly inflate" their actions.[43] A relationship between pro-environmental attitudes and self-reported pro-environmental behavior[44] is more often found in studies that do not investigate the actions themselves. Attitudinal factors generally do better at predicting behavioral intentions (what we intend to do) than what we actually do, although they are not even especially good at predicting intentions.[45]

There are many reasons for this disconnect between attitudes and behavior. First is the broader context of structures and incentives our activities are embedded in. Even those who study the role of values, attitudes, and identity acknowledge that "many environmentally consequential behaviors are strongly influenced by factors outside an individual's control."[46]

Any specific action involves more than just an attitude. If you prioritize recycling but your town has no recycling facilities, it is difficult to act in support of that concern. Organic fruit may not be available in your grocery store, so your options for living up to your attitude favoring green agriculture may be limited.[47] To overcome those barriers, environmentally relevant values would have to be a primary focus of your life. Other factors discussed in chapter 2, like issues of time and distance, can also decrease the behavioral influence of attitudes. The effort to recycle takes place in the middle of a busy workweek, while the benefits are felt collectively in the long term and often far away. Incentives are also likely to point in the wrong direction: if there is organic produce available, it almost certainly costs more. People might have values that support environmental action, all else equal. But all else is rarely equal.

In addition, values, attitudes, and identity are broad.[48] Behavior is specific (you decide whether to take the bus to work this morning, what to eat for dinner, or which washing machine to buy), and the guidance these ethical orientations deliver may not be detailed enough. Attitudes ("I believe in preventing climate change"), though more specific than values, are still general. It may not be clear how a given attitude translates to a specific action or—in the case of deciding whether to take the bus to work—if the suggested action would even have a measurable effect on the issue your attitude is about. Any given attitude could translate to more than one potential behavior. Valuing the lives of animals could lead me to become a vegetarian or to prefer humanely raised meat.

It is also likely that at least some aspects of values, attitudes, or identity conflict with each other, which can make it difficult to draw clear implications for behavior. I have an antipesticide attitude and also a concern for protecting public health; these attitudes offer opposing advice on mosquito control. Whatever I choose to do will conflict with one of those attitudes.

People also have multiple identities. I am a college professor, a woman, a Democrat, a musician, a dog owner, and an environmentalist, among other identities; any of these may have different levels of salience at different points in time, and they can be more or less prominent depending on what decisions I face. It is reasonable to expect that at some points the behavior expected from one identity will conflict with that from another, or at least take priority on a given decision.

A pro-environmental identity can influence behavior in an environmentally preferable direction. But identities of other sorts—as a nurturing parent, an efficient executive, or a thrifty consumer, for instance—may actually work against paying attention to environmental issues. Car drivers who see driving as a part of their identity are less likely to consider using public transportation than those for whom driving is not a core identity.[49]

SO WHY STUDY ATTITUDES?

If there isn't a direct relationship between attitudes and behavior, why even examine them? First, because attitudes are prevalent—we all have lots of evaluative beliefs about a lot of things and we communicate them to others. Even if my specific attitude about something is not a reliable predictor of my behavior on that issue, the collections of attitudes that people have (Is the population concerned about ozone depletion? How do people feel collectively about reintroducing wolves in an area?) can influence the messages that politicians receive and the actions or policy steps they choose to take.[50]

This link to policy can be even more direct. Identity may influence a person's willingness to take political or social action, such as writing to public officials or attending meetings related to environmental issues. One study suggested that 27 percent of this type of activism can be predicted by environmental identity.[51] Another suggested that an identity as an environmentalist predicts a set of activist behaviors (like contributing funding to organizations, signing petitions, or boycotting products for environmental reasons).[52] Identity in this context can help overcome collective action problems, such as voting. Studies have found that people are more likely to vote when they can vote for someone they see as a member of a group that reflects their social identity,[53] or when they see themselves acting as a member of a group.[54]

This identity-behavior link is more important than the role that identity plays in any given individual behavior. If changing the behavior of many people is necessary to prevent environmental harm, the political action that contributes to broader institutional or incentive change is key. People who identify as environmentalists are the ones most likely to put in the work to make that kind of policy or organizational change that drives widespread environmental behavior change socially.

When do values, attitudes, and identity matter? Attitudes that are most likely to influence behavior are those that are stable, easy to recall,[55] and formed from direct experience.[56] When people face time pressure in making decisions, they are more likely to call upon attitudes to inform their choices,[57] because they don't have the leisure to more fully consider options.

Consumer behavior is also linked to identity. Purchasing choices can help create or reflect identities that people want to have, or communicate that information to others.[58] The social aspects of identity will have a greater effect on behavior that is visible (a product one would use in public or a behavior seen by others) than on things used or done in private.[59] That helps account for my willingness to walk back home when I've forgotten my reusable mug on the way to the coffee shop—and suggests that I might be more likely to do that in my own town than in a distant city.

The ability of attitudes to affect behavior is influenced by external conditions. One study evaluated people's attitudes about recycling; at the same time (and outside of the study's control), collection bins were provided to just over a quarter of the people in the study. The greatest recycling was reported in those households that had pro-recycling attitudes and had also received bins, suggesting an interactive effect between attitudes and ease of action.[60] Other studies found similar effects. When recycling was hard, those with pro-recycling attitudes were much more likely to recycle than those without those attitudes; when recycling was made easier, the effect of attitudes nearly disappeared.[61]

Some scholars have posited an inverted-U relationship to characterize this relationship. Where contextual factors are neutral, attitudes may influence behavior. When contextual factors are either strongly positive (essentially compelling behavior) or negative (effectively preventing it), attitudes play little or no role. This U-shaped relationship has been found for recycling,[62] and for household energy conservation,[63] among other behaviors. Studies have found also greater effects of attitudes on things that require little behavioral change (like expressing support for environmental policy) than on things (like engaging in activist behavior) that require more personal sacrifice. Attitudes thus matter the most when the behavior in question has the least consequence environmentally.[64]

If behavior itself plays a role in influencing attitudes, the relationship is circular: attitudes can be created by behavior but may also influence behavior. Calling attention to past behavior relevant to an attitude (for example, reminding people that they have taken public transportation or recycled)[65] can influence the extent to which they report having a particular attitude,[66] and can make an attitude more persistent in the face of challenge. Recalling past attitude-relevant behavior can also reinforce a person's intentions to behave in a way consistent with the attitude in question,[67] though it may not necessarily influence actual behavior.

If environmentalist values, attitudes, and identities motivate people to behave in a pro-environmental way, they do so as a form of intrinsic motivation, rather than requiring external rewards.[68] That relationship is useful to know and can help explain environmental action that happens even when structures or incentives do not make it easy. Environmental attitudes can thus influence the types of tools available for changing behavior, even if they do not always change behavior directly.

Another advantage of focusing on values, attitudes, and identity for influencing environmental behavior is the potential "spillover" effect.[69] If identity and attitudes are created in part by behavior, then changing environmental behavior in one area may contribute similar action taken in other activities. Once I became a vegetarian, I also started thinking about the environmental effects of other behaviors and became an avid recycler. On the other hand, the connection across environmental behaviors may have the opposite effect: taking action on one issue may make people less likely to act beneficially in other areas, as discussed further below. That negative spillover could happen either through a rebound effect (e.g., buying an energy-efficient air conditioner and using it more frequently than before) or through a moral licensing effect, in which people feel that they have done their moral part and thus feel that they are off the hook in their subsequent actions. In either case, creating a green identity could avoid the possibility of these backfire effects.

SACRED VALUES

One subset of values, those considered as "sacred," may be more behaviorally relevant than others. These could include the injunction not to kill animals, for a vegetarian, or the idea that access to core resources—like water—should be universal. Whether or not you behave in a way consistent with these values or the identity they frame, they are held to be incapable of compromise.[70]

Sacred values may have different implications for behavior or policy than other types of values. If your sacred values are at odds with environmental behavior, incentives are unlikely to be sufficient to get you to change.[71] A person who does not care much about the environment might be persuaded to drive a smaller car in the face of a subsidy for fuel-efficient vehicles, or start bicycling to work in the face of a new parking fee. However, parents who drive their children to school out of concern for their safety, which is a sacred value, are unlikely to be affected by these incentives.

That may be an even bigger issue when someone's central values are opposed to certain types of environmental action. An observant Catholic may be unable to consider birth control no matter the environmental implications of population growth or the incentives for using contraception. The same is true of acceptance of policy approaches. Even if they want to act in an environmentally helpful way, free-market absolutists or those who consider property rights to be inviolable may be unwilling to consider the imposition of environmental constraints on what people can do with the property they own.

The phenomenon of sacred values can also help explain environmental choices that committed environmentalists make even when the incentives are aligned against such behavior. I, for instance, have been a vegetarian, for ethical reasons, for most of my life. I am never tempted to "cheat" (as friends often ask me), even when it means there is nothing I can eat at a dinner I'm invited to. For most people, environmental values are not sacred. But for those for whom they are, this factor can motivate action even when—as is so often the case—incentives are aligned against good environmental behavior.

When people's sacred values are threatened, they respond by expressing moral outrage or by undertaking actions that will "reaffirm their solidarity with their moral community."[72] People who are asked to behave (or even contemplate behaving) in a way that violates values they consider to be inviolable will quickly find ways to demonstrate their fealty to those initial values. In one study, people led to consider the cost of a liver transplant in determining which of two lives to save (something that violated their belief that such decisions should not be driven by cost) were more likely to volunteer to work to increase organ donation generally afterward.[73]

Identity functions in similar ways. When people's belief in the validity of their identity is called into question, they may be more likely to act in ways that bolster or signal these identities.[74] They are also more likely to change behavior when the change asked of them does not threaten their identities.[75] People may be more inclined to act in an environmentally friendly way when they "perceive themselves as good environmentalists," something that can be accomplished by drawing their attention to previous environmental activities they have undertaken,[76] or showing them their position relative to others who have been less environmentally involved.[77]

This effect can work both ways. People who feel a threat to their (non-environmental) identity may double down on their actions in environmentally problematic ways. This is similar to the counterintuitive effect, discussed in chapter 4, when people with an antivaccine commitment were given information that showed that their concerns about vaccines were not empirically valid. On the one hand, they responded by agreeing that vaccines were less dangerous than they had previously thought. But they also became less likely to vaccinate their children, which is understandable if they had violated sacred values or a core feature of their identity by acknowledging the lack of vaccine risk. When environmental policy or action conflicts with what some consider to be sacred values or central features of identity, efforts to create change for those people may not only be ineffective, but actually backfire.

Especially difficult is the situation where acting in an antienvironmental manner is an aspect of identity. The phenomenon of climate change denial prominent among Republicans in the United States (and expressed to a lesser degree among conservatives in other countries) has taken on the character of identity marker. Political affiliation is a major determinant of whether or not people profess belief in the basic science of climate change (and, obviously, the extent to which they are concerned about it), and that effect has only increased over time.[78] Because of the importance given in some political contexts to climate change denial, it is clearly seen as a "sacred" aspect of identity for some people, politicians especially, and is thus even more resistant to change than other attitudes.

This attitude/identity polarization creates a feedback loop. People process the information they take in through the ideological frame they have already adopted. Those who have staked a claim to not believing that climate change is a problem are unlikely to pay attention to disconfirming information and may discount any that does not line up with their ideology. That feedback loop is additionally important if climate change-denying politicians succeed in taking action that makes it less likely that climate change will be discussed. This process is apparent in the analogous case of antievolution political action. Policymakers who deny evolution create additional momentum for this position by increasing the extent to which this position is taught in school curricula. People then grow up with this incorrect perspective and are then more likely to vote for politicians or policies that deny evolution.

Climate change denial might also have its roots in values and attitudes. For conservative-leaning people, another reason for potential denial of the broader issue of climate change is the cognitive dissonance it produces with other ideological priorities they espouse, such as a faith in the glories of industrial capitalism.[79] Accepting that climate change is real, dangerous, and due to human activities would require accepting the downsides of this political-economic system and contemplating limits to the market. Those values are almost certainly sacred for those who espouse them, who may respond by being unable to accept the validity of something that would challenge them.

The development of climate change denial into an identity—and perhaps even a social norm—is problematic for the efforts to create political or even widespread individual action on climate change. The idea that politicians need to publicly proclaim their disbelief that climate change is caused by people, or is even a problem, changes political discourse and persuades low-information voters that the issue is not worth attention, much less sacrifice. A bigger problem might arise when holding this position has become a sacred value; challenging it might lead it to be held even more tightly.

Efforts not just to deny the science of climate change but to prevent consideration—or sometimes mention—of it in a political context also point to the efforts to create a social norm of climate change denial, through rules. In the United States, some state governments have prohibited official discussion of climate change. In Florida, the Department of Environmental Protection, likely at the behest of the Republican governor of the state, instructed employees not to use the terms "climate change" or "global warming."[80] More formally, the commission that oversees public lands in the state of Wisconsin formally voted to disallow employees from "engaging in global warming or climate change work" on official time.[81] By state law, North Carolina went so far as to ban using scientific predictions on sea-level rise in making coastal policy, after the coastal commission estimated that the sea level along the state's coast would rise thirty-nine inches over a century.[82]

What is possible with further climate denial at the highest level of US government after the 2016 presidential election is even more worrisome. The United States is not the only country to make these prohibitions. Canada, when Conservative Stephen Harper was prime minister, forbade government meteorologists from mentioning climate change.[83] These rules, ridiculous as they may seem, can have an actual effect, if fewer people come to be aware of the reality of climate change and the problems it creates, and official policy processes are forbidden from taking action to mitigate it.

CHANGING OR PRIMING ATTITUDES, VALUES, AND IDENTITY

Values, attitudes, and identity are useful to study because of their consistency.[84] That makes them much less useful than other factors, however, in changing day-to-day behavior. They are most likely to shift at moments of dramatic changes in circumstances, such as life-changing events or major socioeconomic transition.[85] Paying attention to, and taking advantage of opportunities presented by, these life changes can be a useful strategy.

Attitudes can be influenced by what we do: simply exposing people to something makes them more favorably inclined toward it.[86] Many environmental education programs that take children out into nature implicitly endorse this relationship. Providing opportunities throughout life for people to experience environmentalism or try out a new activity (be it bicycling, political action, or composting) can influence their attitudes and behavior.

But although it can be difficult to change values, attitudes, or identity at most stages of life, they can nevertheless be primed, giving them more or less salience. Experiments show that when people are reminded of values they have, they are more likely to act on them. In one set of studies people had their attention drawn to environmental values (or not) and then (in what was presented as a separate study) asked to make choices about consumer products that varied on characteristics that included environmental impact. Those who had focused in some way on environmental values were more likely to prioritize environmental factors in making their consumer choices. That was especially prominent for people for whom environmental values had been separately determined to be more central.[87]

So although it can be difficult to create new values from scratch, calling attention to preexisting values, attitudes, or identities may increase the likelihood of making environmentally relevant choices by those who have them. In that way, existing values can be used or framed to encourage beneficial environmental behavior. Calling attention to existing attitudes can be done as easily as by asking people about them or mentioning other factors that call them to mind.[88]

Reminding people of past behaviors, or even framing those behaviors as environmentally relevant, can also make a difference. One study found that people in the United States were more likely to support public policy to address climate change when they had been reminded of previous environmental behaviors they had undertaken.[89] One of the reasons that prompts (discussed further in chapter 4) succeed might be that they remind people of attitudes they already hold.

It is also possible to make use of the multiple attitudes or identities all of us have. Which one is salient at any given moment can influence its role, even if that attitude does not rise to the level of consciousness.[90] Holding attitudes that conflict with each other (I am concerned about climate change; I prefer to keep my house warm in the winter) may cause discomfort, which could lead to changing one or the other attitude.[91] But it could also simply lead to emphasizing one over the other,[92] or even rationalizing how the two could coexist (I can't successfully concentrate on writing my book about environmental behavior if I'm too cold, and must therefore keep the thermostat high even though it contributes to climate change).

Attitudes or identities that aren't specifically environment-focused may also be able to be marshaled in the service of environmental behavior. An attitude of frugality has been found to have a greater influence on intentions to conserve gasoline and electricity than environmental concern does.[93] Using those resources has a cost, and increasing efficiency or conservation saves money. Frugal people are also, therefore, likely to be even more concerned about conservation when the cost of gasoline or electricity increases. The incentive reinforces the effect of the attitude. If someone who sees herself as "thrifty" shies away from making more costly choices to affect the environment, framing environmental behavior (such as avoiding waste, repairing and reusing broken things, or growing your own food) as the thrifty alternative may persuade people who identify that way to include positive environmental behavior within that identity.

Similarly, people whose identity as parent might make them most concerned about what is best for their children might be sympathetic to environmentalist concerns about avoiding pesticide use or preventing air or water pollution. People who have place-based identities ("I'm a north woods resident") may be motivated to take particular actions to prevent the degradation of those places via development.[94] One study in Norway found that the extent to which people expressed attachment to a given location as a part of their core identities influenced their opposition to a proposed hydropower project in the area.[95]

Because people have multiple identities, it is possible for those identities to conflict. I see myself as both an environmentalist and a world traveler, and these contradict each other when it comes to the climate change-inducing airplane trips I take to get to faraway locations. What happens when people experience conflicts across their identities? The problem characteristic and incentive difficulties to behaving in environmentally friendly ways suggest that, in case of identity conflict, environmental identities may be the ones to yield.[96] Solutions can involve finding points of reconciliation across divergent identities. A thrifty consumer who is skeptical of the added cost of many environmentally friendly products can be valued for reusing items rather than adding to both cost and waste by buying new ones. Opportunities for purchasing carbon offsets for airplane travel can be presented to world-traveling environmentalists.

Invoking identity in trying to persuade people to take specific actions may thus have a more powerful effect than simply providing information. Consumer marketing has long understood this relationship, invoking identities like "mother" or "American" to remind people of the ways a given purchase fits how they see themselves. Consumers prefer brands that can be seen to fit their identities, and respond to efforts to communicate that relationship.[97] This type of marketing calls the attention of consumers to identities they already hold; they will then be more likely to purchase the products in contexts that have made their identities salient.[98] This effect may be particularly relevant when people are struggling with an identity they want to see themselves as having, and use their choices as a way to reinforce that identity.[99]

Putting too much pressure on people based on identity can backfire. Studies of consumer marketing have found that consumers with an identity (say, environmentalists) were more likely to purchase goods that referenced the identity than those that didn't. These same consumers were less likely, however, to purchase goods that implied that there was only one acceptable way to behave, such as referring to something as "the only good choice for environmentalists."[100] Under those circumstances, the identity referencing backfired.

Invoking identity as a way to influence behavior, therefore, must be undertaken with care. It can nevertheless be a powerful tool that connects values, habit, and behavior. If identity is in part based on actual behavior and, at the same time, influences future behavior, then the importance of getting people to (regularly) engage in environmentally friendly behaviors takes on new significance.

SOCIAL NORMS

Most analysis of environmental behavior comes from a rationalist perspective. It sees people as unitary actors, deciding whether to recycle or take public transportation based on individual calculations of utility. Even discussion of routines or habits, or values or attitudes, generally considers how these factors play into individual decisions. But people are social entities. How others around us behave—and even more important, what their expectations are of how we should behave—influences us in explicitly social ways.

Social norms are "rules and standards that are understood by members of a group," guiding or constraining their behavior without any external obligation.[101] There are different types of social norms, descriptive and injunctive. Descriptive norms are simply observations of how people actually (collectively) behave in situations.[102] The idea that salad generally precedes the meal in the United States and follows the meal in France is a descriptive norm. Injunctive norms, on the other hand, are more clearly prescriptive: they are guidelines to social expectations of how people should act. You should send a thank-you note after you've received a gift. Disposing of a used cigarette butt in a trash receptacle is the right thing to do (rather than dropping it on the ground). Both types can influence environmentally relevant behavior.

Injunctive norms are what most people focus on when they think about the idea of social norms and environmental behavior. These are the things that people *should* do, and that we generally collectively agree that people should do (and that many of us are doing). We can use information about social norms—either existing or aspirational—to persuade people to change their behavior. This approach works because people accept that the underlying goal, whether it be turning out to vote or turning down their thermostats, is a shared goal of the community.

Descriptive norms have been less studied in the context of environmental issues, but they have an enormous effect on behavior. They are the things you don't even think to articulate, because they are simply the way things are done, and you don't think about what other way they could be done. When I moved briefly to a small town in Austria and turned up at the grocery store without bringing my own grocery bags, I discovered that, in this community, the only way you could transport purchases from the grocery store was in whatever conveyance you had brought with you; there simply was no other option available.

Descriptive norms represent an underappreciated opportunity for behavior change. Because we adapt to the situations we find ourselves in, when we find ourselves in places where people behave differently—where they are more likely to walk than drive, or don't use disposable dishware in cafes, or regularly compost their food waste—we tend to adopt those behaviors as well. In some cases, the infrastructure of the location may account for much of the difference; it's more realistic to take public transportation in New York City than it is in Los Angeles, and if you move to a place with separate bike lanes or curbside recycling pickup, it is no surprise that your behavior might change. But the difference goes beyond infrastructure to norms.

Descriptive norms can be simple. It's the fact that when we're in a place where people don't litter, we're much less likely to litter, even if no one is actively telling us not to. Studies even show that when we have experienced a place where littering isn't common, we're less likely to litter elsewhere.[103] The power of descriptive social norms is the power to change other people's behavior simply by the way your actions (especially in the context of similar actions by others in your community) present the "normal" way of behaving in the community, without ever trying actively to persuade anyone of anything.

College campuses are an excellent illustration. Many that have structural similarities have significant differences in campus culture that could affect environmental impact. Campuses of similar sizes may differ dramatically in the extent to which students have bicycles or regularly carry reusable water bottles around. In some cases—or perhaps even initially on some campuses—those decisions are undertaken by students who make those choices out of environmental commitments. But students who matriculate at a college take up its norms, and if this college is one where people carry reusable mugs, even those students without an environmental orientation are likely to do so as well. Conversely, when students encounter dining halls with disposable dishware, they'll take their breakfast cereal in disposable cups without thinking about the implications if they see others on campus doing that as well.

The distinction between the types of social norms isn't always clear, and transgressing what appears to be a descriptive norm can feel like a social faux pas. Likewise, an injunctive social norm is likely to be ineffective if it is not something that a community has collectively adopted. There may, in fact, be a "sweet spot" that balances descriptive and injunctive norms. An injunctive norm is more effectively conveyed when supported by actual behavior. Pointing out how people are behaving, compared to some relevant group, can motivate behavior change. The public nature of information about your own behavior can persuade you to act differently than you otherwise would.

Where do social norms come from? Because they are social they are collectively created, either consciously or not. Norms exist because they fulfill a function for the group that creates them.[104] They generally begin with what people are collectively doing. At some point, they involve some community exhortation, a collective communication of what the community expects on an issue. Information transmission and efforts by the community communicate the norms. Some scholars draw the connection between habits (as individual activities) and social norms, as collective modes of operation that make group actions and behavior work better.[105]

Thomas Heberlein gives an example of an emerging norm of catch-and-release sport fishing in the United States. There had been a common practice of sometimes throwing fish back out of respect for a fish. It was supported by regulations that began to mandate releasing fish under some circumstances, and then expanded, via both a conservation-minded fishing organization and sport-fishing organization that sponsored competitions, into explicit efforts to communicate the norm of generally throwing back fish caught for sport. It is now common among sport fishers, whether in a situation that requires releasing fish or not, to throw back catches.[106]

As this example suggests, rules can contribute to the development of norms. A rule might mandate something that gets taken further than the narrow regulation requires, or a rule might help formalize or expand existing norms. In fact, rules that do not eventually take on the character of social norms—meaning that they gain some collective acceptance of their legitimacy—often fail as rules; witness the widespread disregard for Prohibition in the 1920s in the United States.

Littering and smoking in public are two other examples of the interaction between rules and norms. In each case social norms (against littering or against smoking in certain locations) were formalized by rules and then expanded further. These were upheld via social opprobrium for those who went against the emerging consensus that these are not generally acceptable activities, even in locations where rules were not necessarily in place.[107] And in both cases, there is also widespread variation in the extent to which these are fully accepted social norms, depending on geographic location.

The effectiveness of social norms at changing behavior depends on a number of factors. Norms are most effectively transmitted among a close reference group. For instance, the environmental behavior of adolescents is influenced strongly by the norms within their families.[108] The size of the group exhibiting a norm can make a difference, at least in the range of small groups. In other words, you are more likely to follow the norms of a group of four than three, though once a group reaches large enough numbers the effect of increasing size disappears.

The visibility of the behavior in question matters as well. Social norms are more effective at influencing activities that take place in public. One strategy for social or environmental change is to call public attention to something that might otherwise be private (whether people vote, or how they use energy in their households). The extent to which someone has internalized a norm can make a difference as well, for someone who would experience guilt or shame at violating it,[109] especially if others know.

The salience of the norm—how much attention is called to it—is also important in determining its influence. In a study of the norm against littering that took place in a litter-free parking garage, people were much less likely to litter when they had just seen someone (in this case, a confederate in the study) litter before they decided what to do with a flyer in the windshield of their car.[110] Interestingly, it was the breaking of the norm that called attention to it; those for whom the confederate simply walked by, rather than littering, were 26 percent more likely to litter.

There are numerous examples of situations where social norms influence environmental action. People whose friends or neighbors recycle are much more likely to do so as well.[111] Farmers are likely to make plans to use sustainable agricultural practices when they believe that other farmers in their communities use these practices.[112]

In this context, comparing someone's behavior to that of others is particularly effective in changing behavior. For example, when hotel guests were given different messages about why to reuse towels, those who received the request to "join your fellow guests in helping to save the environment" were 25 percent more likely to reuse their towels than those asked to "show your respect for nature."[113] Similarly, a study in San Marcos, California, examined efforts to persuade residents to use fans instead of air conditioning, using four different messages about why. Groups urged to use fans because of how much money they could save, or how much greenhouse gas they would refrain from emitting, or even how socially responsible it would be, reduced their energy use by more than 3 percent compared to a control group. The group that was asked to do so because 77 percent of their neighbors already did and it was their "community's popular choice!" reduced consumption by 10 percent.[114]

The reverse is true as well: people are motivated by what they think others will know about their behavior. For example, people are more likely to vote when told that the record of whether or not they voted will be made available to their neighbors,[115] though efforts to make political use of this insight in the 2016 presidential primaries in the United States demonstrated the dangers of such an approach.[116]

Social norms can even affect people you would expect to be unlikely to care about the environment. Narcissists, people who have an inflated view of themselves and focus on their own importance, are unlikely to prioritize decisions that have broadly beneficial social consequences but some degree of personal inconvenience. They would seem to be unlikely, therefore, to take the environment into consideration when making personal choices, and studies have confirmed this tendency.[117] But because they are concerned with how they are perceived by others, if environmental concern is a prevailing social norm, it can affect their behavior even if they do not care about environmental protection for its own sake, but instead simply want to be seen as valued members of a community.[118]

This characteristic can lead those with narcissistic tendencies to make green consumer choices. In one study, people in two groups ranking low or high on narcissism were given the option to purchase a desktop computer or a laptop computer; each option came in a "green" and "nongreen" version. In both cases the nongreen option was rated higher in performance and luxury, but the green one had a less problematic environmental effect. Those without narcissistic tendencies were equally likely to choose the green alternative whether they were buying a laptop or a desktop computer. But the narcissistic consumers were much more likely to choose the green alternative if they were buying a laptop, which would be seen by others, than if they were buying a desktop, which would not.[119] When choosing a product that others would see, those who wanted the high regard of others (even if they were not concerned about the environment) chose the greener option.

Similarly, in a study that allowed people to choose green or nongreen purchases when they shopped either online or in a store, those without narcissistic tendencies were equally likely to purchase green no matter the purchasing location. But narcissists were much more likely to make the green choice when their purchases were in public (at a store).[120]

Price was also a factor, but not in the way one might expect. In another study, when offered the choice between a green or nongreen backpack (something, again, that would be seen in public) at varied prices, nonnarcissists were more likely to choose the green option when it was cheaper than when it was more expensive. Narcissists, however, were the opposite: they were less likely to choose the green option when it was cheaper and more likely to choose it when it was more expensive. The willingness to pay a higher price could be used to signal their environmentally conscious credentials.[121]

Even those who are not concerned about protecting the environment can thus be persuaded to make choices with environmentally beneficial consequences in social contexts. This effect would only hold in a societal setting in which acting in an environmentally conscious way is considered to be a positive thing. It suggests in those settings that calling attention to the greenness of choices and providing the opportunity to make those decisions in a public way (or call attention to them publicly) will help persuade some people to choose better environmental options. Even those without narcissistic personality traits may benefit from positive social reinforcement, so there is little downside to these strategies.

People want to uphold norms they believe already exist in their communities. Letting people know that others will be informed of their shirt color choices would not be an effective way to influence behavior, because people have not internalized a belief that shirt color choice says something normative about their basic character. So most uses of social norms focus on calling attention to behavior that might not be in line with a collective belief about how you should behave, and how people generally act (or try to act) within a community, rather than creating those norms from scratch.

Alternatively, calling public attention to something done in private can help develop a public understanding of a community norm and thus change the behavior of others. A composting effort in a Nova Scotia community where 56 percent of the community was already composting asked those who were composting to make that activity visible—by placing a decal on the waste receptacles—in order to indicate to others that composting was a community norm.[122]

There are some dangers in using social norms to try to change behavior. First, giving people information about how others in their community behave is more likely to achieve the desired result for those whose behavior is worse than the expressed norm. If you give information about a norm to people whose behavior is better than the community norm, they might decrease their "good" behavior (observed, for instance, in the case of energy conservation), a so-called boomerang effect.[123] This is where an explicit appeal to injunctive, rather than simply descriptive, norms may be helpful—indicating to people what the desired behavior is, rather than what the existing behavior is.

The second danger is that people don't like to be told what to do. So while people try to fit in with community expectations, an active effort to persuade people to line their behavior up with expectations—especially if those expectations are not, yet, universally shared—can backfire. That may be even more true when people feel that they ought to be behaving in a certain way and aren't. They feel cognitive dissonance because of the difference between their behavior and the norm. An effort to resolve that conflict so they can see themselves as good people can lead them to devalue the norm or the people practicing it. This "anticipated reproach"[124]—the concern that others are judging you negatively for your behavior—can actually make you turn against the behavior that is seen as the ethical choice. This effect can be seen even if a moral leader makes no effort to change anyone's behavior, or even mentions it; people's fear that they would be judged is enough to cause a backlash.

As a longtime vegetarian I have regularly been on the receiving end of such judgments. While I never attempt to persuade anyone to make the food choices I make, I constantly find people dogmatically justifying their meat consumption (and even, it sometimes seems, increasing it, in my presence) once they find out I don't eat meat. The same is true of some environmental behavior, like choosing to bring a reusable mug. In these cases, it is precisely the "normative," rather than "normal," aspect of a norm that causes the problem, and the problem seems most common when the practice in question is still a minority practice. Since that is precisely the moment at which efforts to create and espouse social norms often begin, it suggests caution about our ability to persuade people to do what we see as ethically preferred, whether we are actively attempting to communicate that preference or not.

Appeals to social norms can be an important policy tool when other options are unavailable—for instance, when political inaction prevents incentivizing preferred behavior. Social norms can also serve as the building blocks for eventual policy action. A community that has already reduced its use of disposable grocery bags is much less likely to stand in the way of policy action to eliminate or tax the remaining use. Policy at local levels—where it has a much greater chance at influencing norms because of the closer connection between people and the ability to see what others are doing[125]—can then increase support for policy at higher levels of government, precisely through changing of social norms.

Social norms also can help determine the type of policy options realistically available. When a social norm supports a course of action, coercive regulatory measures are seen as acceptable by the community, whereas in the absence of a social norm, the community is less likely to accept such action; incentives for good behavior (rather than rules against bad behavior) may be the only realistic option.[126]

Social norms can respond to policy as well. The increasing social norm of accepting marriage equality can be attributed at least in part to its legal acceptability. In many communities increasing social acceptance came about as same-sex couples began to get married (rather than the other way around). Likewise, when attitudes appear to change quickly, the change may come from the change in social norms that then affect the underlying attitude. People who see same-sex married couples accepted in their communities recognize that this acceptance is what is expected in the community. Participating in that social norm can then help change the underlying attitude.

Social norms can also help create the broader community that is seen as key to overcoming collective action problems, particularly tragedies of the commons.[127] Norms favor collective outcomes rather than egoistic approaches.[128] They can increase the odds that people will be able to reach a collective outcome.[129] That effect is especially important in contexts—as is generally the case for environmental problems—where the incentive structure does not favor environmental action.

This effect is specific to social norms rather than values or attitudes, which are individually held ethical framings and are less able to help (and in some cases may even hinder) collective behavior. You may decide to act in a socially or environmentally beneficial way because of an ethical concern for the environment. But if you are the only person who makes that choice, you are unlikely to influence the behavior of others in the desired direction, and in some cases might even increase the likelihood of problematic action by others who do not share that personal moral framing. Imagine the hunter who refrains from killing an endangered animal, only to make the population of available specimens greater for those without such moral qualms.

If one of the reasons that people do not contribute to addressing collective problems is that they can't be assured that others will also behave in cooperative ways, then a community norm that supports the behavior in question can increase confidence that any potential individual sacrifice for an environmental purpose will not be in vain, as the ethical hunter's action, described above, would be.

Those who participate in collective action on an environmental issue, impelled by their own values- or identity-based reasons that make them willing to sacrifice for their environmental goals, might help to create the very social norms that help others to overcome collective action problems.[130] That suggests that a valuable strategy to move from individual to collective action is engaging in those behaviors in a visible way, and attempting to move others—however difficult that might be—in the context of a shared social identity. And it suggests that some types of collective action (where you can see the actions of others and use them to choose how you will act) might be more amenable than others to shaping by social norms.

MORAL LICENSING

An approach to changing people's behavior by persuading them to do the right, or socially desirable, thing may sometimes succeed, but it may run into problems. Psychologists observe that when we focus hard on doing something good, succeeding can have unintended consequences, through a mechanism that has come to be known as "moral licensing," or sometimes just "licensing." The idea is that if you make the effort to make what you see as the normatively better choice in one context, you are more likely to make a subsequent decision that is less normatively good.

Studies have examined this phenomenon in a wide variety of contexts. People who were directed to recall previous acts of generosity were 60 percent less likely to donate to a charitable organization than those who had not had their attention focused on good deeds they had done.[131] Men who had the opportunity to present themselves as nonsexist were more likely to express a preference for hiring a male candidate than those men who had not had an opportunity to present themselves as nonsexist. The same was true for racial hiring preferences by white Americans. These results held even when the two stages—establishing nondiscriminatory identities and making hiring decisions—happened across separate experiments.[132]

This tendency has been examined in the context of environmental behavior. In a business simulation, those managers who were directed to recall good deeds they had previously done were less likely to invest in pollution control measures than those who had not thought about ethical choices they had made.[133] Acting environmentally may also decrease your likelihood of taking additional beneficial action. People who purchased "green" products in a store were less likely to act altruistically in a subsequent cooperation game than those who had purchased conventional products.[134] People in the grocery store who use a reusable bag are more likely to buy junk food.[135]

There are several underlying mechanisms that could account for this effect. The first is the idea that we see our choices as relative or contingent. An initial positive act establishes your credentials as someone who behaves in a morally upstanding manner. After an initially virtuous act, you feel justified in behaving in a more self-indulgent way in a subsequent context, having already established your self-image as someone behaving altruistically.[136] This has been referred to as the "moral credentials" model. In other words, the good action establishes your credentials as a good person.[137] If you have already shown yourself to be environmentally concerned, this new less environmentally positive action should be reinterpreted in that light: you, as a concerned environmentalist, would not actually make bad environmental choices.

A second type of explanation sees decisions reflecting how close we are to living up to our intentions. People who are making progress toward a goal or a commitment may decide that it is therefore okay to do something inconsistent with that goal, as a reward or as an acknowledgment of being close to achieving their intentions. They can afford to ease up and not worry so much about what they are supposed to be doing. People closer to fulfilling their intentions or achieving their goals are more likely to do something contrary to their stated way of behaving (like hanging out with friends instead of studying, for those focused on academic success) the more progress they have made toward fulfilling their goals.[138]

Doing something that makes you feel good about yourself makes you less vigilant in guarding against other problematic actions you might take. This "self-completion theory" also suggests that the balancing act works the other way; people who have their attention drawn to some nonvirtuous way they have acted might be more likely to act in a virtuous way to reaffirm the positive view they want to have of themselves or their progress toward their goal.[139]

In both these views, we are essentially constantly navigating a behavioral balancing act, in which behaving well makes us feel virtuous enough that we give ourselves the license to give in to less noble desires. These explanations also suggest the weaknesses in an identity- or values-based approach to creating environmentally good behavior, since framing something as the ethically correct way to behave also engenders or enables the balancing "incorrect" behavior.

A third way to explain the licensing effect is the role of willpower, which has been shown in some contexts to be a depletable resource, at least temporarily. If you exercise willpower (to, say, keep you from eating something unhealthy but yummy), evidence suggests that you are less likely to be able to resist temptation later. Another way to think about the same process is to see self-control as a form of work. Making an intentional choice to behave differently than you otherwise would (and usually, given the existing problem characteristics and incentives, in ways that are legitimately harder or more costly) takes effort, perhaps physical, and certainly mental. The effort that you put into those decisions or those actions counts in the way that any effort does. It depletes your reserves, making it less likely that you will muster the effort to prioritize the environmental choice in your subsequent actions.[140]

This concept is related to—and might actually account for some of the effect of—the Jevons paradox, discussed in chapter 3. The paradox, also known as a rebound effect, happens as innovation allows a resource (such as energy) to be used more efficiently. It will then be used more extensively; additional use of that resource will cancel out some part of the efficiency gains. Most of this paradox is explained by the decreasing costs that accompany efficiency that thus allow expanding use in ways that wouldn't previously have been possible.

But there are almost certainly licensing components to what happens. If you feel virtuous because of your new fuel-efficient car, you might be more likely to drive it longer distances than you otherwise would; after all, you've already done your part to decrease the environmental effects of driving (and any additional mile in such a vehicle causes less damage than would otherwise come from a car). If your office uses 100 percent recycled paper, you might be less likely to worry about any additional printing you do, since you have already taken steps to improve the problem. When I tried to get my local juice shop to make my beverage in a reusable cup, they told me they recycle the disposable cups they use.

There are several practical implications of the licensing effect. The most important of these is that if you want to change behavior, it's best to figure out a way to reorient what you are doing—systematically changing how you act, in a way that doesn't allow for exception—rather than relying on episodic and frequent decisions to do the right thing. I have a friend who, for moral and health reasons, has decided that he shouldn't eat meat. So he tries really hard to avoid eating meat and feels good about himself when he succeeds. And then inevitably he gives in to his desire, usually after a stretch of time of being "good." He feels bad about his action and then returns to his daily struggle to avoid eating meat, until the next temptation comes after a stretch of successful avoidance. If he actually wants to give up eating meat, he'd be better off to simply put it categorically off-limits than to have to fight a daily struggle to determine whether *this* time he's going to eat those chicken wings.

If there are good reasons for framing environmentally friendly behavior as the ethical choice, finding ways to decrease the number of repeated individual decisions people have to engage in to fulfill that mission will be helpful. The kind of moral willpower needed to repeatedly make the right choice may be in finite supply; not only will it sometimes fail, but investing that effort in one action may result in lack of availability in other contexts. You'll consistently make an effort to sort the recycling and then increase your odds of driving rather than taking the bus.

The licensing phenomenon more broadly also calls into question the value of framing environmentally beneficial actions as virtuous or ethically preferable. Ironically, framing beneficial environmental behavior as "good" makes it more likely that people will reward themselves for their noble actions by allowing "bad" behavior. The issue goes beyond willpower to the broader framing of issues in a moral context. Being good gives us license to reward ourselves by doing something we consider to be indulgent or bad. It may even be that assigning moral significance to a behavior actually makes us feel more ambivalent about doing it and less likely to do it consistently.[141] And similarly, focusing too much on people's identity can backfire as well, since framing their actions generally as environmentally friendly may give them license to make environmentally bad choices.

More dangerous is the possibility that a focus on the virtues of environmental concern as a motivation for action leads people toward behavior that makes them feel good about demonstrating their concern, regardless of the actual environmental benefit. A report by the American Psychological Association's Task Force on the Interface Between Psychology and Global Climate Change noted that people derive a psychological benefit from actions that they "believe address the climate problem—even if the actual effect on climate is minimal or nonexistent."[142] Will a focus on "doing the right thing" actually result in useful environmental action, or will people be satisfied that they have demonstrated their concern (even if they have not improved the environment) and go no further?

It is even more important to remember that, if you are the type of person whose identity or value system is formed around making environmentally beneficial choices in your daily action, you are likely the exception. Most people, even if they are generally in favor of environmental protection and willing to sacrifice a bit to contribute to it, do not frame most of their daily decisions around making the best environmental choice. Those for whom environmental behavior is a core part of their identity or value structure (including most environmental activists) might thus err in projecting their reasons for action onto the general population. If your primary orientation is toward behavior that will not cause environmental harm, you may overestimate (for example) the role that information plays in persuading people to take action, assuming that anyone who learns that a behavior is environmentally problematic will choose to avoid that behavior.

ATTITUDES AND NORMS
AND ENVIRONMENTAL CHOICES

Because values, attitudes, and identities are formed early and are generally stable, they do not provide many opportunities for quick changes in behavior. That is even more true because they are also only tenuously linked to behavior—for some people on some issues, they can make a difference, but for most of us on most of our daily actions, our underlying attitudes don't play a major role in our environmental choices. That also means that they are not the primary explanations for our undesirable environmental behavior. So although it might be useful over the long term to work toward a society in which more people are concerned about the environment, doing so is unlikely to have a major effect on many daily choices we make.

Framing environmental behavior as the morally correct thing to do can even backfire. We resent being told what to do. And even when we are receptive to these messages, we may allow ourselves to backslide once we have done some environmentally noble acts. We should therefore be cautious when framing environmental behavior as the ethically preferable choice.

These attitudinal factors may matter more in efforts to make broader policy changes to address environmental issues. The people most willing to devote time and effort to making these social and political changes are likely to be those whose identity or values are framed around environmental protection. The more the attitudes of the general population support or accept protection of the environment as an important goal, the more politically possible this change is. So in the bigger picture and the long run, these factors may matter a lot even if they play only a small role in individual daily choices.

The reverse is also true: attitudes are at least as likely to be caused by behavior as to cause it. So larger social changes caused by social norms, or even by policy requirements that induce behavior, can create attitudes favorable to the norm or behavior. Social norms, which can be changed more quickly than values, attitudes, or identity, are thus important in both causing and changing these environmental choices.

What to Do About It

It makes sense that we behave in ways that harm the environment, even if we're good people and care deeply about protecting the planet. Understanding that our actions are influenced by the systems and structures we find ourselves in helps explain why information about the harm we are causing or about the dire state of the environment so frequently fails to create widespread change, and why caring about the environment isn't enough to prevent us from doing things that contribute to environmental harm. Most people care about the environment and would prefer to protect it. And yet we all, on a regular basis, do things that cause environmental harm, even if we know and even if we care.

Arguing that our behavior makes sense is not a call for complacency or inaction. It's an argument that if we don't recognize the reasons behind our behavior, we will be powerless, individually or collectively, to change it in a meaningful way. And make no mistake: we need to change the impact people are having on the planet. I have not spent much time in this book making this case, because it is not the purpose of this analysis, and so many others make that case more compellingly than I can.[1] But attempting to change our behavior to prevent real environmental harm, without recognizing that there are reasons for our actions that help create that harm, is a recipe for failure.

I wrote this book, and I teach environmental politics, because I want us to be wise in the ways we choose to tackle environmental problems. I've seen too many generations of students and other activists dispirited when their efforts to tell people the right way to behave environmentally fail to achieve the change they hope for. It turns out that behavior change of any kind is difficult, and the deck is usually stacked against making environmentally beneficial choices.

We should not lose hope about our ability to change behavior and address environmental problems. At the same time, though, naive hope is likely to backfire. Figuring out how to work effectively for change will create more enthusiastic activists who do not burn out when they fail to score easy victories. The same is true for the actual behavior change. Environmental fixes that require people to sacrifice might make them feel momentarily noble when they undertake those sacrifices, but are unlikely to persist over time.

The preceding chapters have examined what accounts for—and what doesn't—the behavior we collectively engage in that harms the environment, and what the resulting implications are for how we change collective behavior. This chapter first reviews the primary arguments from those chapters, before making cross-cutting observations and broader recommendations for pursuing change.

PROBLEM CHARACTERISTICS

Environmental problems have characteristics that decrease the odds that individuals—and often communities or states—will make wise environmental choices. Many of those difficulties are inherent in the nature of environmental problems. Environmental problems are externalities—unintended, unpriced, consequences of something else that people want to do. Almost by definition, taking action to prevent externalities will be more costly than not doing so, at least initially. Externalities are felt by people other than (or in addition to) those who create them; I get all the individual advantages of my action, but the environmental downsides are primarily felt by others. Those people are frequently quite far away in both space and time, perhaps even in other political jurisdictions or generations. Their potential concerns will rarely be taken into consideration when engaging in an activity.

Almost all environmental issues are common pool resource problems, in which a given resource is accessible to many people and its use by some people affects its usability by others. It is difficult to exclude those who use or degrade the resource, and anyone who can access it has the ability to diminish it. So externalities happen in a context in which it is difficult to keep people from creating them, and they are experienced by others in the system. These difficulties also make it hard to work collectively to address environmental problems; if you cannot be sure that others will undertake difficult and costly action to prevent environmental damage, it can be foolish to do so yourself, since the nature of the problems means you are unable to address or prevent them alone. All of these characteristics are naturally present in environmental issues in the world as it is currently structured, rather than relating to individual choices or governing decisions. But they make it difficult for individuals or societies to make individually and collectively beneficial environmental decisions.

Even more important are the societal-level structures within which we live our lives and conduct our business. The choices we face are constrained in ways that do not allow us to exercise the full range of options we might desire. From where I live, it is either impossible or impractical to take public transportation to many of the places I regularly go. The choices narrow much further for someone in a less privileged situation. Plenty of people don't have the resources to prioritize minimizing environmental harm or can't afford to run the risk of being the only one to take action and thereby failing to make meaningful environmental progress while bearing a personal cost. It is far more important to work to create realistic transportation alternatives (for instance) than to guilt-trip someone into taking expensive or inconvenient forms of transportation.

We can make structural difficulties more or less problematic. Collective action is difficult to engage in. Precisely because of that, there are opportunities for people focused on bringing together community or political action to help create it. Changing the problem characteristics—giving access to amenities only to those who have agreed to help protect or create them—can decrease the problems of free riding. Help people see how the effects of environmental problems are affecting them here and now, even if many of the problems are faced far away and in the future.

The biggest problem of environmental issues—that they are externalities of other things we are trying to accomplish—is also their biggest opportunity. No one is trying to cause environmental problems, so working to give people a way to address their underlying needs and interests in a way that doesn't harm the environment is likely to be embraced.

INCENTIVES

Getting the incentives right may not always be sufficient to persuade people to take the right environmental actions, and there are even instances when using economic incentives to change behavior can be counterproductive in the long run. But as a starting point, ensuring that the right environmental choice is easier and less costly than the harmful option in a given situation can go a long way toward shaping good environmental behavior.

Inherent characteristics of environmental problems create some of the incentives that make poor environmental choices seem sensible. If environmental harm is an externality, then I may experience no cost from the harm my actions create for others. Preventing those harms, by forgoing a desired action, or by taking additional steps to prevent the environmental damage, is likely more difficult and more costly. Even if that may not be true in the long run or at the societal level, for any individual choice the incentives do not favor the environment.

Plenty of other factors contribute to counterproductive incentives. Subsidies abound, preventing those who use natural resources or create pollution from being responsible for the direct economic—to say nothing of the environmental—costs of their damaging behavior. Policy measures put into place to encourage one type of behavior create unintended environmental effects. Zoning requirements that mandate certain numbers of parking spaces to avoid congestion prioritize automobile use and decrease the call for transportation alternatives, for example.

Not all incentives are purely monetary. When the preferred environmental outcome is more difficult—if recycling involves cleaning and sorting waste or even a separate trip to a recycling facility—it is easy to understand why people with full lives and busy schedules will not allocate the extra time and effort to make the environmentally preferable choice.

In some cases, changing incentives may be simple. Removing barriers to action can make environmentally preferred action more likely. Recycling rates are higher when there is curbside pickup and limited requirements to sort. Anything that can be done to make the better choice easier or less expensive will help change behavior.

People prefer positive incentives (benefits for doing the right thing) but are more likely to change their behavior to respond to negative incentives (penalties for doing the wrong thing), and the latter incentives are less costly to apply in policy terms. It's possible that people who change their behavior solely in response to incentives will revert to their old way of doing things if those incentives change, but there are ways to decrease this effect. Subsidies for major infrequent purchases may have long-term effects because once you've bought the efficient vehicle or energy-saving appliance, you will use it for a long time. By the time you're making the next purchase technology is likely to have evolved such that more efficient options are cost-effective without a subsidy. That evolution may even be helped along by the market created by those of us who buy the more energy-efficient option, perhaps prodded by those initial subsidies.

Incentives are not all-powerful. People regularly make choices based on the well-being of others, and for some people acting in support of the environment is its own reward. In other cases, incentives may cause rebound effects, like driving your fuel-efficient car longer distances because it costs less to do so or you feel like you've already done your part to protect the environment. But as a starting point, incentives both help to explain some of why we behave in environmentally unfriendly ways, and provide simple opportunities for changing behavior. In the longer run, those changes in incentives may even contribute to changing social structures, as systems evolve based on new behavior.

INFORMATION

It's easy to assume that what is needed for environmental change is a fully informed public. But while there are aspects of information that are important for addressing environmental problems—it's difficult to solve a problem if you don't know what is causing it or what actions would improve the situation—educating people about a problem and the desired behavior is rarely enough to change behavior. Knowing the basics may be necessary for environmental action, but it's not sufficient. Once the public in general is aware of environmental problems and factors that contribute to them, further information may not help.

Information fails to achieve the desired environmental change in part because of the powerful role of problem characteristics and incentives and other social structures: knowing that your behavior contributes to environmental damage may not influence it if you are meeting important short-term needs by your action or if the desired behavior is much harder or more expensive.

There are also key psychological factors that prevent us from fully acting on information relating to environmental problems. We have cognitive biases that make it difficult to fully understand uncertainty and risk. Our emotional responses to environmental problems hinder our ability to act. Certain ways of communicating information can leave people believing that their actions are insignificant compared to what is needed and make action less likely. Dire warnings about environmental problems can decrease our motivation to take action to address them because coping mechanisms lead us to deny the problems or to mistrust information that contradicts our worldview.

There are nevertheless important ways that informing people can usefully change behavior. Providing procedural knowledge—practical information about how to do the desired activity (on which day recycling is collected, or how to clean the bottom of your boat to prevent transfer of invasive species)—makes it more likely that people will engage in it. Feedback so that people know what their actual behavior is—both in contexts in which that information may not have been clear or otherwise presented in a usable form, and in situations when people simply might not be paying attention—can make change more likely. Prompts, such as reminders about a specific behavior (a sign on the exit door that asks, "Have you turned your computer off?") at the time and location when that behavior would be most useful, can serve a similar function.

HABITS AND OTHER ROUTINES

Analysis of environmental behavior—including in this book—frequently begins by assuming our actions are fully rational considerations of the complete range of alternatives. But nearly half of our daily actions are habitual; in businesses and organizations even more activities are routine. These habits and routines are adaptive; they are themselves adopted because routinized behavior is more efficient and serves some purpose. At the same time, addressing environmental problems generally requires acting differently than standard behavior, and routinized behavior is by definition difficult to change.

Because routines and habits are resistant to change, setting up new ones that integrate positive environmental behavior is an excellent way to affect behavior in a consistent and long-term way. For businesses these changes might even make economic sense. Doing so, though, requires serious intentional intervention.

Easier to change are systems that are set up with a default choice. If the default can be set up as the better environmental action (e.g., your electricity comes from renewable sources unless you choose otherwise, or your department's paper order is 100 percent recycled), most people will simply accept the default option. Anyone who feels strongly retains the option to choose differently, but the system both communicates and implements the preference for the better environmental choice.

ATTITUDES AND NORMS

We frequently think of environmental behavior as a moral issue, but hav-ing pro-environmental values or attitudes rarely translates into action. They are not entirely unrelated—at minimum, environmentally con-cerned attitudes and identities influence intentions to behave in environ-mental friendly ways. Attitudes that are the most salient (on their own or because of being primed) are most likely to influence behavior. These aspects are more likely to have an effect when external conditions mean that environmental behavior is not especially difficult.

Committed environmental activists also err in thinking that most of the rest of the world (or the country, or their community) is like them. Although the public generally favors environmental protection and expresses some level of support for personal sacrifices to bring it about, that support is reasonably shallow—it is almost no one's first priority. If environmental stewardship is a central part of your identity (which it is for many committed activists), it may be difficult to understand the extent to which that is simply not the frame through which most people make most decisions.

Some people do have values or identities for which environmental behavior is of central importance, however. For those people these ori-entations do help determine action. More importantly, these may be the people willing to help organize collective action to change structures and incentives for the rest of us, so that environmental behavior is more likely to change across society.

More important are social norms. We prefer to fit in with how others in our communities behave, and when that behavior is environmentally friendly and our attention is called to it, we may likewise act in an envi-ronmentally friendly manner. One lesson that comes from the normative effect of how we happen to do things is that we can adapt pretty easily to new ways of doing things if they are seen as just how things are done. If we move to a city where the standard way to get around is by bicycle, we're likely to take up cycling, and if curbside recycling is the thing to do in our new city, we'll do that.

The same insight can apply to newly adopted measures in the area we're already living in. Despite the likely griping if a city adopts a no-plastic-bag law or begins to require composting (or your office sets its winter temperature lower), once the plan is in place, people get used to it fairly quickly. A visit to a community that doesn't do things that way will feel odd. Recognizing that we do adapt reasonably quickly can help guard against the predicted backlash from a new policy or practice. It should encourage those who advocate such policies to do what they can to get them implemented, safe in the understanding that most times the policy will quickly become the norm. Of course, the converse is also true: we adjust quickly to changes to our situations in ways that are problematic for the environment. That forested area on the edge of a neighborhood that gets cut down to make new housing might seem a shock at first, but with not too much time it feels like that is how the neighborhood has always been.

There are some potential downsides in framing environmental action as the morally preferably choice, including the possibility that once people have established their moral credentials or made progress toward an ethical goal, they will relax their standards or even backslide. And for those of us—the ones who think to read a book about environmental behavior in the first place—for whom a focus on doing the right thing environmentally is central, we do need to remember that for many other people it is not central, and that there may be other routes to influencing their behavior.

CROSS-CUTTING THEMES

These strategies don't exist in a vacuum; they interact with each other. A regulation provides the incentive that creates the habit. Information changes the behavior of a business that then changes its routines or the choices available to consumers. Social norms are most powerful when they are consistent with values or attitudes we already hold or identities we want to have. Norms, which can change faster than attitudes, can lead to attitude change, as people infer their attitudes from how they are behaving. Incentives to do something can create procedural knowledge about how to do it, so that even if the incentive disappears, it may have become a habit or at least something we are able to undertake. Getting people to do something—whether by incentives or some other method—helps shape their attitudes in support of that action. If enough of us are doing it, it becomes a norm; others start doing it, simply because it's how people act in this community.

There are also commonalities across the concepts. How you frame things can make a difference. People are loss-averse and so are more likely to change their behavior to avoid penalties than to get a bonus. It's easier to make a habit about what you do than about what you avoid doing. People accept the default option in part to avoid making an active decision that might turn out to be the wrong choice.

Moments of change create opportunities. It's hard to form new habits and it's rare to develop new attitudes, but when we move to a new home, change our family structure, or start a new job or school, these are the best opportunities to make changes that might persist.

Systematizing behavior at any level is easier than putting in the mental or logistical energy to make every decision anew. Habits, routines, or rules of thumb create change across time or populations. Social norms are similar: we tend to do what everyone else does. Make the desired action the standard way to do things.

Values or attitudes may not succeed on their own at influencing behavior, but they make it more likely that, if the incentives or structures do not stand in the way, we will make good environmental decisions. They can help with the motivation to create habits, make people more receptive to procedural information, and make people more interested in fitting in with a social norm. And, perhaps most importantly, people whose identities or attitudes strongly support environmental protection are the ones most likely to set out to help create the broader social and institutional changes that lead the rest of us to make better environmental choices.

RULES OF (GREEN) THUMB

Because shorthand approaches make it easier to create desired action without the need to fully analyze every decision, some rules of thumb, derived from the analysis in this book, may be useful for approaching efforts to influence environmental behavior. As with more general rules of thumb, there are always exceptions, but these provide a good starting point for standard ways to approach efforts to change environmental behavior for the better, regardless of the environmental issue or the social context.

- Make the better environmental choice easier and cheaper than the alternatives.
- Avoid scaring or depressing people or using guilt or shame. These approaches are at best ineffective and at worst counterproductive.
- The best kind of information is procedural: show people how to do the things that will make an environmental difference. (Better yet, find ways to get them to experience doing them.)
- Behavior can change attitudes; get people to act in an environmentally friendly way and they are more likely to support environmental action.
- Willpower can be a depletable resource; make the preferred option automatic or habitual, or obligatory, rather than a constant moral decision.
- Change the systems (social, economic, or legal) rather than the individuals. People will respond to the systems they operate within.
- Recognize that people's behavior happens for a reason. Find out what they are trying to accomplish, and figure out a way for that need or goal to be met in a less environmentally damaging way.

HOW TO GET GOOD PEOPLE TO DO GOOD ENVIRONMENTAL THINGS

What does all the preceding information suggest about how we should approach environmental problems more generally? There are lessons both big and small for activists, planners, and policymakers.

It's worth applying these concepts to specific types of behaviors to understand what could make people behave in ways that are better for the environment in actual daily activities. Here I give four examples of behaviors we all regularly engage in that frequently contribute to environmental degradation: commuting, using household energy, producing and disposing of household waste, and purchasing food. For each of them there are lessons about options for how to improve individual and collective behavior environmentally.

Activists or policymakers may choose different points of intervention based on their own assessments of which factor contributes the most to the choices people make, which are easiest to change, or which align with other values they pursue or skills they bring. And, of course, approaches that can work to address several underlying contributors to problematic behavior simultaneously may be especially effective.

Commuting

How we get to and from work has environmental implications. Driving a car burns fossil fuels that contribute to particulate air pollution and to climate change. Most buses and trains run on fossil fuels as well, though they account for fewer emissions per person than solo automobile travel does. We could decrease the environmental impact from commuting by using different fuels in vehicles, by commuting in ways that use less fossil fuel per person (or, even better, none at all), and by traveling shorter distances.

If we focus on *problem characteristics and social structures*, we will put our energies toward creating a transportation infrastructure that makes it possible for us to commute in environmentally friendly ways. We should prioritize building bike lines or walking paths (and showers and bike storage at workplaces) that make nonvehicle commuting possible. We should work to create public transit options and to remove regulatory constraints (like mandated parking spots or zoning policies that separate residential from commercial spaces) that benefit those who travel by car.

Working with *incentives* for better commuting behavior involves making environmentally friendly commuting cheaper and easier and fossil fuel-intensive commuting more difficult and costlier. We should find ways to charge for parking and subsidize public transit passes or provide shuttles (perhaps using the revenue gained from parking charges). Create carpool lanes, preferred parking for efficient vehicles, or offer rebates to people who agree to forgo onsite parking.

At the broader societal level, work for tax rebates or other subsidies for efficient vehicles, which make them cheaper than they would otherwise be and increase the number of people who choose to buy these vehicles. Although there are dangers of creating new subsidies, subsidizing newly available technology to encourage widespread adoption can allow for an eventual decrease in price even as subsidies disappear, as was true of hybrid vehicles in the United States. Subsidies on purchases (like cars) that people make only infrequently are less likely to run into difficulties when the subsidy is removed—a car bought with a subsidy is likely to be operational for more than a decade. People who buy vehicles that are less environmentally harmful will decrease their environmental harm over the lifetime of the vehicle, giving a one-time incentive a long-term effect. Support the elimination of fossil fuel subsidies that make climate-problematic commuting less costly than it would otherwise be. Even better would be to tax gasoline additionally to internalize the environmental externalities it causes (and decrease the incentives for using it). If driving or parking is expensive or inconvenient, people are more likely to prioritize finding homes near where they work or near public transportation lines.

What *information* is most useful for encouraging better environmental commuting choices? We should ensure that people know about any existing incentives for better commuting, as well as how transit systems work, especially when new options become available. Hand out maps of bike routes and locations of shower facilities. At the broader societal level, support mandating information about the costs of vehicle commuting (such as gas mileage information translated into fuel costs over time) and the benefits of alternatives.

Providing information in a such a way that people can easily use it makes it more likely to influence behavior. Mandated information on gas mileage of cars at the point of sale makes it easier to consider the comparative effects of driving different cars. Even better is when that information is translated into average annual fuel costs for the car, or the environmental effects are presented in a standardized comparative metric. Mandating provision and form of this information is key. Otherwise people trying to sell you a car are likely to "greenwash" information, presenting incorrect or misleading information about its gas mileage or environmental effect.

Because *habit* plays a central role in our commuting behavior, interrupting environmentally problematic commuting habits or developing good ones can have a powerful effect. Moments of life change provide the best opportunities to change or form habits. Ensure that it is routine for a firm to give out information about public transportation or bike routes to new hires, or for real estate agents or town welcome committees to deliver it to new renters or homeowners. If we want to change our own commuting habits, we need to find ways to prompt the behavior we want to develop, to avoid falling into old patterns. Put the car keys in an inaccessible place, lay out your bike helmet by the coffee maker, and make an implementation intention for what you will do if it's raining in the morning when you're heading out to the train.

A focus on *attitudes and norms* may not provide many opportunities for quick behavior change, but there are a few possibilities. Find ways to communicate community preferences for commuting in environmentally benign ways (highlighting a company's target for noncar commuting and progress toward it, or making a town goal for increased public transit ridership). In the right context, badges or window decals given to those who buy transit passes or forgo parking can identify them as environmentally friendly commuters and make others aware that there is a social value in this behavior. Anything that can be done over the medium or long term to increase the social advantage people experience from better commuting choices will support the development of the general practice, and social expectation, of green commuting. And because of the power of descriptive norms, simply living in a community where people commute in environmentally friendly ways, especially if you are aware of it, will entice you to do the same to fit in.

The most effective approaches are likely to be those that cut across these different methods of behavior change. Providing free transit passes for a month or two creates an initial incentive to try that method of commuting. It also transmits procedural information—you learn how to take public transportation by doing it. If the initial incentive lasts long enough, you may develop a habit of commuting that way. This initial incentive may also help to create a norm—"This is how people in this community travel"—or even send a message that this is a socially preferred method of commuting. If enough people begin to commute this way, other social structures may change as well: more demand for public transportation may lead to the development of additional transit lines or more frequent service.

Similarly, incentives (like tax breaks, preferred parking, or carpool-lane access) for the purchase of high-efficiency or alternative fuel vehicles increase the likelihood that people will buy them. Those incentives are key to creating necessary social and economic structures—like a viable market at the beginning of a new product line, or a sufficient number of electric vehicle charging stations that people will be willing to buy such a vehicle because they know they'll be able to charge it. Widespread adoption of these technologies contributes to a social norm that favors them (and mandated labeling of them as "zero emission" or "high efficiency" vehicles makes more people aware that they exist and are socially preferred).

Household Energy

Most houses in most places derive heat and electricity from the burning of fossil fuels, like coal, oil, or natural gas. These energy sources contribute to local and regional air pollution and acid rain and are a significant contributor to climate change. Most of us could make a big difference in our energy use by undertaking some actions to use less energy overall or prioritizing getting our energy from sources with lower environmental effects, and yet few of us do.

To make household energy use more efficient or generated from less polluting sources, change the *problem characteristics and social structures* within which energy provision happens. Regulatory structures are key here: if energy providers are required to make use of renewable sources of energy or pursue energy efficiency measures, the options available to individual energy consumers will change. Existing infrastructure in most places relies on fossil fuel energy sources, so making it possible (either technically or in terms of regulation) to connect alternative energy generation to the existing electric grid, or to make houses more able to be heated or cooled by alternative energy, changes the choices households can make.

A focus on *incentives* involves making preferred energy choices cheaper and easier than the alternative. If possible, subsidize alternative energy so that it costs less, rather than more, than that from fossil fuels. In the long run, work to decrease the subsidization of fossil fuels. Make use of the existing natural incentive for energy efficiency: the less energy you use, the less it costs you, and communicating to people the cost savings from energy efficiency measures can increase their willingness to undertake them. Better yet, because of our loss aversion, communicate how much money we are losing by not undertaking conservation measures. At the same time, we need to recognize that economic incentives (especially if the cost is in the present and the savings accrue later in time) are not always sufficient to entice energy-saving measures. Make it as easy as possible to schedule an energy audit and act on the cost-saving opportunities presented.

Likewise, we should work to create incentives for alternative energy. Make it possible for users of solar energy to connect their systems to the grid and to benefit from "selling" the energy their houses generate back to the utility. Anything that can be done (by companies or governments) to help consumers offset the short-term costs of energy efficiency or alternative energy choices that have long-term economic (and environmental) benefits increases the incentive to adopt them. Offer low-interest loans or cover the upfront costs of installing solar panels that will pay off over time. Make it easy for energy consumers to sign up for renewable electricity or to change their heating systems to use environmentally preferable fuel.

Some types of *information* can change energy decisions. Make sure that people have easy access to usable information about their energy consumption and its costs. Although we might be able to access that information if we go looking for it, finding ways to place it in front of us, in units we intuitively understand, will better get our attention. Help people learn how to be efficient in their energy consumption: provide information on which appliances or practices use the most energy (or even real-time feedback as we use energy).

Some of that information can come in the form of mandated labels on appliances so that we know which ones will be more energy efficient (and, ideally, translate that information not only into environmental effects but also into operational costs). Procedural information is key: teach people how to use programmable thermostats and how to save energy (for instance) by strategic uses of shades or by turning off or unplugging appliances when not in use.

Within our broader energy choices, we can help create *habits* that can, at least at the margins, change how much energy we use. These may be less central than the type of energy sources we use or ensuring a well-insulated house, but helping people develop habits of turning off lights and unplugging appliances when not in use can, in the aggregate, decrease energy use.

Defaults may be even more valuable. If a town provides a choice of electricity from renewable sources, work to make it the default option, even if people are able to select conventional energy sources if they prefer. Set thermostats in offices low in winter (and high in summer) and return them to those settings regularly. Even if people can adjust them to meet their needs, the settings will default back to energy savings, and many people will simple adapt rather than adjust.

To work with *norms*, find ways to make environmentally preferable energy choices publicly visible: provide window decals for households that have adopted renewable energy; communicate town-wide adoption of this choice, alongside a message about joining your neighbors in reducing the environmental effects of the town's energy choices. Use energy bills to communicate a norm of energy efficiency and how well a household is fitting in with this community goal.

Many of these concepts can usefully be aggregated. Mandating that energy providers increase efficiency makes it likely that they will offer free energy audits to consumers. These audits provide information to households about the most cost-effective ways to decrease their energy costs. The economic incentives to act on this information can be augmented by subsidizing upfront costs of actions (like better insulation or improved windows) that have longer-term payoffs, perhaps even with loans that could be paid back out of the savings. Help with nonmonetary incentives, like providing clear information about how to access the services to do the recommended work, or even providing access to services like firms that clean out attics to make insulation possible.

Subsidies for alternative energy not only can help provide an incentive to make it easier for people to adopt these energy sources, but also help create the market for alternative energy. As businesses providing environmentally preferable energy grow, the long-term cost of technology or providing energy in these new ways decreases, making it more broadly accessible even without subsidies.

These concepts are inherently linked in other ways. Information strategies that help people become more energy efficient work best in a context when there are real incentives to decreasing energy use. The more expensive environmentally problematic energy choices are, the greater these incentives, and thus the impact of information, will be.

Household Waste

Waste is, in some ways, a double externality. We generate it incidental to something else we're trying to do—it's the packaging on the toy for the kids or the part of the apple we don't eat. Our secondary intention, once it is generated, is to get rid of it. We rarely see the effects of our waste; often it is picked up by someone and taken away to a landfill, incinerator, or recycling facility. These landfills take up natural space that could be used for other purposes; the waste within them can contribute to water pollution, and its decomposition creates natural gas that, if not captured, contributes to climate change. Incineration of waste creates air pollution. Even though recycling is generally preferable to simply discarding waste, it uses energy and water, in some cases intensively. Addressing the problems of household waste can most usefully be done by generating less of it in the first place, and by repurposing or recycling the waste that we do create.

If we're concerned about the environmental implications of household waste, we can work to change *problem characteristics and social structures* that privilege problematic disposal of waste. That would involve things like ensuring that infrastructure exists to easily recycle waste; for instance, is recyclable waste picked up in the same way that trash is?

Addressing the extent of waste generation requires attention to deeper structures of the political economy so that businesses responsible for the generation of things that are later discarded are held responsible for the waste-related externalities they create. Ultimately the structures of the political economy that contribute most to the extent of household waste generated is the logic of market capitalism that encourages constantly replacing items and increasing consumption. These structures are the hardest to change, and any change is likely to be slow and difficult, though useful.

An *incentive*-based approach to addressing problems of household waste would focus on making preferable disposal options cheaper and easier than more environmentally harmful ones. Recycling should be at least as easy as trash disposal, and ideally free. Charging (per weight or per volume) for household trash provides a twin incentive to reduce generation and to recycle or compost things that can be disposed of that way. Additional individual small-scale incentives (such as charging for bags or disposable containers) make some difference in reducing the waste that people accumulate. Nonmonetary incentives matter as well: it's not just the cost of waste that influences how we generate or dispose of it, but the ease. Making recycling the easiest option makes it more likely that people will recycle.

More important, however, is the incentive to businesses and other major organizations to reduce the generation of waste. Such an incentive can be created by a requirement that business take back any packaging waste—or, more radically, anything that they have made that people are ready to discard. Such requirements give businesses the incentive to reduce packaging and to manufacture items in ways that can be disassembled, reused, or recycled. It could lead to redesign of products to make them more modular, so that one section (say, a piece of stained carpeting) can be replaced without having to purchase an entirely new rug. Although these approaches regulate businesses, they have a major effect on consumers and thus on how much household waste is generated. If waste disposal at the household level were made especially expensive, the consumer pressure for lower-waste purchases would give an incentive to those businesses that could meet that demand.

The primary kind of *information* people lack about household waste is procedural. We need to ensure that everyone has adequate information about recycling processes—what can be recycled and how. That procedural information can be simplified if procedures are set up in ways that are easy to keep track of: recycling and trash picked up every time, on the same day, or at least in predictable patterns that are easy to describe and remember.

Information may be less useful for addressing the generation of waste. While most of us probably have no idea how much waste we dispose of overall, absent any particular incentive (like a per-unit waste charge), delivering that information will probably make little difference. At the margin things like prompts to bring reusable bags (possibly even in the parking lot of a grocery store, as a reminder to bring them in from the car) can have small effects on the amounts of waste we accumulate, but most of the household waste we generate comes from deeper structures of the political economy over which we have little individual control. On the plus side, there is little reason to assume that information about waste would backfire.

It is easy to see how developing a *habit* of recycling or composting could contribute to better handling of household waste; once those practices are in place, people simply act automatically to do them. The trick is how to help develop that kind of habitual behavior. Create processes of recycling that allow people to engage in it without thinking about it. Systematize waste and recycling collection so that it happens on a regular schedule that doesn't require effort to determine whether or how to do it. At the margin, creation of purchasing habits (always bringing reusable bags or cups, for instance) can help with accumulation of household waste in the first place, but habit is unlikely to make a major difference in this aspect of waste.

Household waste is rarely the focus of values or attitudes; our identities are much less likely to be wrapped up in our waste-generation behavior than in the other examples examined here. Working to build good community *norms* on waste disposal may be the most productive of the normative approaches. Make recycling efforts visible (if there is curbside pickup, bins of different colors or shapes for recycling help neighbors identify recycling behavior) and present a community expectation that recycling is what local residents do. At the same time, we should be on guard for a licensing effect, especially if efforts at recycling lead us to worry less about the overall amounts of waste generated.

Because the generation of household waste is embedded in aspects that are part of the structures of the political economy, there are few individual or short-term ways that attitudes or norms can easily overcome these. Although an overturning of the market capitalism that underpins the generation of waste may not be likely in the foreseeable future, a more plausible (if limited) approach would be to work for social norms that value reuse and limiting consumerism. These would have benefits not only in reducing waste, but in addressing environmental harms caused by global capitalism more broadly.

As with any issue, approaches that can invoke pathways to behavior change can be especially effective. Rules requiring the recycling and composting of household waste can reverberate across different aspects that influence behavior. A regulatory structure that requires households to recycle incentivizes recycling. So does charging for trash and not for recycling. Both policies simultaneously would be even better. The act of recycling becomes habitual with enough repetition, especially if the processes set up are systematic enough to allow people to recycle without having to remember complex information. And the act of regularly recycling itself may then contribute to values or attitudes in favor, and a social norm (descriptive, and probably injunctive) will come about when most people in an area recycle and doing so is seen as a community expectation. These new norms are likely to translate to other areas as well, with people more likely to recycle in other contexts. Good habits or rules prioritizing better forms of waste management may even lead to efforts to minimize waste generation, if they persuade people to avoid packaging or unnecessary purchases they would then bear the cost of disposing.

Likewise, incentives for reducing trash, like waste fees or charging extra for disposable items, help to better align incentives with desired behavior. These are likely to be far more effective than the generally small charge would suggest. These fees help to create a message about what the desired behavior is, and thus a social norm that magnifies the effect.

Food Purchasing

What food we purchase has significant consequences environmentally. How crops are grown affects land use and biodiversity and contributes to deforestation. Industrial agriculture, especially the raising of animals, is a major contributor to climate change. Food production is water-intensive and also contributes to pollution of lakes, rivers, and oceans. Decreasing the environmental effects of our food purchasing can come from changing what we eat to food with smaller ecological footprints.

Although *problem characteristics* and *social structures* help frame our food purchasing choices, they don't present easy solutions. Perhaps the most important one that could be changed is the market capitalism that leads to higher profits for companies the more processed and packaged and commodified is the food we purchase. It may be that this social structure is nearly as difficult to change as the inherent externalities that underlie the environmental problems our food choices present. In other words, understanding these structures may help us frame other approaches for influencing behavior to decrease the negative environmental effect of food purchasing, though they do not present us with readily available tools for making that change.

Focusing on the *incentives* that drive our food purchases suggests that efforts to internalize externalities—usually through policy measures that make producers pay for the environmental harms they cause or require them to reduce those harms—will remove at least some of the economic advantage for food made in ways that cause environmental harms. Removing subsidies, though politically difficult to do, will decrease the advantage that currently makes environmentally harmful food options cheaper.

At the individual level, it may be difficult to create incentives that actively encourage food choices with lower environmental harms, as opposed to removing the incentives that give an advantage to harmful choices. But other options are available at the level of businesses producing food, including farmers and fishers. Subsidies or policy measures can encourage better environmental behavior that presents consumers with choices that are themselves more environmentally friendly.

There are some good strategies for using *information* to influence food purchases. Primary among these are labels that provide unbiased information about the environmental effects of food purchases. These are especially effective when mandated or at least officially sanctioned. A similar approach gives certification to foods caught or processed in environmentally benign ways. These approaches simply give people information, so unless they are combined with other incentives or social structures, they require that people prioritize minimizing the environmental harm of their food purchases.

Because many of our food-purchasing decisions are governed by *habit*, we are unlikely to make conscious decisions to minimize the environmental impact of our choices. Our best option is to find ways to interrupt our habits and replace them with others that are based on our environmental preferences. Rules of thumb, like eating low on the food chain, prioritizing organically or locally grown food, or even choosing food with fewer ingredients or less packaging, can provide quick frameworks to select food options likely to have a better environmental effect. Once new purchasing behavior becomes habitual, it systematizes decisions we regularly make, increasing their reach.

Food purchasing, although generally an individual act, is likely influenced by the descriptive *attitudes and norms* of the communities we are part of. Changes in values—such as when someone becomes vegetarian or prioritizes purchasing organic food—can be deep and even identity-defining experiences. But for many people whose attitudes favor minimizing environmental damage, it can be difficult to translate this experience into food-purchasing decisions that minimize environmental damage. For individuals, shifts in values that are central enough might matter, but we need broader reach.

For communities, figuring out how to shift or communicate norms is key, especially because most food-purchasing actions take place out of the public eye. Because food purchasing generally takes place at commercial venues, there might be some opportunity for communication about these norms, but only if the interests of the businesses are not threatened by these community messages. A proliferation of farmers' markets in communities might signal some level of social preference for less commodified or organic food choices. At best, this kind of descriptive norm ("This is where we buy food") may become an injunctive norm ("This is the best kind of food to buy").

Opportunities abound for combining approaches to encouraging purchases of more environmentally sustainable food. Certification programs (such as the Marine Stewardship Council certification of sustainably caught seafood) are nominally information strategies. They give consumers the information to allow those who prioritize sustainability, frequently as a moral choice, to know which purchases to make. At the same time, these programs provide incentives to fishers to fish sustainably so that they can gain certification and perhaps a price premium in markets that value this sustainability. More importantly, when stores agree to stock only MSC-certified seafood, they create a structure in which all those purchasing seafood, no matter what their attitudes toward sustainability, will be making a responsible environmental choice.

GETTING (NOT SO) GOOD PEOPLE TO DO GOOD ENVIRONMENTAL THINGS

Some environmentalists want to change hearts and minds, to persuade us all of the value of the natural world and the necessity of living within its limits. I want to change the context in which people operate so even those who don't care or don't know will decrease their harmful environmental effects. There are too many people with too many priorities and too many daily actions, and the necessity for change is too great, for it to happen one person and one action at a time. One of the most important advantages of fixing social structures and incentives, or addressing habits, routines, or social norms, is that these approaches don't require people to have good intentions in order to act in environmentally positive ways.

These approaches also don't require haranguing people about their environmental choices. It's no fun being an environmental scold (nor is it enjoyable to be the one being scolded). As the preceding chapters have demonstrated, scolding is not necessarily productive and can even backfire. We should be able to go about our daily lives without having to dwell on whether or not our actions are causing environmental harms, because better environmental choices are simply a part of how things are done.

The best way to change a lot of behavior of a lot of people reasonably quickly is for that change to be structural or systemic. Some of the problem characteristics examined in this book—the physical characteristics of environmental problems as externalities that are often felt by people distant in space or time—may not be amenable to alteration. But the incentives created by those characteristics can be changed. Implementing policy to add a cost to doing things that are environmentally problematic (to make up for the unpriced nature of the externality) eliminates some of the advantage to doing bad environmental things. Creating infrastructure that makes the better environmental choice possible, or easier, has a similarly large effect.

Creating infrastructure, regulations, or other incentives isn't always easy, but once they are in place they affect many people, regardless of their level of environmental concern. This institutionalization need not always be done by policy: community norms or even collective habits (made possible by how we structure the opportunities available to people) can change behavior in lasting ways reasonably efficiently. I want to work for a world in which people's level of concern about the environment isn't the primary determinant of their level of environmentally friendly behavior, one in which making the right choice for the environment is either the only or the easiest option, and even people who have other priorities, or who are unaware that they are benefiting the environment, make that choice.

To be clear: I am not arguing that you shouldn't care about the environment or undertake difficult or costly endeavors to implement that concern. I do all those things. I'm not even arguing that you should not try to persuade people to care about the environment and act on that concern. It's just too slow for that to be the only, or even primary, approach to changing widespread behavior. I want—and the world needs us—to be able to change the behavior of people with other priorities and other concerns, and perhaps even those who don't believe in or care about environmental harm.

There are some ways in which individual and collective concern is key, however: unless some of us do care "a whole awful lot,"[2] the changes that need to happen to create the structures, incentives, habits, and norms capable of changing collective behavior are unlikely to happen. This is where I choose to put my focus.

NOTES

CHAPTER 1

1. Intergovernmental Panel on Climate Change, "Climate Change 2014: Synthesis Report, Summary for Policy Makers," in *Fifth Assessment Report* (Geneva: IPCC, 2014).

2. C. P. Baldé, F. Wang, R. Kuehr, and J. Huisman, *The Global E-Waste Monitor—2014* (Bonn: United Nations University IAS—SCYCLE, 2015).

3. Alina Bradford, "Deforestation: Facts, Causes & Effects," *LiveScience*, March 4, 2015.

4. Theodore Seuss Geisel (Dr. Seuss), *The Lorax* (New York: Random House, 1971).

5. Erik Assardourian and Christopher Flavin, *State of the World 2004: A Worldwatch Institute Report on Progress toward a Sustainable Society, Special Focus: The Consumer Society* (New York: Norton, 2004).

6. Intergovernmental Panel on Climate Change, *Climate Change 2014: Mitigation of Climate Change*, Contribution of Working Group III to the Fifth Assessment Report of the Intergovernmental Panel on Climate Change (New York: Cambridge University Press, 2014).

7. Daniel Hoornweg and Perinaz Bhada-Tata, "What a Waste: A Global Review of Solid Waste Management," Urban Development Series Knowledge Papers No. 15, World Bank, March 2015. The statistic represents OECD countries.

8. As represented in places like 50 Ways to Help, "50 Ways to Help the Planet and Environment," 50waystohelp.com; The Guardian, "50 Easy Ways to Save the Planet," TheGuardian.com, August 22, 2002; Sara Olsher, "50 Ways to Save the Environment," *JustGive* blog, September 18, 2012; JustGive, "50 Ways to Save the Environment," *JustGive* website, or, for a while, the Environmental Defense Fund's annual calendar.

9. Michael F. Maniates, "Individualization: Plant a Tree, Buy a Bike, Save the World?," *Global Environmental Politics* 1(3) (August 2001), pp. 31–52.

10. Paul F. Steinberg, *Who Rules the Earth? How Social Rules Shape Our Planet and Our Lives* (Oxford: Oxford University Press, 2015).

11. Maniates, "Individualization," p. 33.

12. Even then, the case is not always clear: looking across the entire life cycle of a product there are times when recycling it requires far more energy than not doing so, and there may be a case against recycling if that energy is from an environmentally problematic source. In most cases, though, recycling is probably a good choice.

CHAPTER 2

1. Tom Tietenberg, *Environmental and Natural Resource Economics*, 5th ed. (Boston: Addison-Wesley, 2000); Kenneth Gillingham and James Sweeney, "Market Failure and the Structure of Externalities," in Boaz Moselle, Jorge Padilla, and Richard Schmalensee, eds., *Harnessing Renewable Energy in Electric Power Systems* (Washington, DC: Earthscan, 2010), pp. 69–91.

2. Ronald H. Coase, "The Problem of Social Cost," *Journal of Law and Economics* 3 (October 1960), pp. 1–44.

3. Adam B. Jaffe, Richard G. Newell, and Robert N. Stavins, "Environmental Policy and Technological Change," *Environmental and Resource Economics* 22 (2002), pp. 41–69; Michael E. Porter and Claas van der Linde, "Green and Competitive: Ending the Stalemate," *Harvard Business Review*, Reprint No. 95507 (1995).

4. Jennifer Clapp, *Toxic Exports: The Transfer of Hazardous Wastes from Rich to Poor Countries* (Ithaca, NY: Cornell University Press, 2001).

5. Michael Rauscher, "Tall Smokestacks and Transfrontier Pollution: A Tale for Orestia and Trebeisia," in Rüdiger Pethig and Michael Rauscher, *Challenges to the World Economy* (Berlin: Springer, 2003), pp. 356–366.

6. Arjun Makhijani and Kevin R. Gurney, *Mending the Ozone Hole* (Cambridge, MA: MIT Press, 1995), pp. 101–105.

7. Zachary A. Smith, *The Environmental Policy Paradox*, 2nd ed. (Englewood Cliffs, NJ: Prentice Hall, 1995), pp. 46–47.

8. Stephen M. Gardiner, "The Global Warming Tragedy and the Dangerous Illusion of the Kyoto Protocol," *Ethics and International Affairs* 18(1) (2004), pp. 23–39.

9. There is also a lot of disagreement about what the appropriate discount rate is for environmental issues. J. Samuel Barkin, "Discounting the Discount Rate: Ecocentrism and Environmental Economics," *Global Environmental Politics* 6(4) (November 2006), pp. 56–72.

10. Emily C. Lawrance, "Poverty and the Rate of Time Preference: Evidence from Panel Data," *Journal of Political Economy* 99(1) (February 1991), pp. 54–77.

11. The potential problems of collective action are a different issue, discussed later in this chapter.

12. Jerry A. Hausman, "Individual Discount Rates and the Purchase and Utilization of Energy-Using Durables," *Bell Journal of Economics* 10(1) (Spring 1979), pp. 33–54.

13. Dermot Gately, "Individual Discount Rates and the Purchase and Utilization of Energy-Using Durables: Comment," *Bell Journal of Economics* 11(1) (Spring 1980), pp. 373–374.

14. Mancur Olson, *The Logic of Collective Action* (Cambridge, MA: Harvard University Press, 1971), p. 2.

15. Robert Axelrod and William D. Hamilton, "The Evolution of Cooperation," *Science* 211 (March 1981), pp. 1390–1396; Charles Lipson, "International Cooperation in Economic and Security Affairs," *World Politics* 37 (1984), pp. 1–23.

16. John Tierney, "A Tale of Two Fisheries," *New York Times Magazine*, August 27, 2000.

17. Olson, *Logic of Collective Action*, pp. 9–16; Gerald Marwell and Pamela Oliver, *The Critical Mass in Collective Action: A Micro-social Theory* (Cambridge: Cambridge University Press, 1993).

18. Olson, *Logic of Collective Action*, pp. 28–30; Russel Hardin, *Collective Action* (Baltimore: Johns Hopkins University Press, 1982), pp. 40–41.

19. Bert Klandermans, "Union Action and the Free-Rider Dilemma," in L. Kriesberg and B. Misztal, eds., *Research in Social Movements, Conflict and Change*, vol. 10, *Social Movements as a Factor of Change in the Contemporary World* (Greenwich, CT: JAI Press, 1988), pp. 77–92.

20. Kenneth A. Oye and James H. Maxwell, "Self-Interest and Environmental Management," in Robert O. Keohane and Elinor Ostrom, eds., *Local Commons and Global Interdependence* (London: Sage, 1995), pp. 191–221.

21. Pamela Oliver, "'If You Don't Do it, Nobody Else Will': Active and Token Contributors to Local Collective Action," *American Sociological Review* 49(5) (October 1984), pp. 601–610; Steven Finkel, Edward N. Muller, and Karl-Dieter Opp, "Personal Influence, Collective Rationality, and Mass Political Action," *American Political Science Review* 83(3) (September 1989), pp. 885–903.

22. Finkel, Muller, and Opp, "Personal Influence," pp. 892–894; Stephen J. Zaccaro, Virginia Blair, Christopher Peterson, and Michelle Zazanis, "Collective Efficacy," in J. E. Maddux, ed., *Self-Efficacy, Adaptation, and Adjustment* (New York: Plenum Press, 1995), pp. 305–328.

23. Hardin, *Collective Action*, p. 32.

24. Elinor Ostrom, *Governing the Commons: The Evolution of Institutions for Collective Action* (Cambridge: Cambridge University Press, 1990).

25. Ostrom, *Governing the Commons*.

26. Elinor Ostrom, "Collective Action and the Evolution of Social Norms," *Journal of Economic Perspectives* 14(3) (Summer 2000), pp. 137–158.

27. Gerald Marwell and Ruth E. Ames, "Experiments on the Provision of Public Goods I: Resources, Interests, Group Size, and the Free-Rider Problem," *American Journal of Sociology* 84(6) (May 1979), pp. 1335–1360.

28. Gerald Marwell and Ruth Ames, "Economists Free Ride, Does Anyone Else? Experiments on the Provision of Public Goods, IV," *Journal of Public Economics* 15(3) (June 1981), pp. 295–310.

29. Robert H. Frank, Thomas Gilovich and Dennis T. Regan, "Does Studying Economics Inhibit Cooperation?," *Journal of Economic Perspectives* 7(2) (Spring 1993), pp. 159–171.

30. Ostrom, "Collective Action."

31. Nancy N. Rabalais, R. Eugene Turner, and William J. Wiseman Jr., "Gulf of Mexico Hypoxia, a.k.a. 'The Dead Zone,'" *Annual Review of Ecology and Systematics* 33 (2002), pp. 235–263.

32. Garrett Hardin, "The Tragedy of the Commons," *Science* 162 (December 13, 1968), 1243–1248.

33. Elizabeth R. DeSombre, "Globalization, Competition and Convergence: Shipping and the Race to the Middle," *Global Governance* 14(2) (April–June 2008), pp. 179–198.

34. Paul C. Stern, "Information, Incentives, and Proenvironmental Consumer Behavior," *Journal of Consumer Policy* 22 (1999), p. 461.

CHAPTER 3

1. Paul C. Stern, "Information, Incentives, and Proenvironmental Consumer Behavior," *Journal of Consumer Policy* 22 (1999), p. 474.

2. Bente Halvorsen, "Effects of Norms and Opportunity Cost of Time on Household Recycling," *Land Economics* 84(3) (August 2008), pp. 501–516.

3. Marcelo Ostria, "How U.S. Agricultural Subsidies Harm the Environment, Taxpayers, and the Poor," Issue Briefs—Energy and Natural Resources No. 126, National Center for Policy Analysis, August 7, 2013.

4. Chris Nelder, "Reframing the Transportation Debate," *SmartPlanet*, October 19, 2011; Management Information Services, "60 Years of Energy Incentives: Analysis of Federal Expenditures for Energy Development," paper prepared for the Nuclear Energy Institute, Washington, DC, October 2011.

5. Stephan Barg, "Eliminating Perverse Subsidies: What's the Problem?," in OECD, *Subsidies and Environment: Exploring the Linkages* (Paris: OECD, 1996), pp. 23–42.

6. Robert Samuelson, "Why (Sigh!) Farm Subsidies Survive," *Real Clear Politics*, June 13, 2013.

7. It should be noted that other, explicit or implicit subsidies have now been applied to photovoltaic technology that might help tip the balance back.

8. Elizabeth R. DeSombre, "The Experience of the Montreal Protocol: Particularly Remarkable and Remarkably Particular," *UCLA Journal of Environmental Law and Policy* 19 (2000), pp. 49–81.

9. Garrett Hardin, "The Tragedy of the Commons," *Science* 162 (1968), pp. 1243–1248.

10. Mark Sagoff, "At the Shrine of Our Lady of Fatima, or Why Political Questions Are Not All Economic," in W. Michael Hoffman and Jennifer Mills Moore, eds., *Business Ethics: Readings and Cases in Corporate Morality*, 2nd ed. (New York: McGraw-Hill, 1992), pp. 494–503; Michael J. Sandel, "It's Immoral to Buy the Right to Pollute," *New York Times*, December 15, 1997, p. A29.

11. See, for instance, James D. Reschovsky and Sarah E. Stone, "Market Incentives to Encourage Household Waste Recycling: Paying for What You Throw Away," *Journal of Policy Analysis and Management* 13(1) (Winter 1994), pp. 120–139.

12. Kelly Sims Gallagher and Erich Muehlegger, "Giving Green to Get Green? Incentives and Consumer Adoption of Hybrid Vehicle Technology," *Journal of Environmental Economics and Management* 61 (2011), pp. 1–15; Ambarish Chandra, Sumeet Gulati, and Milind Kandlikar, "Green Drivers or Free Riders? An Analysis of Tax Rebates for Hybrid Vehicles," *Journal of Environmental Economics and Management* 60 (2010), pp. 78–93.

13. Lyubov Kurkalova, Catherine Kling, and Jinhua Zhao, "Green Subsidies in Agriculture: Estimating the Adoption Costs of Conservation Tillage from Observed Behavior," *Canadian Journal of Agricultural Economics* 54 (2006), pp. 247–267.

14. Adam B. Jaffe, Richard G. Newell, and Robert N. Stavins, "Environmental Policy and Technological Change," *Environmental and Resource Economics* 22 (2002), pp. 41–69.

15. Andrew Green, "You Can't Pay Them Enough: Subsidies, Environmental Law, and Social Norms," *Harvard Environmental Law Review* 30 (2006), pp. 407–440; Jan

HM Pieters, "Subsidies and the Environment: What Subsidies and Tax Incentives Affect Production Decisions to the Detriment of the Environment," in Kai Schlegelmilch, ed., *Green Budget Reform in Europe* (Berlin: Springer, 1999), pp. 259–265.

16. Paul C. Stern, "What Economics Doesn't Say about Energy Use," *Journal of Policy Analysis and Management* 5(2) (Winter 1986), pp. 200–227.

17. Stern, "Information, Incentives," pp. 461–478.

18. Ernst Fehr and Armin Falk, "Psychological Foundations of Incentives," *European Economic Review* 46 (2002), pp. 687–724.

19. Thomas A. Heberlein and G. Keith Warriner, "The Influence of Price and Attitude on Shifting Residential Electricity Consumption from On- to Off-Peak Periods," *Journal of Economic Psychology* 4(1) (1983), pp. 107–130.

20. Katri Bennhold, "The Ministry of Nudges," *New York Times*, December 8, 2013, pp. B1, B4.

21. Timothy D. Ludwig, Timothy W. Gray, and Allison Rowell, "Increasing Recycling in Academic Buildings: A Systematic Replication," *Journal of Applied Behavior Analysis* 31(4) (Winter 1998), pp. 683–686.

22. See, for example, Mancur Olson, *The Logic of Collective Action* (Cambridge, MA: Harvard University Press, 1971), p. 51 n. 72.

23. Matthia Sutter, Stefan Haigner, and Martin Kocher, "Choosing the Carrot or the Stick: Endogenous Institutional Choice in Social Dilemma Situations," Working Papers in Economics and Statistics No. 2008-07, University of Innsbruck, 2008.

24. Özgur Gürek, Bernd Irlenbusch, and Betting Rockenbach, "Motivating Teammates: The Leader's Choice between Positive and Negative Incentives," *Journal of Economic Psychology* 30 (2000), pp. 591–607.

25. Jean-Jacques Laffont and Jean Tirole, "The Dynamics of Incentive Contracts," *Econometrica* 56(5) (September 1988), pp. 1153–1175.

26. Tony N. Docan, "Positive and Negative Incentives in the Classroom: An Analysis of Grading Systems and Student Motivation," *Journal of Scholarship of Teaching and Learning* 6(2) (October 2006), pp. 21–40.

27. Daniel Kahneman, Jack L. Knetsch, and Richard H. Thaler, "The Endowment Effect, Loss Aversion, and Status Quo Bias," *Journal of Economic Perspectives* 5(1) (Winter 1999), pp. 193–206.

28. Pamela Oliver, "Rewards and Punishments as Selective Incentives for Collective Action: Theoretical Investigations," *American Journal of Sociology* 85(6) (May 1980), 1356–1375.

29. Oliver, "Rewards and Punishments."

30. World Bank, *Curbing the Epidemic: Governments and the Economics of Tobacco Control* (Washington, DC: World Bank, 1999).

31. Oliver, "Rewards and Punishments," p. 1365.

32. Bruno S. Frey, "On the Relationship between Intrinsic and Extrinsic Work Motivation," *International Journal of Industrial Organization* 15(4) (July 1997), pp. 427–439.

33. Edward L. Deci and Richard M. Ryan, *Intrinsic Motivation and Self-Determination in Human Behavior* (New York: Plenum Press, 1985).

34. Richard M. Titmuss, *The Gift Relationship: From Human Blood to Social Policy* (London: Allen and Unwin, 1970); Carl Mellström and Magnus Johannesson, "Crowding Out in Blood Donation: Was Titmuss Right?," *Journal of the European Economic Association* 6(4) (June 2008), pp. 845–863.

35. Edward L. Deci, "The Effects of Contingent and Noncontingent Rewards and Controls on Intrinsic Motivation" *Organizational Behavior and Human Performance* 8(2) (1972), pp. 217–229.

36. Sigmund Koch, "Behavior as 'Intrinsically' Regulated: Work Notes towards a Pre-theory of Phenomena Called 'Motivational,'" in *Nebraska Symposium on Motivation*, vol. 4 (Lincoln: University of Nebraska Press, 1956).

37. Mark Lepper, David Greene, and Robert Nisbett, "Undermining Children's Intrinsic Interest with Extrinsic Rewards: A Test of the 'Overjustification' Hypothesis," *Journal of Personality and Social Psychology* 28(1) (1973), pp. 129–137.

38. Edward I. Deci, Richard Ryan, and Richard Koestner, "A Meta-analytic Review of Experiments Examining the Effects of Extrinsic Rewards on Intrinsic Motivation," *Psychological Bulletin* 125(6) (1999), pp. 627–688.

39. Daniel H. Pink, *Drive: The Surprising Truth about What Motivates Us* (New York: Riverhead Books, 2009), p. 54.

40. Anton Suvorov, "Addiction to Rewards," Toulouse School of Economics, November 2003, available online at http://www.nes.ru/public-presentations/suvorov_js-08-12-03.pdf.

41. Oliver, "Rewards and Punishments," p. 1367.

42. Lynn Levitt and Gloria Leventhal, "Little Reduction: How Effective Is the New York State Bottle Bill?," *Environment and Behavior* 18 (1986), pp. 467–479.

43. Daniel Engber, "A Nickel Isn't Worth a Cent: Why the Bottle Deposit Should Be Much, Much Higher," *Slate*, August 27, 2013, available at http://www.slate.com/articles/health_and_science/science/2013/08/bottle_deposit_should_keep_up_with_inflation_time_to_raise_fee_from_a_nickel.html.

44. Engber, "Nickel Isn't Worth a Cent."

45. Uri Gneezy and Aldo Rustichini, "A Fine Is a Price," *Journal of Legal Studies* 29 (January 2000), pp. 1–17.

46. Urs Fischbacher, Simon Gächter, and Ernst Fehr, "Are People Conditionally Cooperative? Evidence from a Public Goods Experiment," *Economics Letters* 71(3) (2001), pp. 397–404.

47. Fehr and Falk, "Psychological Foundations of Incentives," pp. 687–724.

48. Frey, "Relationship between Intrinsic and Extrinsic."

49. Frey, "Relationship between Intrinsic and Extrinsic."

50. Nicola Lacetera and Mario Macias, "Motivating Altruism: A Field Study," Institute for the Study of Labor Discussion Paper No. 3770, October 28, 2008.

51. Dan Ariely, Uri Gneezy, George Loewenstein, and Nina Mazar, "Large Stakes and Big Mistakes," *Review of Economic Studies* 76(2) (2009), pp. 451–469.

52. Anton U. Pardini and Richard D. Katzev, "The Effect of Strength of Commitment on Newspaper Recycling," *Journal of Environmental Systems* 13(3) (1983), pp. 245–254.

53. Teresa M. Amabile, *Creativity in Context* (Boulder: Westview Press, 1996).

54. Sam Glucksberg, "The Influence of Strength of Drive on Functional Fixedness and Perceptual Recognition," *Journal of Experimental Psychology* 63 (1962), pp. 36–41.

55. Edward L. Deci, Richard Koestner, and Richard M. Ryan, "Extrinsic Rewards and Intrinsic Motivation in Education: Reconsidered Once Again," *Review of Educational Research* 71(1) (2001), pp. 1–27.

56. Pardini and Katzev, "Effect of Strength," pp. 245–254.

57. William Stanley Jevons, *The Coal Question: An Inquiry Concerning the Progress of the Nation, and the Possible Exhaustion of Our Coal-Mines* (New York: Augustus Kelly, 1865).

58. Blake Alcott, "Jevons' Paradox," *Ecological Economics* 54 (2005), pp. 9–21.

59. Steve Sorrell, "Jevons' Paradox Revisited: The Evidence for Backfire from Improved Energy Efficiency," *Energy Policy* 37 (2009), pp. 1456–1469.

60. Dale Jamieson, "Scientific Uncertainty and the Political Process," *Annals of the American Academy of Political and Social Sciences* 545 (May 1996), pp. 35–43.

61. Jevons, "The Coal Question," p. 141.

62. David Owen, "The Efficiency Dilemma," *New Yorker*, December 2010, pp. 78–85.

63. Stan Cox, *Losing Our Cool: Uncomfortable Truths about Our Air-Conditioned World* (New York: New Press, 2010); Owen, "The Efficiency Dilemma," pp. 80–81.

64. Kenneth A. Small and Kurt van Dender, "If Cars Were More Efficient, Would We Use Less Fuel?," *Access* 31 (Fall 2007), pp. 8–13.

65. Richard York, "Ecological Paradoxes: William Stanley Jevons and the Paperless Office," *Human Ecology Review* 13(2) (2006), pp. 143–147.

66. Keith Bradsher, *High and Mighty: SUVs—the World's Most Dangerous Vehicles and How They Got That Way* (New York: Public Affairs, 2002).

67. Vaclav Smil, *Energy at the Crossroads: Global Perspectives and Uncertainties* (Cambridge, MA: MIT Press, 2003).

68. Abigail J. Sellen and Richard H. R. Harper, *The Myth of the Paperless Office* (Cambridge, MA: MIT Press, 2002), p. 11.

69. Vaclav Smil, "Worldwide Transformation of Diets, Burdens of Meat Production and Opportunities for Novel Food Proteins," *Enzyme and Microbial Technology* 30 (200), pp. 305–311.

70. Kelly Vaughn, "Jevons Paradox: The Debate That Just Won't Die," *RMI Outlet*, Rocky Mountain Institute, March 20, 2012.

71. Amory B. Lovins, "On the Rebound: A Letter in Response to David Owen's Article," *New Yorker*, January 17, 2011.

72. Quoted in Owen, "The Efficiency Dilemma," p. 79.

73. Owen, "The Efficiency Dilemma," p. 80.

CHAPTER 4

1. Matthias Finger calls it the "dominant paradigm" and cites many who proceed from this assumption. Finger, "From Knowledge to Action? Exploring the Relationships between Environmental Experiences, Learning, and Behavior," *Journal of Social Issues* 50(3) (1994), pp. 141–160.

2. Thomas A. Heberlein, *Navigating Environmental Attitudes* (Oxford: Oxford University Press, 2012), p. 70.

3. Gerald T. Gardner and Paul C. Stern, *Environmental Problems and Human Behavior*, 2nd ed. (Boston: Pearson Custom Publishing, 2002), p. 75.
4. P. Wesley Schultz, "Knowledge, Information, and Household Recycling: Examining the Knowledge-Deficit Model of Behavior Change," in Thomas Dietz and Paul C. Stern, eds., *New Tools for Environmental Protection: Education, Information, and Voluntary Measures* (Washington, DC: National Academy Press, 2002), pp. 67–82.
5. Paul C. Stern, "Information, Incentives, and Proenvironmental Consumer Behavior," *Journal of Consumer Policy* 22 (4) (1999), pp. 461–478.
6. Schultz, "Knowledge, Information," pp. 69–70.
7. Finger, "From Knowledge to Action," p. 143.
8. Barbara Connolly, "Asymmetrical Rivalry in Common Pool Resources and European Responses to Acid Rain," in J. Samuel Barkin and George E. Shambaugh, eds., *Anarchy and the Environment* (Albany: SUNY Press, 1999), p. 130.
9. Riley E. Dunlap and Peter J. Jacques, "Climate Change Denial Books and Conservative Think Tanks: Exploring the Connection," *American Behavioral Scientist* 57(6) (2013), pp. 699–731; Peter J. Jacques, Riley E. Dunlap, and Mark Freeman., "The Organisation of Denial: Conservative Think Tanks and Environmental Scepticism," *Environmental Politics* 17(3) (2008), pp. 349–385.
10. Karl T. Ulrich, "The Environmental Paradox of Bicycling," working paper, Department of Operations and Information Management, Wharton School, July 2006, available online at http://opim.wharton.upenn.edu/~ulrich/documents/ulrich-cycling-enviro-jul06.pdf.
11. John Tierney, "How Virtuous Is Ed Begley Jr.?," *TierneyLab* blog, *New York Times*, February 25, 2008, available online at http://tierneylab.blogs.nytimes.com/2008/02/25/how-virtuous-is-ed-begley-jr/. There are a number of questionable assumptions in that analysis, including the idea that someone bicycling or walking would be eating the full number of calories burned and doing so via animal protein and fat. Peer-reviewed analysis by Paul A. T. Higgins concludes that biking or walking for recommended levels of exercise instead of driving those distances would result in dramatic reductions in oil production and carbon dioxide emissions. "Exercise-Based Transportation Reduces Oil Dependence, Carbon Emissions and Obesity," *Environmental Conservation* 32(3) (2005), pp. 197–202.
12. CNW Marketing, "Dust to Dust: The Energy Cost of New Vehicles from Concept to Disposal" (2007). This report is no longer available on the Web.
13. Peter Gleick, "Hummer versus Prius: 'Dust to Dust' Report Misleads the Media and Public with Bad Science," Pacific Institute, 2007, available online at www.pacinst.org/wp-content/.../hummer_vs_prius3.pdf; Heidi Hauenstein and Laura Schewel, "Checking Dust to Dust's Assumptions about the Prius and the Hummer," Rocky Mountain Institute, 2007, available online at http://www.evworld.com/library/rmi_hummerVprius.pdf.
14. Jennifer Clapp, "The Rising Tide against Plastic Waste: Unpacking the Industry Attempts to Influence the Debate," in Stephanie Foote and Elizabeth Mazzolini, eds., *Histories of the Dustheap* (Cambridge, MA: MIT Press, 2012), pp. 199–225.
15. Naomi Oreskes and Erik M. Conway, *Merchants of Doubt: How a Handful of Scientists Obscured the Truth on Issues from Tobacco Smoke to Global Warming* (New York: Bloomsbury Publishing, 2010).

16. Michaël Aklin and Johannes Urpelainen, "Perceptions of Scientific Dissent Undermine Public Support for Environmental Policy," *Environmental Science and Policy* 38 (2014), pp. 173–177.

17. Howard Leventhal, Robert Singer, and Susan Jones, "Effects of Fear and Specificity of Recommendation upon Attitudes and Behavior," *Journal of Personality and Social Psychology* 2(1) (1965), pp. 20–29.

18. Howard Leventhal, Jean C. Watts, and Francia Pagano, "Effects of Fear and Instructions on How to Cope with Danger," *Journal of Personality and Social Psychology* 6(3) (1967), pp. 313–321.

19. Jacob Hornik, Joseph Cherian, Michelle Madansky, and Chem Narayana, "Determinants of Recycling Behavior: A Synthesis of Research Results," *Journal of Socio-economics* 24(1) (1995), pp. 105–127.

20. Schultz, "Knowledge, Information," p. 70.

21. Sean Duffy and Michelle Verges, "It Matters a Hole Lot: Perceptual Affordances of Waste Containers Influence Recycling Compliance," *Environment and Behavior* 41(5) (2009), pp. 741–749.

22. Schultz, "Knowledge, Information," p. 73.

23. Gardner and Stern, *Environmental Problems*, p. 83.

24. Sarah Darby, "Energy Feedback in Buildings: Improving the Infrastructure for Demand Reduction," *Building Research & Information* 36(5) (2008), pp. 499–508.

25. Sarah Darby, "Making It Obvious: Designing Feedback into Energy Consumption," in Paolo Bertoldi, Andrea Ricciardi, and Aníbal T. de Almeida, eds., *Energy Efficiency in Household Appliances and Lighting* (Berlin: Springer, 2001), pp. 685–696.

26. Tom Hargreaves, Michael Nye, and Jacqueline Burgess, "Making Energy Visible: A Qualitative Field Study of How Householders Interact with Feedback from Smart Energy Monitors," *Energy Policy* 38(10) (2010), pp. 6111–6119.

27. W. Fred van Raaij and Theo M. M. Verhallen, "Patterns of Residential Energy Behavior," *Journal of Economic Psychology* 4(1) (1983), pp. 85–106.

28. Darby, "Making It Obvious," 2001.

29. Harold Wilhite and Rich Ling, "Measured Energy Savings from a More Informative Energy Bill," *Energy and Buildings* 22(2) (1995), pp. 145–155.

30. See, for example, Hargreaves, Nye, and Burgess, "Making Energy Visible."

31. Edwin A. Locke, Norman Cartledge, and Jeffrey Koeppel, "Motivational Effects of Knowledge of Results: A Goal-Setting Phenomenon?," *Psychological Bulletin* 70(6) (1968), pp. 474–485.

32. Lawrence J. Becker, "Joint Effect of Feedback and Goal Setting on Performance: A Field Study of Residential Energy Conservation," *Journal of Applied Psychology* 63(4) (1978), pp. 428–433.

33. L. T. McCalley and Cees J. H. Midden, "Energy Conservation through Product-Integrated Feedback: The Roles of Goal-Setting and Social Orientation," *Journal of Economic Psychology* 23(5) (2002), pp. 589–603.

34. Deborah Simmons and Ron Widmar, "Motivations and Barriers to Recycling: Toward a Strategy for Public Education," *Journal of Environmental Education* 22(1) (1990), pp. 13–18.

35. Darby, "Making It Obvious," pp. 503–504.

36. Charles M. Farmer and JoAnn K. Wells, "Effect of Enhanced Seat Belt Reminders on Driver Fatality Risk," *Journal of Safety Research* 41(1) (2010), pp. 53–57.

37. Dennis H. Reid, Paul D. Luyben, Robert J. Rawers, and Jon S. Bailey, "Newspaper Recycling Behavior: The Effects of Prompting and Proximity of Containers," *Environment and Behavior* 8(3) (1976), pp. 471–482.

38. Doug McKenzie-Mohr, "Promoting Sustainable Behavior: An Introduction to Community-Based Social Marketing," *Journal of Social Issues* 56(3) (2000), pp. 543–554.

39. Robert B. Cialdini, "Crafting Normative Messages to Protect the Environment," *Current Directions in Psychological Science* 12(4) (2003), pp. 105–109.

40. Doug McKenzie-Mohr, *Fostering Sustainable Behavior: An Introduction to Community-Based Social Marketing* (Gabriola Island, BC: New Society Publishers, 2011).

41. Duffy and Verges, "It Matters a Hole Lot," pp. 741–749.

42. C. Samuel Craig and John M. McCann, "Assessing Communication Effects on Energy Conservation," *Journal of Consumer Research* 5(2) (1978), pp. 82–88.

43. Paul C. Stern, "Changing Behavior in Households and Communities: What Have We Learned?," in Thomas Dietz and Paul C. Stern, eds., *New Tools for Environmental Protection: Education, Information, and Voluntary Measures* (Washington, DC: National Academy Press, 2002) pp. 201–211.

44. Cohn & Wolfe, Lander Associates, Penn, Schoen & Berland, "Green Brands Survey," http://www.cohnwolfe.com/en/ideas-insights/white-papers/green-brands-survey-2011.

45. Charlotte Leire and Åke Thidell, "Product-Related Environmental Information to Guide Consumer Purchases: A Review and Analysis of Research on Perceptions, Understanding and Use among Nordic Consumers," *Journal of Cleaner Production* 13(10) (2005), pp. 1061–1070.

46. Julian Morris, *Green Goods? Consumers, Product Labels and the Environment* (London: IEA Environment Unit, 1997).

47. John Thøgersen, "Promoting 'Green' Consumer Behavior with Eco-Labels," in Thomas Dietz and Paul C. Stern, eds., *New Tools for Environmental Protection: Education, Information, and Voluntary Measures* (Washington, DC: National Academy Press, 2002) pp. 83–104.

48. Jacob Jacoby, "Perspectives on Information Overload," *Journal of Consumer Research* 10(4) (1984), pp. 432–435.

49. Morris, *Green Goods*, p. 13.

50. OECD, "Eco-Labeling: Actual Effects of Selected Programmes," OECD/GD(97)/105, Paris, 1997.

51. See, for example, CONE Communications/ECHO, "Global CSR Study," 2013 (available online at http://www.conecomm.com/2013-global-csr-study-report), in which 88 percent of consumers around the world indicated that they feel "a responsibility to purchase products they think are socially and environmentally responsible" (p. 23).

52. Environment Committee, House of Commons, *Eco-labeling: Eighth Report of the House of Commons* (London: HMSO, 1991).

53. Douadia Bougherara, Gilles Grolleau, and Luc Thiébaut, "Can Labelling Policies do More Harm Than Good? An Analysis Applied to Environmental Labelling Schemes," *European Journal of Law and Economics* 19(1) (2005), pp. 5–16.

54. Ibon Galarraga Gallastegui, "The Use of Eco-Labels: A Review of the Literature," *European Environment* 12(6) (2002), pp. 316–331.

55. R. Bruce Hutton, "Advertising and the Department of Energy's Campaign for Energy Conservation," *Journal of Advertising* 11(2) (1982), pp. 27–39.

56. Elizabeth R. DeSombre and J. Samuel Barkin, *Fish* (Cambridge, MA: Polity Press, 2011), pp. 149–155.

57. Resource Conservation Alliance and Government Purchasing Project, "Focus on Government Purchasing," Using Less Wood: Quick Facts Series, http://www.gpp.org/gpp.pdf.

58. Graham Bullock, "The Poor Man's Strategy? Information-Based Environmental Governance in Hard Times," paper presented at the American Political Science Association Annual Meeting, 2010; available online at http://ssrn.com/abstract=1664703.

59. David Sarokin and Warren Muir, "Too Little Toxic Waste Data," *New York Times*, October 7, 1985, p. A31.

60. Margaret M. Jobe, "The Power of Information: The Example of the US Toxics Release Inventory," *Journal of Government Information* 26(3) (1999), pp. 287–295.

61. Shameek Konar and Mark A. Cohen, "Information as Regulation: The Effect of Community Right to Know Laws on Toxic Emissions," *Journal of Environmental Economics and Management* 32(1) (1997), pp. 109–124.

62. Jobe, "The Power of Information," p. 291; Madhu Khanna, Wilma Rose H. Quimio, and Dora Bojilova, "Toxics Release Information: A Policy Tool for Environmental Protection," *Journal of Environmental Economics and Management* 36(3) (1998), pp. 243–266.

63. Ronald B. Outen, "Designing Information Rules to Encourage Better Environmental Performance," paper presented at the conference "On Environmental Policies in the New Millennium: Incentive-Based Approaches," 1999.

64. US General Accounting Office, "Toxic Chemicals: EPA's Toxics Release Inventory Is Useful but Can Be Improved," GAO/RCED-91-121, 1991.

65. Sara N. Bleich, Julia A. Wolfson, and Marian P. Jarlenski, "Calorie Changes in Chain Restaurant Menu Items: Implications for Obesity and Evaluations of Menu Labeling," *American Journal of Preventive Medicine* 48(1) (2015), pp. 70–75.

66. Alexandre Mas, "Does Transparency Lead to Pay Compression?," National Bureau of Economic Research Paper No. w20558, 2014, available online at https://www.princeton.edu/~amas/papers/transparency.pdf.

67. Jake Rosenfeld and Patrick Denice, "The Power of Transparency: Evidence from a British Workplace Survey," *American Sociological Review* 80(5) (2015), pp. 1045–1068.

68. Quoted in Claire Cain Miller, "What We Can Do to Close the Pay Gap," *New York Times* (Business), January 17, 2016, p. 6.

69. Konar and Cohen, "Information as Regulation."

70. Bradley C. Karkkainen, "Information as Environmental Regulation: TRI and Performance Benchmarking, Precursor to a New Paradigm," *Georgetown Law Journal* 89 (2000), pp. 257–370.

71. I. B. Vasi and M. Macy, "The Mobilizer's Dilemma: Crisis, Empowerment and Collective Action," *Social Forces*, 81(3) (2003), pp. 979–998.

72. Vasi and Macy, "The Mobilizer's Dilemma."

73. Amara Brook, "Ecological Footprint Feedback: Motivating or Discouraging?," *Social Influence* 6(2) (2011), pp. 113–128.

74. Tom Jacobs, "Environmental Footprints May Produce Backlash," *Miller-McCune*, May 2, 2011, http://www.miller-mccune.com/culture-society/environmental-footprints-may-produce-backlash-30769/.

75. Robert H. Frank, Thomas Gilovich, and Dennis T. Regan, "Does Studying Economics Inhibit Cooperation?," *Journal of Economic Perspectives* 7(2) (1993), pp. 159–171.

76. Susanne C. Moser and Lisa Dilling, "Making Climate Hot," *Environment: Science and Policy for Sustainable Development* 46(10) (2004), pp. 32–46.

77. Matthew Feinberg and Robb Willer, "Apocalypse Soon? Dire Messages Reduce Belief in Global Warming by Contradicting Just-World Beliefs," *Psychological Science* 22(1) (2011), pp. 34–38.

78. Robert A. C. Ruiter, Charles Abraham, and Gerjo Kok, "Scary Warnings and Rational Precautions: A Review of the Psychology of Fear Appeals," *Psychology and Health* 16(6) (2001), pp. 613–630.

79. Brendan Nyhan, Jason Reifler, Sean Richey, and Gary L. Freed, "Effective Messages in Vaccine Promotion: A Randomized Trial," *Pediatrics* 133(4) (March 3, 2014), peds. 2013-2365.

80. Akiva Liberman and Shelly Chaiken, "Defensive Processing of Personally Relevant Health Messages," *Personality and Social Psychology Bulletin* 18(6) (1992), pp. 669–679.

81. Saffron O'Neill and Sophie Nicholson-Cole, "Fear Won't Do It: Promoting Positive Engagement with Climate Change through Visual and Iconic Representations," *Science Communication* 30(3) (2009), pp. 355–379.

82. Kim Witte, "Putting the Fear Back into Fear Appeals: The Extended Parallel Process Model," *Communications Monographs* 59(4) (1992), pp. 329–349.

83. Kim Witte and Mike Allen, "A Meta-analysis of Fear Appeals: Implications for Effective Public Health Campaigns," *Health Education and Behavior* 27(5) (2000), pp. 591–615.

84. Ronald W. Rogers and C. Ronald Mewborn, "Fear Appeals and Attitude Change: Effects of a Threat's Noxiousness, Probability of Occurrence, and the Efficacy of Coping Responses," *Journal of Personality and Social Psychology* 34(1) (1976), pp. 54–61.

85. Melvin J. Lerner, *The Belief in a Just World: A Fundamental Delusion* (New York: Plenum Press, 1980).

86. Matt Kaplan, "Why Dire Climate Warnings Boost Skepticism," *Nature News*, January 4, 2011, http://www.nature.com/news/2011/110104/full/news.2011.701.html.

87. Feinberg and Willer, "Apocalypse Soon," 2011.

88. Brendan Nyhan, Jason Reifler, and Peter A. Ubel, "The Hazards of Correcting Myths about Health Care Reform," *Medical Care* 51(2) (2013), pp. 127–132.

89. Dan M. Kahan, Donald Braman, John Gastil, Paul Slovic, and C. K. Mertz, "Culture and Identity-Protective Cognition: Explaining the White-Male Effect in Risk Perception," *Journal of Empirical Legal Studies* 4(3) (2007), pp. 465–505.

90. Ziva Kunda, "The Case for Motivated Reasoning," *Psychological Bulletin* 108(3) (1990), pp. 480–498.

91. Kari Edwards and Edward E. Smith, "A Disconfirmation Bias in the Evaluation of Arguments," *Journal of Personality and Social Psychology* 71(1) (1996), pp. 5–24; Brendan Nyhan and Jason Reifler, "When Corrections Fail: The Persistence of Political Misperceptions," *Political Behavior* 32(2) (2010), pp. 303–330.

92. Charles S. Taber and Milton Lodge, "Motivated Skepticism in the Evaluation of Political Beliefs," *American Journal of Political Science* 50(3) (2006), pp. 755–769.

93. Howard Leventhal, "Findings and Theory in the Study of Fear Communications," *Advances in Experimental Social Psychology* 5 (1970), pp. 119–186.

94. Joseph W. Thompson, Shirley Tyson, Paula Card-Higginson, Richard F. Jacobs, J. Gary Wheeler, Pippa Simpson, James E. Bost, Kevin W. Ryan, and Daniel A. Salmon, "Impact of Addition of Philosophical Exemptions on Childhood Immunization Rates," *American Journal of Preventive Medicine* 32(3) (2007), pp. 194–201.

95. The perception issues are examined here, rather than issues in which people may choose to value the trade-offs between risks and actions, which is a different phenomenon. See Gardner and Stern, *Environmental Problems*, pp. 213–217.

96. Paul Slovic, Baruch Fischhoff, and Sarah Lichtenstein, "Accident Probabilities and Seat Belt Usage: A Psychological Perspective," *Accident Analysis and Prevention* 10 (1978), pp. 281–285.

97. Paul Slovic, Baruch Fischhoff, Sarah Lichtenstein, Bernard Corrigan, and Barbara Combs, "Preference for Insuring against Probable Small Losses: Insurance Implications," *Journal of Risk and Insurance* 44(2) (1977), pp. 237–258.

98. Slovic, Fischhoff, and Lichtenstein, "Accident Probabilities."

99. John Wittenbraker, Brenda Lynn Gibbs, and Lynn R. Kahle, "Seat Belt Attitudes, Habits, and Behaviors: An Adaptive Amendment to the Fishbein Model," *Journal of Applied Social Psychology* 13(5) (1983), pp. 406–421.

100. David M. DeJoy, "The Optimism Bias and Traffic Accident Risk Perception," *Accident Analysis and Prevention* 21(4) (1989), pp. 333–340.

101. Neil D. Weinstein, "Why It Won't Happen to Me: Perceptions of Risk Factors and Susceptibility," *Health Psychology* 3(5) (1984), pp. 431–457.

102. Paul Slovic, Baruch Fischhoff, and Sarah Lichtenstein, "Rating the Risks," *Environment* 21(3) (1979), pp. 14–39.

103. Richard Stanley Lazarus and Susan Folkman, *Stress, Appraisal, and Coping* (New York: Springer, 1984).

104. Darrin R. Lehman and Shelley E. Taylor, "Date with an Earthquake: Coping with a Probable, Unpredictable Disaster," *Personality and Social Psychology Bulletin* 13(4) (1987), pp. 546–555.

105. Robert W. Kates, "Hazard and Choice Perception in Flood Plain Management," Research Paper 78, Department of Geography, University of Chicago, 1962.

106. Patricia A. Rippetoe and Ronald W. Rogers, "Effects of Components of Protection-Motivation Theory on Adaptive and Maladaptive Coping with a Health Threat," *Journal of Personality and Social Psychology* 52(3) (1987), pp. 596–604.

107. James Flynn, Paul Slovic, and Chris K. Mertz, "Gender, Race, and Perception of Environmental Health Risks," *Risk Analysis* 14(6) (1994), pp. 1101–1108.

108. Aaron M. McCright and Riley E. Dunlap, "Cool Dudes: The Denial of Climate Change among Conservative White Males in the United States," *Global Environmental Change* 21(4) (2011), pp. 1163–1172.

109. Herbert A. Simon, "Theories of Decision-Making in Economics and Behavioral Science," *American Economic Review* 49(3) (1959), pp. 253–283.

110. Paul Slovic, Baruch Fischhoff, and Sarah Lichtenstein, "Characterizing Perceived Risk," in Robert W. Kates, Christoph Hohenemser, and Jeanne X. Kasperson, eds. *Perilous Progress: Managing the Hazards of Technology* (Boulder: Westview Press, 1985), pp. 91–125.

111. Daniel Goleman, "Hidden Rules Often Distort Ideas of Risk," *New York Times*, February 1, 1994, p. C1.

112. Dale Griffin and Amos Tversky, "The Weighing of Evidence and the Determinants of Confidence," *Cognitive Psychology* 24 (1992), p. 411.

113. Sarah Lichtenstein, Paul Slovic, Baruch Fischhoff, Mark Layman, and Barbara Combs, "Judged Frequency of Lethal Events," *Journal of Experimental Psychology: Human Learning and Memory* 4(6) (1978), pp. 551–578.

114. Amos Tversky and Daniel Kahneman, "Judgment under Uncertainty: Heuristics and Biases," *Science* 185(4157) (1974), pp. 1124–1131.

115. Timothy D. Wilson, Christopher E. Houston, Kathryn M. Etling, and Nancy Brekke, "A New Look at Anchoring Effects: Basic Anchoring and Its Antecedents," *Journal of Experimental Psychology: General* 125(4) (1996), pp. 387–402.

116. Wilson et al., "New Look," pp. 387–402.

117. Jack L. Knetsch and John A. Sinden, "Willingness to Pay and Compensation Demanded: Experimental Evidence of an Unexpected Disparity in Measures of Value," *Quarterly Journal of Economics* 99(3) (1984), pp. 507–521.

118. Richard Thaler, "Toward a Positive Theory of Consumer Choice," *Journal of Economic Behavior and Organization* 1(1) (1980), pp. 39–60.

119. Daniel Kahneman, Jack L. Knetsch, and Richard H. Thaler, "Experimental Tests of the Endowment Effect and the Coase Theorem," *Journal of Political Economy* 98(6) (December 1990), pp. 1325–1348.

120. Ann Fisher, Gary H. McClelland, and William D. Schulze, "Measures of Willingness to Pay versus Willingness to Accept: Evidence, Explanations, and Potential Reconciliation," in George L. Peterson, Beverly L. Driver, and Robin Gregory, eds., *Amenity Resource Valuation: Integrating Economics with Other Disciplines* (State College, PA: Venture, 1988), pp. 127–134.

121. Thaler, "Toward a Positive Theory."

122. Robin Gregory, Sarah Lichtenstein, and Donald MacGregor, "The Role of Past States in Determining Reference Points for Policy Decisions," *Organizational Behavior and Human Decision Processes* 55(2) (1993), pp. 195–206.

123. Gardner and Stern, *Environmental Problems*, p. 234.

124. Gardner and Stern, *Environmental Problems*, pp. 92–93.

125. Theodore Mead Newcomb, Kathryn E. Koenig, Richard Flacks, and Donald P. Warwick, *Persistence and Change: Bennington College and Its Students after 25 Years* (New York: Wiley, 1967).

126. See, for example, Detra Dettmann-Easler and James L. Pease, "Evaluating the Effectiveness of Residential Environmental Education Programs in Fostering Positive Attitudes toward Wildlife," *Journal of Environmental Education* 31(1) (1999), pp. 33–39.

127. Julie Ann Pooley and Moira O'Connor, "Environmental Education and Attitudes: Emotions and Beliefs Are What Is Needed," *Environment and Behavior* 32(5) (2000), pp. 711–723.

128. Louise Chawla and Debra Flanders Cushing, "Education for Strategic Environmental Behavior," *Environmental Education Research* 13(4) (2007), pp. 437–452.

129. Heberlein, *Navigating Environmental Attitudes*.

130. Gardner and Stern, *Environmental Problems*, p. 73.

CHAPTER 5

1. For discussion of these assumptions, see Richard R. Nelson and Sidney G. Winter, *An Evolutionary Theory of Economic Change* (Cambridge, MA: Belknap Press of Harvard University Press, 1982), pp. 6–10.

2. Herbert A. Simon, *Models of Bounded Rationality: Empirically Grounded Economic Reason*, vol. 3 (Cambridge, MA: MIT Press, 1997).

3. Irving L. Janis and Leon Mann, *Decision Making: A Psychological Analysis of Conflict, Choice, and Commitment* (New York: Free Press, 1977); Lee Roy Beach and Terence R. Mitchell, "A Contingency Model for the Selection of Decision Strategies," *Academy of Management Review* 3(3) (1978), pp. 439–449.

4. Icek Ajzen, *From Intentions to Actions: A Theory of Planned Behavior* (Berlin: Springer, 1985).

5. Benjamin Gardner, Gert-Jan de Bruijn, and Phillippa Lally, "A Systematic Review and Meta-analysis of Applications of the Self-Report Habit Index to Nutrition and Physical Activity Behaviours," *Annals of Behavioral Medicine* 42(2) (2011), pp. 174–187.

6. Bas Verplanken and Wendy Wood, "Interventions to Break and Create Consumer Habits," *Journal of Public Policy and Marketing* 25(1) (2006), pp. 90–103.

7. Wendy Wood, Jeffrey M. Quinn, and Deborah A. Kashy, "Habits in Everyday Life: Thought, Emotion, and Action," *Journal of Personality and Social Psychology* 83(6) (2002), pp. 1281–1297; John A. Bargh and Tanya L. Chartrand, "The Unbearable Automaticity of Being," *American Psychologist* 54(7) (1999), pp. 462–479.

8. Wood, Quinn, and Kashy, "Habits in Everyday Life."

9. Jeremy Dean, *Making Habits, Breaking Habits: Why We Do Things, Why We Don't, and How to Make Any Change Stick* (Boston: Da Capo, 2013).

10. Michael Athay and John M. Darley, "Toward an Interaction-Centered Theory of Personality," in Nancy Cantor and John F. Kihlstrom, eds., *Personality, Cognition, and Social Interaction* (New York: Routledge, 1981), pp. 281–308.

11. Tommy Gärling, Satoshi Fujii, and Ole Boe, "Empirical Tests of a Model of Determinants of Script-Based Driving Choice," *Transportation Research Part F: Traffic Psychology and Behaviour* 4(2) (2001), pp. 89–102.

12. Shu Fai Cheung, Darius K.-S. Chan, and Zoe S.-Y. Wong, "Reexamining the Theory of Planned Behavior in Understanding Wastepaper Recycling," *Environment and Behavior* 31(5) (1999), pp. 587–612; Jennifer Boldero, "The Prediction of Household Recycling of Newspapers: The Role of Attitudes, Intentions, and Situational Factors," *Journal of Applied Social Psychology* 25(5) (1995), pp. 440–462.

13. Gary D. Gregory and Michael Di Leo, "Repeated Behavior and Environmental Psychology: The Role of Personal Involvement and Habit Formation in Explaining Water Consumption," *Journal of Applied Social Psychology* 33(6) (2003), pp. 1261–1296.

14. Bas Verplanken, Henk Aarts, and Ad van Knippenberg, "Habit, Information Acquisition, and the Process of Making Travel Mode Choices," *European Journal of Social Psychology* 27(5) (1997), pp. 539–560; Henk Aarts, Bas Verplanken, and Ad van Knippenberg, "Habit and Information Use in Travel Mode Choices," *Acta Psychologica* 96(1) (1997), pp. 1–14.

15. Christian A. Klöckner, Ellen Matthies, and Marcel Hunecke, "Problems of Operationalizing Habits and Integrating Habits in Normative Decision-Making Models," *Journal of Applied Social Psychology* 33(2) (2003), p. 400.

16. Judith A. Ouellette and Wendy Wood, "Habit and Intention in Everyday Life: The Multiple Processes by Which Past Behavior Predicts Future Behavior," *Psychological Bulletin* 124(1) (1998), pp. 54–74.

17. Charles Duhigg, *The Power of Habit: Why We Do What We Do in Life and Business* (New York: Random House, 2012), p. 19.

18. Henry H. Yin and Barbara J. Knowlton, "The Role of the Basal Ganglia in Habit Formation," *Nature Reviews Neuroscience* 7(6) (2006), pp. 464–476.

19. Bas Verplanken and Henk Aarts, "Habit, Attitude, and Planned Behaviour: Is Habit an Empty Construct or an Interesting Case of Goal-Directed Automaticity?" *European Review of Social Psychology* 10(1) (1999), pp. 101–134.

20. Aarts, Verplanken, and van Knippenberg, "Habit and Information Use."

21. Unna N. Danner, Henk Aarts, and Nanne K. Vries, "Habit vs. Intention in the Prediction of Future Behaviour: The Role of Frequency, Context Stability and Mental Accessibility of Past Behaviour," *British Journal of Social Psychology* 47(2) (2008), pp. 245–265.

22. Giuseppe Carrus, Paola Passafaro, and Mirilia Bonnes, "Emotions, Habits and Rational Choices in Ecological Behaviours: The Case of Recycling and Use of Public Transportation," *Journal of Environmental Psychology* 28(1) (2008), pp. 51–62.

23. Bas Verplanken, Henk Aarts, Ad Knippenberg, and Carina Knippenberg, "Attitude versus General Habit: Antecedents of Travel Mode Choice," *Journal of Applied Social Psychology* 24(4) (1994), pp. 285–300.

24. Aarts, Verplanken, and Knippenberg, "Habit and Information Use."

25. Sebastian Bamberg, "The Promotion of New Behavior by Forming an Implementation Intention: Results of a Field Experiment in the Domain of Travel Mode Choice," *Journal of Applied Social Psychology* 30(9) (2000), pp. 1903–1922.

26. Sebastian Bamberg and Peter Schmidt, "Theory-Driven Subgroup-Specific Evaluation of an Intervention to Reduce Private Car Use," *Journal of Applied Social Psychology* 31(6) (2001), pp. 1300–1329.

27. Satoshi Fuji and Ryuichi Kitamura, "What Does a One-Month Free Bus Ticket Do to Habitual Drivers?," *Transportation* 30 (2003), pp. 81–95.

28. Louise Eriksson, Jörgen Garvill, and Annika M. Nordlund, "Interrupting Habitual Car Use: The Importance of Car Habit Strength and Moral Motivation for Personal Car Use Reduction," *Transportation Research Part F: Traffic Psychology and Behaviour* 11(1) (2008), pp. 10–23.

29. Bamberg and Schmidt, "Theory-Driven Subgroup-Specific Evaluation," p. 1322.

30. Charles M. Farmer and Allan F. Williams, "Effect on Fatality Risk of Changing from Secondary to Primary Seat Belt Enforcement," *Journal of Safety Research* 36(2) (2005), pp. 189–194.

31. Verplanken et al., "Attitude versus General Habit"; Banwari Mittal, "Achieving Higher Seat Belt Usage: The Role of Habit in Bridging the Attitude-Behavior Gap," *Journal of Applied Social Psychology* 18(12) (1988), pp. 993–1016.

32. Gunilla Fhanér and Monica Hane, "Seat Belts: Opinion Effects of Law-Induced Use," *Journal of Applied Psychology* 64(2) (1979), pp. 205–212.

33. Paschal Sheeran, "Intention—Behavior Relations: A Conceptual and Empirical Review," *European Review of Social Psychology* 12(1) (2002), pp. 1–36.

34. Victoria Stillwell, "The Value of Redirection," *Positively: The Future of Dog Training*, available online at https://positively.com/victorias-blog/the-value-of-redirection/.

35. Alan R. Andreasen, "Life Status Changes and Changes in Consumer Preferences and Satisfaction," *Journal of Consumer Research* 11(3) (1984), pp. 784–794; Anil Mathur, George P. Moschis, and Euehun Lee, "A Longitudinal Study of the Effects of Life Status Changes on Changes in Consumer Preferences," *Journal of the Academy of Marketing Science* 36(2) (2008), pp. 234–246.

36. Wendy Wood, Leona Tam, and Melissa Guerrero Witt, "Changing Circumstances, Disrupting Habits," *Journal of Personality and Social Psychology* 88(6) (2005), pp. 918–933.

37. Bas Verplanken, Ian Walker, Adrian Davis, and Michaela Jurasek, "Context Change and Travel Mode Choice: Combining the Habit Discontinuity and Self-Activation Hypotheses," *Journal of Environmental Psychology* 28(2) (2008), pp. 121–127.

38. This number most likely comes from a 1960 book by Maxwell Maltz, who found that amputees took twenty-one days to adjust to the loss of a limb. Melissa Dahl, "Think It'll Take 21 Days to Make your Resolution a Habit? Try Tripling That," *Today*, January 1, 2014, http://www.today.com/news/think-itll-take-21-days-make-your-resolution-habit-try-2D11826051.

39. Mindy F. Ji and Wendy Wood, "Purchase and Consumption Habits: Not Necessarily What You Intend," *Journal of Consumer Psychology* 17(4) (2007), pp. 261–276.

40. Anna-Lisa Cohen, Ute C. Bayer, Alexander Jaudas, and Peter M. Gollwitzer, "Self-Regulatory Strategy and Executive Control: Implementation Intentions Modulate Task Switching and Simon Task Performance," *Psychological Research* 72(1) (2008), pp. 12–26.

41. Marieke A. Adriaanse, Gabriele Oettingen, Peter M. Gollwitzer, Erin P. Hennes, Denise T. D. De Ridder, and John B. F. De Wit, "When Planning Is Not Enough: Fighting Unhealthy Snacking Habits by Mental Contrasting with Implementation Intentions (MCII)," *European Journal of Social Psychology* 40(7) (2010), pp. 1277–1293.

42. Mark E. Bouton, "Context, Ambiguity, and Unlearning: Sources of Relapse after Behavioral Extinction," *Biological Psychiatry* 52(10) (2002), pp. 976–986.

43. Michele Reilly, "Eat Lower—and Better—on the Food Chain," *AgMag* blog, October 25, 2010, http://www.ewg.org/agmag/2010/10/eating-lower-and-better-food-chain.

44. Michael Pollan, *Food Rules: An Eater's Manual* (New York: Penguin Group, 2009).

45. Eric J. Johnson, John Hershey, Jacqueline Meszaros, and Howard Kunreuther, *Framing, Probability Distortions, and Insurance Decisions* (Dordrecht: Springer, 1993).

46. Eric J. Johnson, Steven Bellman, and Gerald L. Lohse, "Cognitive Lock-In and the Power Law of Practice," *Journal of Marketing* 67 (2003), pp. 62–75.

47. Eric J. Johnson and Daniel Goldstein, "Do Defaults Save Lives?," *Science* 302 (21 November 2003), pp. 1338–1339.

48. Eric J. Johnson and Daniel G. Goldstein, "Defaults and Donation Decisions," *Transplantation* 78(12) (December 27, 2004), pp. 1713–1716.

49. Johnson and Goldstein, "Do Defaults Save Lives," p. 1338.

50. James J. Choi, David Laibson, Brigitte C. Madrian, and Andrew Metrick, "Defined Contribution Pensions: Plan Rules, Participant Choices, and the Path of Least Resistance," in *Tax Policy and the Economy*, vol. 16 (Cambridge, MA: MIT Press, 2002), pp. 67–114.

51. James J. Choi, David Laibson, Brigitte C. Madrian, and Andrew Metrick, "Defined Contribution Pensions: Plan Rules, Participant Choices, and the Path of Least Resistance," in *Tax Policy and the Economy*, vol. 16 (Cambridge, MA: MIT Press, 2002), p. 79.

52. See, for example, Shlomo Benartzi and Richard H. Thaler, "Heuristics and Biases in Retirement Savings Behavior," *Journal of Economic Perspectives* 21(3) (2007), pp. 81–104; Gabriel D. Carroll, James J. Choi, David Laibson, Brigitte C. Madrian, and Andrew Metrick, "Optimal Defaults and Active Decisions," *Quarterly Journal of Economics* 124(4) (2009), pp. 1639–1674.

53. Brigitte C. Madrian and Dennis F. Shea, "The Power of Suggestion: Inertia in 401(i) Participation and Savings Behavior," *Quarterly Journal of Economics* 116(4) (November 2001), pp. 1149–1187.

54. Daniel Kahneman and Amos Tversky, "Prospect Theory: An Analysis of Decision under Risk," *Econometrica* 47 (1979), pp. 263–292.

55. William Samuelson and Richard Zeckhauser, "Status Quo Bias in Decision Making," *Journal of Risk and Uncertainty* 1 (1988), pp. 7–59.

56. Richard H. Thaler and Cass R. Sunstein, "Libertarian Paternalism," *American Economic Review* 93(2) (2003), pp. 175–179.

57. Johnson and Goldstein, "Do Defaults Save Lives."

58. Johnson and Goldstein, "Do Defaults Save Lives."

59. Jonathan Baron and Ilana Ritov, "Reference Points and Omission Bias," *Organizational Behavior and Human Decision Processes* 59 (1994), pp. 475–498.
60. Kahneman and Tversky, "Prospect Theory."
61. Eric J. Johnson, John Hershey, Jacqueline Meszaros, and Howard Kunreuther, "Framing, Probability Distortions, and Insurance Decisions," *Journal of Risk and Uncertainty* 7 (1993), pp. 35–51.
62. Julie R. Irwin and Jonathan Baron, "Response Mode Effects and Moral Values," *Organizational Behavior and Human Decision Processes* 84(2) (2001), pp. 177–197.
63. Daniel Pichert and Konstantinos V. Katsikopoulos, "Green Defaults: Information Presentation and Pro-environmental Behaviour," *Journal of Environmental Psychology* 28 (2008), pp. 63–73.
64. Pichert and Katsikopoulos, "Green Defaults"; Christina L. Brown and Aradhna Krishna, "The Skeptical Shopper: A Metacognitive Account for the Effects of Default Options on Choice," *Journal of Consumer Research* 31(3) (December 2004), pp. 529–539.
65. Craig R. M. McKenzie, Michael J. Liersch, and Stacey R. Finkelstein, "Recommendations Implicit in Policy Defaults," *Psychological Science* 17 (2006), pp. 414–420.
66. Shlomi Sher and Craig R. M. McKenzie, "Information Leakage from Logically Equivalent Frames," *Cognition* 101(3) (2006), pp. 467–494.
67. Simon Hedlin, "Is Guilt a Good Motivator for Pro-social Behaviour?" *Angle Journal*, October 9, 2015.
68. Johnson and Goldstein, "Do Defaults Save Lives"; Madrian and Shea, "The Power of Suggestion."
69. McKenzie, Liersch, and Finkelstein, "Recommendations."
70. Nelson and Winter, *Evolutionary Theory*, p. viii.
71. Connie J. G. Gersick and J. Richard Hackman, "Habitual Routines in Task-Performing Groups," *Organizational Behavior and Human Decision Processes* 47(1) (1990), pp. 65–97.
72. Fritz Machlup, "Marginal Analysis and Empirical Research," *American Economic Review* 36 (1946), pp. 519–554.
73. Nelson and Winter, *Evolutionary Theory*, p. 14.
74. Richard M. Cyert and James G. March, *A Behavioral Theory of the Firm* (Englewood Cliffs, NJ: Prentice Hall, 1963).
75. Nelson and Winter, *Evolutionary Theory*, pp. 56, 73.
76. Michael Polanyi, *The Tacit Dimension* (Garden City, NY: Anchor Books, 1967).
77. Alejandro Drexler, Greg Fischer, and Antoinette Schoar, "Keeping It Simple: Financial Literacy and Rules of Thumb," *American Economic Journal: Applied Economics* 6(2) (2014), pp. 1–31.
78. Gersick and Hackman, "Habitual Routines," p. 71.
79. Thomas W. Malone and Kevin Crowston, "The Interdisciplinary Study of Coordination," *ACM Computing Surveys (CSUR)* 26(1) (1994), pp. 87–119.
80. H. Landis Gabel and Bernard Sinclair-Desgagné, "The Firm, Its Routines, and the Environment," INSEAD Working Paper 97/05/EPS, Fontainbleau, 1997; Martha S.

Feldman and Brian T. Pentland, "Reconceptualizing Organizational Routines as a Source of Flexibility and Change," *Administrative Science Quarterly* 48(1) (2003), pp. 94–118.

81. Michel Crozier, *The Bureaucratic Phenomenon: An Examination of Bureaucracy in Modern Organizations and Its Cultural Setting in France* (Chicago: University of Chicago Press, 1964).

82. Gabel and Sinclair-Desgagné, "The Firm."

83. Gabel and Sinclair-Desgagné, "The Firm."

84. Cyert and March, "Behavioral Theory," pp. 133–134.

85. Torsten Reimer, Anne-Louise Bornstein, and Klaus Opwis, "Positive and Negative Transfer Effects in Groups," in Tilmann Betsch and Susanne Haberstroh, eds., *The Routines of Decision Making* (New York: Psychology Press, 2012), pp. 175–192.

86. Gabel and Sinclair-Desgagné, "The Firm."

87. Michael E. Porter, "America's Green Strategy," *Scientific American* 264(4) (April 1991), p. 168.

88. Michael E. Porter and Claas van der Linde, "Toward a New Conception of the Environment-Competitiveness Relationship," *Journal of Economic Perspectives* 9(4) (1995), pp. 97–118.

89. Porter and van der Linde, "Toward a New Conception," p. 99.

90. Among those in support: Smita B. Brunnermeier and Mark A. Cohen, "Determinants of Environmental Innovation in U.S. Manufacturing Industries," *Journal of Environmental Economics and Management* 45(2) (2003), pp. 278–293; among those opposed: Marcus Wagner, *The Porter Hypothesis Revisited: A Literature Review of Theoretical Models and Empirical Tests* (Leuneburg: Center for Sustainability Management, 2003); Adam B. Jaffe, Steven R. Peterson, Paul R. Portney, and Robert N. Stavins, "Environmental Regulation and the Competitiveness of U.S. Manufacturing: What Does the Evidence Tell Us?," *Journal of Economic Literature* 33(1) (1995), pp. 132–163. An excellent overview of the efforts to evaluate the hypothesis theoretically and empirically is Stefan Ambec, Mark A. Cohen, Stewart Elgie, and Paul Lanoie, "The Porter Hypothesis at 20: Can Environmental Regulation Enhance Innovation and Competitiveness?," *Review of Environmental Economics and Policy* 7(1) (2013), pp. 2–22.

91. Gabel and Sinclair-Desgagné, "The Firm," pp. 1–2.

92. Gabel and Sinclair-Desgagné, "The Firm," p. 3.

93. Xiaoping Wu, Shuai Deng, Xiaohong Du, and Jing Ma, "Green-Wave Traffic Theory Optimization and Analysis," *World Journal of Engineering and Technology* 2(3) (2014), pp. 14–19.

94. UPS, "Big Data = Wins for the Environment," 2013, available online at http://www.community.ups.com/media/UPS-Big-Data-Infographic.pdf.

95. Peter Dauvergne and Jane Lister, *Eco-Business: A Big-Brand Takeover of Sustainability* (Cambridge, MA: MIT Press, 2013).

96. Dina Spector, "18 Facts about Walmart That Will Blow Your Mind," *Business Insider*, November 15, 2012, available online at http://www.businessinsider.com/crazy-facts-about-walmart-2012-11.

97. MSNBC News Services, "Is Wal-mart Going Green?," NBCNews.com, October 25, 2005, available online at http://www.nbcnews.com/id/9815727/ns/us_news-environment/t/wal-mart-going-green.

98. Walmart, "Environmental Sustainability—Truck Fleet," http://corporate.walmart.com/global-responsibility/environment-sustainability/truck-fleet.

99. Edward Humes, *Force of Nature: The Unlikely Story of Wal-Mart's Green Revolution* (New York: HarperCollins, 2011).

CHAPTER 6

1. Axel Franzen and Dominikus Vogl, "Two Decades of Measuring Environmental Attitudes: A Comparative Analysis of 33 Countries," *Global Environmental Change* 23(5) (2013), pp. 1001–1008.

2. Franzen and Vogl, "Two Decades," p. 1004.

3. Jennifer E. Givens and Andrew K. Jorgenson, "Individual Environmental Concern in the World Polity: A Multilevel Analysis," *Social Science Research* 42(2) (2013), pp. 418–431.

4. Riley E. Dunlap and Aaron M. McCright, "Social Movement Identity: Validating a Measure of Identification with the Environmental Movement," *Social Science Quarterly* 89(5) (2008), pp. 1045–1065. Their analysis refers specifically to the United States.

5. Martin Fishbein and Icek Ajzen, *Belief, Attitude, Intention and Behavior: An Introduction to Theory and Research* (Reading, MA: Addison-Wesley, 1975).

6. Icek Ajzen, "The Theory of Planned Behavior," *Organizational Behavior and Human Decision Processes* 50(2) (1991), pp. 179–211.

7. Paul Sparks and Richard Shepherd, "Self-Identity and the Theory of Planned Behavior: Assessing the Role of Identification with 'Green Consumerism,'" *Social Psychology Quarterly* 55(4) (1992), pp. 388–399.

8. André Hansla, Amelie Gamble, Asgeir Juliusson, and Tommy Gärling, "The Relationships between Awareness of Consequences, Environmental Concern, and Value Orientations," *Journal of Environmental Psychology* 28(1) (2008), pp. 1–9.

9. Paul C. Stern, Thomas Dietz, Troy D. Abel, Gregory A. Guagnano, and Linda Kalof, "A Value-Belief-Norm Theory of Support for Social Movements: The Case Of Environmentalism," *Human Ecology Review* 6(2) (1999), pp. 81–97.

10. Thomas A. Heberlein, *Navigating Environmental Attitudes* (Oxford: Oxford University Press, 2012), p. 16.

11. Lorraine Whitmarsh and Saffron O'Neill, "Green Identity, Green Living? The Role of Pro-environmental Self-Identity in Determining Consistency across Diverse Pro-environmental Behaviours," *Journal of Environmental Psychology* 30(3) (2010), pp. 305–314.

12. Peggy A. Thoits and Lauren K. Virshup, "Me's and We's: Forms and Functions of Social Identities," in Richard D. Ashmore and Lee Jussim, eds., *Self and Identity: Fundamental Issues* (Oxford: Oxford University Press, 1997), pp. 106–136.

13. Lucia Mannetti, Antonio Pierro, and Stefano Livi, "Recycling: Planned and Self-Expressive Behaviour," *Journal of Environmental Psychology* 24(2) (2004), pp. 227–236.

14. P. Wesley Schultz, Valdiney V. Gouveia, Linda D. Cameron, Geetika Tankha, Peter Schmuck, and Marek Franěk, "Values and Their Relationship to Environmental Concern and Conservation Behavior," *Journal of Cross-Cultural Psychology* 36(4) (2005), pp. 457–475.

15. Susan Clayton, "Environmental Identity: A Conceptual and Operational Definition," in Susan Clayton and Susan Opotow, eds., *Identity and the Natural Environment: The Psychological Significance of Nature* (Cambridge, MA: MIT Press, 2003), pp. 45–65.

16. Meg J. Rohan, "A Rose by Any Name? The Values Construct," *Personality and Social Psychology Review* 4(3) (2000), pp. 255–277.

17. Mark P. Zanna and John K. Rempel, "Attitudes: A New Look at an Old Concept," in Daniel Bar-Tal and Arie W. Kruglanski, eds., *The Social Psychology of Knowledge* (New York: Cambridge University Press, 1988), pp. 315–334.

18. Martin Fishbein, "A Consideration of Beliefs, and Their Role in Attitude Measurement," in Fishbein, ed., *Readings in Attitude Theory and Measurement* (New York: Wiley, 1967), pp. 257–266.

19. See, for example, Michael R. Cohen, "Environmental Information versus Environmental Attitudes," *Journal of Environmental Education* 5(2) (1973), pp. 5–8. This observation has not held across all studies, however.

20. Russell H. Fazio and Mark P. Zanna, "Direct Experience and Attitude-Behavior Consistency," *Advances in Experimental Social Psychology* 14 (1981), pp. 161–202.

21. Thomas Gilovich, "Secondhand Information and Social Judgment," *Journal of Experimental Social Psychology* 23(1) (1987), pp. 59–74.

22. Fishbein, "Consideration of Beliefs," pp. 257–266.

23. Gregory R. Maio, James M. Olson, Mark M. Bernard, and Michelle A. Luke, "Ideologies, Values, Attitudes, and Behavior," in John Delamater, ed., *Handbook of Social Psychology* (New York: Kluwer Academic / Plenum Publishers, 2003), pp. 283–308.

24. Lichang Lee, Jane Allyn Piliavin, and Vaughn R. A. Call, "Giving Time, Money, and Blood: Similarities and Differences," *Social Psychology Quarterly* 62(3) (1999), pp. 276–290.

25. Daryl J. Bem, "Self-Perception Theory," in Leonard Berkowitz, ed., *Advances in Experimental Social Psychology*, vol. 6 (New York: Academic Press, 1972), pp. 1–62.

26. Benjamin Gardner, Gert-Jan de Bruijn, and Phillippa Lally, "Habit, Identity, and Repetitive Action: A Prospective Study of Binge-Drinking in UK Students," *British Journal of Health Psychology* 17(3) (2012), pp. 565–581.

27. Paul Norman, "The Theory of Planned Behavior and Binge Drinking among Undergraduate Students: Assessing the Impact of Habit Strength," *Addictive Behaviors* 36 (2011), pp. 502–507.

28. Erik H. Erikson, *Identity: Youth and Crisis* (New York: Norton, 1994).

29. Richard J. Shavelson and Roger Bolus, "Self-Concept: The Interplay of Theory and Methods," *Journal of Educational Psychology* 74(1) (1982), pp. 3–17.

30. Shan-Shan Chung and Monica Miu-Yin Leung, "The Value-Action Gap in Waste Recycling: The Case of Undergraduates in Hong Kong," *Environmental Management* 40(4) (2007), pp. 603–612; Stewart Barr and Andrew Gilg, "Sustainable

Lifestyles: Framing Environmental Action in and around the Home," *Geoforum* 37(6) (2006), pp. 906–920.

31. Allan W. Wicker, "Attitudes versus Actions: The Relationship of Verbal and Overt Behavioral Responses to Attitude Objects," *Journal of Social Issues* 25(4) (1969), pp. 41–78.

32. P. Wesley Schultz and Lynnette C. Zelezny, "Values and Proenvironmental Behavior: A Five-Country Survey," *Journal of Cross-Cultural Psychology* 29(4), (1998), pp. 540–558, among many similar studies.

33. Jeffrey A. Joireman, Terell P. Lasane, Jennifer Bennett, Diana Richards, and Salma Solaimani, "Integrating Social Value Orientation and the Consideration of Future Consequences within the Extended Norm Activation Model of Proenvironmental Behaviour," *British Journal of Social Psychology* 40(1) (2001), pp. 133–155.

34. Jeffrey A. Joireman, Paul A. M. van Lange, and Mark van Vugt, "Who Cares about the Environmental Impact of Cars? Those with an Eye toward the Future," *Environment and Behavior* 36(2) (2004), pp. 187–206.

35. Wicker, "Attitudes versus Actions."

36. Icek Ajzen and Martin Fishbein, "Attitude-Behavior Relations: A Theoretical Analysis and Review of Empirical Research," *Psychological Bulletin* 84(5) (1977), pp. 888–918.

37. Jody M. Hines, Harold R. Hungerford, and Audrey N. Tomera, "Analysis and Synthesis of Research on Responsible Environmental Behavior: A Meta-analysis," *Journal of Environmental Education* 18(2) (1987), pp. 1–8.

38. Thomas A. Heberlein and J. Stanley Black, "Attitudinal Specificity and the Prediction of Behavior in a Field Setting," *Journal of Personality and Social Psychology* 33(4) (1976), pp. 474–479.

39. Aline Kühl et al., "The Role of Saiga Poaching in Rural Communities: Linkages between Attitudes, Socio-economic Circumstances and Behaviour," *Biological Conservation* 142(7) (2009), pp. 1442–1449.

40. Charles R. Tittle and Richard J. Hill, "Attitude Measurement and Prediction of Behavior: An Evaluation of Conditions and Measurement Techniques," *Sociometry* 30(2) (June 1967), pp. 199–213.

41. Clayton, "Environmental Identity," pp. 45–65.

42. Jan E. Stets and Chris F. Biga, "Bringing Identity Theory into Environmental Sociology," *Sociological Theory* 21(4) (November 12, 2003), pp. 398–423.

43. Clayton, "Environmental Identity," p. 55.

44. Brent S. Steel, "Thinking Globally and Acting Locally? Environmental Attitudes, Behavior and Activism," *Journal of Environmental Management* 47(1) (1996), pp. 27–36.

45. Thomas A. Heberlein, "Navigating Environmental Attitudes," *Conservation Biology* 26(4) (2012), pp. 583–585.

46. Thomas Dietz, Amy Fitzgerald, and Rachael Shwom, "Environmental Values," *Annual Review of Environment and Resources* 30(1) (2005), pp. 335–372.

47. Carmen Tanner and Sybille Wölfing Kast, "Promoting Sustainable Consumption: Determinants of Green Purchases by Swiss Consumers," *Psychology and Marketing* 20(10) (2003), pp. 883–902.

48. Paul C. Stern, Linda Kalof, Thomas Dietz, and Gregory A. Guagnano, "Values, Beliefs, and Proenvironmental Action: Attitude Formation toward Emergent Attitude Objects," *Journal of Applied Social Psychology* 25(18) (1995), pp. 1611–1636.

49. Stephen Stradling, "Persuading People out of Their Cars," Inaugural Lecture, Napier University, March 27, 2002.

50. Douglas K. Reiter, Mark W. Brunson, and Robert H. Schmidt, "Public Attitudes toward Wildlife Damage Management and Policy," *Wildlife Society Bulletin* 27(3) (1999), pp. 746–758.

51. Willett Kempton and Dorothy C. Holland, "Identity and Sustained Environmental Practice," in Susan Clayton and Susan Opotow, eds., *Identity and the Natural Environment: The Psychological Significance of Nature* (Cambridge, MA: MIT Press, 2003), pp. 317–341.

52. Joanne Dono, Janine Webb, and Ben Richardson, "The Relationship between Environmental Activism, Pro-environmental Behaviour and Social Identity," *Journal of Environmental Psychology* 30(2) (2010), pp. 178–186.

53. Avi Ben-Bassat and Momi Dahan, "Social Identity and Voting Behavior," *Public Choice* 151(1–2) (2012), pp. 193–214.

54. Carole Jean Uhlaner, "'Relational Goods' and Participation: Incorporating Sociability into a Theory of Rational Action," *Public Choice* 62(3) (1989), pp. 253–285. This finding is notable, because rational choice theory would predict the opposite.

55. Russell H. Fazio and Carol J. Williams, "Attitude Accessibility as a Moderator of the Attitude-Perception and Attitude-Behavior Relations: An Investigation of the 1984 Presidential Election," *Journal of Personality and Social Psychology* 51(3) (1986), pp. 505–514.

56. Laura R. Glasman and Dolores Albarracín, "Forming Attitudes That Predict Future Behavior: A Meta-analysis of the Attitude-Behavior Relation," *Psychological Bulletin* 132(5) (2006), pp. 778–822; Jörg Doll and Icek Ajzen, "Accessibility and Stability of Predictors in the Theory of Planned Behavior," *Journal of Personality and Social Psychology* 63(5) (1992), pp. 754–765.

57. David W. Jamieson and Mark P. Zanna, "Need for Structure in Attitude Formation and Expression," in Anthony R. Pratkanis, Steven J. Breckler, and Anthony G. Greenwald, eds., *Attitude Structure and Function* (New York: Psychology Press, 1989), pp. 383–406.

58. Russell W. Belk, "Possessions and the Extended Self," *Journal of Consumer Research* 15(2) (1988), pp. 139–168.

59. William O. Bearden and Michael J. Etzel, "Reference Group Influence on Product and Brand Purchase Decisions," *Journal of Consumer Research* 9 (September 1982), pp. 183–94.

60. Gregory A. Guagnano, Paul C. Stern, and Thomas Dietz, "Influences on Attitude-Behavior Relationships: A Natural Experiment with Curbside Recycling," *Environment and Behavior* 27(5) (1995), pp. 699–718.

61. Henning Best and Thorsten Kneip, "The Impact of Attitudes and Behavioral Costs on Environmental Behavior: A Natural Experiment on Household Waste Recycling," *Social Science Research* 40(3) (2011), pp. 917–930.

62. Guagnano, Stern, and Dietz, "Influences on Attitude-Behavior Relationships."

63. J. Stanley Black, Paul C. Stern, and Julie T. Elworth, "Personal and Contextual Influences on Household Energy Adaptations," *Journal of Applied Psychology* 70(1) (1985), pp. 3–21.

64. Paul C. Stern, "Toward a Coherent Theory of Environmentally Significant Behavior," *Journal of Social Issues* 56(3) (2000), pp. 407–424.

65. Gert Cornelissen, Mario Pandelaere, Luk Warlop, and Siegfried Dewitte, "Positive Cueing: Promoting Sustainable Consumer Behavior by Cueing Common Environmental Behaviors as Environmental," *International Journal of Research in Marketing* 25(1) (2008), pp. 46–55.

66. Gerald R. Salancik and Mary Conway, "Attitude Inferences from Salient and Relevant Cognitive Content about Behavior," *Journal of Personality and Social Psychology* 32(5) (1975), pp. 829–840.

67. Michael Ross, Cathy McFarland, Michael Conway, and Mark P. Zanna, "Reciprocal Relation between Attitudes and Behavior Recall: Committing People to Newly Formed Attitudes," *Journal of Personality and Social Psychology* 45(2) (1983), pp. 257–267.

68. Ellen van der Werff, Linda Steg, and Kees Keizer, "It Is a Moral Issue: The Relationship between Environmental Self-Identity, Obligation-Based Intrinsic Motivation and Pro-environmental Behaviour," *Global Environmental Change* 23(5) (2013), pp. 1258–1265.

69. Whitmarsh and O'Neill, "Green Identity, Green Living."

70. Philip E. Tetlock, Orie V. Kristel, S. Beth Elson, Melanie C. Green, and Jennifer S. Lerner, "The Psychology of the Unthinkable: Taboo Trade-offs, Forbidden Base Rates, and Heretical Counterfactuals," *Journal of Personality and Social Psychology* 78(5) (2000), pp. 853–870.

71. Jeremy Ginges and Scott Atranm, "Noninstrumental Reasoning over Sacred Values: An Indonesian Case Study," *Psychology of Learning and Motivation* 50 (2009), pp. 193–206.

72. Tetlock et al., "Psychology of the Unthinkable," p. 855.

73. Tetlock et al., "Psychology of the Unthinkable."

74. Leilei Gao, S. Christian Wheeler, and Baba Shiv, "The 'Shaken Self': Product Choices as a Means of Restoring Self-View Confidence," *Journal of Consumer Research* 36(1) (2009), pp. 29–38.

75. Niamh Murtagh, Birgitta Gatersleben, and David Uzzell, "Self-Identity Threat and Resistance to Change: Evidence from Regular Travel Behaviour," *Journal of Environmental Psychology* 32(4) (2012), pp. 318–326.

76. Ellen van der Werff, Linda Steg, and Kees Keizer, "The Value of Environmental Self-Identity: The Relationship between Biospheric Values, Environmental Self-Identity and Environmental Preferences, Intentions and Behaviour," *Journal of Environmental Psychology* 34 (2013), pp. 55–63.

77. Kimberly A. Wade-Benzoni, Min Li, Leigh L. Thompson, and Max H. Bazerman, "The Malleability of Environmentalism," *Analyses of Social Issues and Public Policy* 7(1) (2007), pp. 163–189.

78. Aaron M. McCright and Riley E. Dunlap, "The Politicization of Climate Change and Polarization in the American Public's Views of Global Warming, 2001–2010," *Sociological Quarterly* 52(2) (2011), pp. 155–194.

79. Peter Jacques, "The Rearguard of Modernity: Environmental Skepticism as a Struggle of Citizenship," *Global Environmental Politics* 6(1) (2006), pp. 76–101.

80. Tom McCarthy, "Florida Banned State Workers from Using 'Climate Change'— Report," *The Guardian*, March 8, 2015, http://www.theguardian.com/us-news/2015/mar/08/florida-banned-terms-climate-change-global-warming.

81. Tim McDonnell, "Another State Agency Just Banned the Words 'Climate Change,'" *Mother Jones*, April 8, 2015, http://www.motherjones.com/blue-marble/2015/04/another-state-agency-just-banned-words-climate-change.

82. Alon Harish, "New Law in North Carolina Bans Latest Scientific Predictions of Sea-Level Rise," *ABC News*, August 2, 2012, http://abcnews.go.com/US/north-carolina-bans-latest-science-rising-sea-level/story?id=16913782.

83. Emily Atkin, "The Canadian Government Doesn't Let Its Meteorologists Talk about Climate Change," *Climate Progress*, May 28, 2014, http://thinkprogress.org/climate/2014/05/28/3442208/meteorologists-climate-change/.

84. Heberlein, *Navigating Environmental Attitudes*, p. 5.

85. Boyka Bratanova, Steve Loughnan, and Birgitta Gatersleben, "The Moral Circle as a Common Motivational Cause of Cross-Situational Pro-environmentalism," *European Journal of Social Psychology* 42(5) (2012), pp. 539–545.

86. Robert Boleslaw Zajonc, "Social Facilitation," *Science* 149(3681) (1965), pp. 269–274.

87. Bas Verplanken and Rob W. Holland, "Motivated Decision Making: Effects of Activation and Self-Centrality of Values on Choices and Behavior," *Journal of Personality and Social Psychology* 82(3) (2002), pp. 434–447.

88. See, for example, Jennifer R. Steele and Nalini Ambady, "'Math Is Hard!': The Effect of Gender Priming on Women's Attitudes," *Journal of Experimental Social Psychology* 42(4) (2006), pp. 428–436.

89. Katherine Lacasse, "The Importance of Being Green: The Influence of Green Behaviors on Americans' Political Attitudes toward Climate Change," *Environment and Behavior* 47(7) (2014), pp. 1–28.

90. William A. Cunningham, Kristopher J. Preacher, and Mahzarin R. Banaji, "Implicit Attitude Measures: Consistency, Stability, and Convergent Validity," *Psychological Science* 12(2) (2001), pp. 163–170.

91. Andrew J. Elliot and Patricia G. Devine, "On the Motivational Nature of Cognitive Dissonance: Dissonance as Psychological Discomfort," *Journal of Personality and Social Psychology* 67(3) (1994), pp. 382–394.

92. Joshua Aronson, Hart Blanton, and Joel Cooper, "From Dissonance to Disidentification: Selectivity in the Self-Affirmation Process," *Journal of Personality and Social Psychology* 68(6) (1995), pp. 986–996.

93. Satoshi Fujii, "Environmental Concern, Attitude toward Frugality, and Ease of Behavior as Determinants of Pro-environmental Behavior Intentions," *Journal of Environmental Psychology* 26(4) (2006), pp. 262–268; it should be noted that the study focused only on intentions and not actual behavior.

94. Patrick Devine-Wright, "Rethinking NIMBYism: The Role of Place Attachment and Place Identity in Explaining Place-Protective Action," *Journal of Community and Applied Social Psychology* 19(6) (2009), pp. 426–441.

95. Marit Vorkinn and Hanne Riese, "Environmental Concern in a Local Context: The Significance of Place Attachment," *Environment and Behavior* 33(2) (2001), pp. 249–263.

96. Whitmarsh and O'Neill, "Green Identity, Green Living."

97. Americus Reed, Mark R. Forehand, Stefano Puntoni, and Luk Warlop, "Identity-Based Consumer Behavior," *International Journal of Research in Marketing* 29(4) (2012), pp. 310–21.

98. Americus Reed, "Activating the Self-Importance of Consumer Selves: Exploring Identity Salience Effects on Judgments," *Journal of Consumer Research* 31(2) (2004), pp. 286–295.

99. Robyn A. LeBoeuf, Eldar Shafir, and Julia Belyavsky Bayuk, "The Conflicting Choices of Alternating Selves," *Organizational Behavior and Human Decision Processes* 111(1) (2010), pp. 48–61; Mark R. Forehand, Rohit Deshpandé, and Americus Reed II, "Identity Salience and the Influence of Differential Activation of the Social Self-Schema on Advertising Response," *Journal of Applied Psychology* 87(6) (2002), pp. 1086–1099.

100. Amit Bhattacharjee, Jonah Berger, and Geeta Menon, "When Identity Marketing Backfires: Consumer Agency in Identity Expression," *Journal of Consumer Research* 2(4) (August 2014), pp. 294–309.

101. Robert B. Cialdini and Melanie R. Trost, "Social Influence: Social Norms, Conformity and Compliance," in Daniel T. Gilbert, Susan T. Fiske, and Gardner Ed Lindzey, eds., *The Handbook of Social Psychology,* 4th ed., vol. 2 (New York: McGraw-Hill, 1998), pp. 151–192.

102. Aronson, Blanton, and Cooper, "From Dissonance to Disidentification," p. 596.

103. Robert B. Cialdini, Raymond R. Reno, and Carl A. Kallgren, "A Focus Theory of Normative Conduct: Recycling the Concept of Norms to Reduce Littering in Public Places," *Journal of Personality and Social Psychology* 58(6) (1990), pp. 1015–1026.

104. Norbert L. Kerr, "Norms in Social Dilemmas," in David A. Schroeder, ed., *Social Dilemmas: Perspectives on Individuals and Groups* (Westport, CT: Greenwood Publishing Group, 1995), pp. 31–47.

105. Kerr, "Norms in Social Dilemmas," pp. 33ff.

106. Heberlein, *Navigating Environmental Attitudes*, pp. 102–105.

107. Karine Nyborg and Mari Rege, "On Social Norms: The Evolution of Considerate Smoking Behavior," *Journal of Economic Behavior and Organization* 52(3) (2003), pp. 323–340.

108. Alice Grønhøj and John Thøgersen, "Action Speaks Louder Than Words: The Effect of Personal Attitudes and Family Norms on Adolescents' Pro-environmental Behaviour," *Journal of Economic Psychology* 33(1) (2012), pp. 292–302.

109. Jon Elster, "Social Norms and Economic Theory," *Journal of Economic Perspectives* 3(4) (1989), pp. 99–117.

110. Raymond R. Reno, Robert B. Cialdini, and Carl A. Kallgren, "The Transsituational Influence of Social Norms," *Journal of Personality and Social Psychology* 64(1) (1993), pp. 104–112.

111. Stuart Oskamp et al., "Factors Influencing Household Recycling Behavior," *Environment and Behavior* 23(4) (1991), pp. 494–519.

112. Kelly S. Fielding, Deborah J. Terry, Barbara M. Masser, and Michael A. Hogg, "Integrating Social Identity Theory and the Theory of Planned Behaviour to Explain Decisions to Engage in Sustainable Agricultural Practices," *British Journal of Social Psychology* 47(1) (2008), pp. 23–48.

113. Noah J. Goldstein, Robert B. Cialdini, and Vladas Griskevicius, "A Room with a Viewpoint: Using Social Norms to Motivate Environmental Conservation in Hotels," *Journal of Consumer Research* 35(3) (2008), pp. 472–482.

114. Jessica M. Nolan, P. Wesley Schultz, Robert B. Cialdini, Noah J. Goldstein, and Vladas Griskevicius, "Normative Social Influence Is Underdetected," *Personality and Social Psychology Bulletin* 34(7) (2008), pp. 913–923.

115. Sasha Issenberg, *The Victory Lab: The Secret Science of Winning Campaigns* (New York: Crown Publishers, 2012).

116. Republican candidate Ted Cruz faced a backlash after having sent mailers during the primaries in Iowa that looked like official information indicating "voting violations," and reminding people that whether they participated in caucuses is public information. Ryan Lizza, "Ted Cruz's Iowa Mailers Are More Fraudulent Than Everyone Thinks," *New Yorker*, January 31, 2016, http://www.newyorker.com/news/news-desk/ted-cruzs-iowa-mailers-are-more-fraudulent-than-everyone-thinks.

117. Iman Naderi and David Strutton, "I Support Sustainability but Only When Doing So Reflects Fabulously on Me: Can Green Narcissists Be Cultivated?," *Journal of Macromarketing* 35(1) (2013), pp. 1–14.

118. Harry M. Wallace and Roy F. Baumeister, "The Performance of Narcissists Rises and Falls with Perceived Opportunity for Glory," *Journal of Personality and Social Psychology* 82(5) (2002), pp. 819–834.

119. Iman Naderi and David Strutton, "Can Normal Narcissism Be Managed to Promote Green Product Purchases? Investigating a Counterintuitive Proposition," *Journal of Applied Social Psychology* 44(5) (2014), pp. 375–391.

120. Naderi and Strutton, "Normal Narcissism," pp. 381–383.

121. Naderi and Strutton, "Normal Narcissism," pp. 383–386.

122. Doug McKenzie-Mohr, "Promoting Sustainable Behavior: An Introduction to Community-Based Social Marketing," *Journal of Social Issues* 56(3) (2000), pp. 543–554.

123. P. Wesley Schultz, Jessica M. Nolan, Robert B. Cialdini, Noah J. Goldstein, and Vladas Griskevicius, "The Constructive, Destructive, and Reconstructive Power of Social Norms," *Psychological Science* 18(5) (2007), pp. 429–434.

124. Julia A. Minson and Benoît Monin, "Do-Gooder Derogation: Disparaging Morally Motivated Minorities to Defuse Anticipated Reproach," *Social Psychological and Personality Science* 3(2) (2012), pp. 200–207.

125. Richard A. Posner, "The Problematics of Moral and Legal Theory," *Harvard Law Review* (1998), pp. 1637–1717.

126. Judith I. M. De Groot and Geertje Schuitema, "How to Make the Unpopular Popular? Policy Characteristics, Social Norms and the Acceptability of Environmental Policies," *Environmental Science and Policy* 19–20 (2012), pp. 100–107.

127. Elinor Ostrom, *Governing the Commons* (Cambridge: Cambridge University Press, 1990).

128. Anders Biel and John Thøgersen, "Activation of Social Norms in Social Dilemmas: A Review of the Evidence and Reflections on the Implications for Environmental Behaviour," *Journal of Economic Psychology* 28(1) (2007), pp. 93–112.

129. Christophe Boone, Carolyn H. Declerck, and Sigrid Suetens, "Subtle Social Cues, Explicit Incentives and Cooperation in Social Dilemmas," *Evolution and Human Behavior* 29(3) (2008), pp. 179–188.

130. James S. Coleman, "Free Riders and Zealots: The Role of Social Networks," *Sociological Theory* 6(1) (1988), pp. 52–57.

131. Sonya Sachdeva, Rumen Iliev, and Douglas L. Medin, "Sinning Saints and Saintly Sinners: The Paradox of Moral Self-Regulation," *Psychological Science* 20(4) (2009), pp. 523–528.

132. Benoît Monin and Dale T. Miller, "Moral Credentials and the Expression of Prejudice," *Journal of Personality and Social Psychology* 81(1) (2001), pp. 33–43.

133. Sachdeva, Iliev, and Medin, "Sinning Saints," pp. 525–527.

134. Nina Mazar and Chen-Bo Zhong, "Do Green Products Make Us Better People?," *Psychological Science* 21(4) (2010), pp. 494–498.

135. Uma R. Karmarkar and Bryan Bollinger, "BYOB: How Bringing Your Own Shopping Bags Leads to Treating Yourself and the Environment," *Journal of Marketing* 79(4) (2015), pp. 1–15.

136. Uzma Khan and Ravi Dhar, "Licensing Effect in Consumer Choice," *Journal of Marketing Research* 43(2) (2006), pp. 259–266.

137. Anna C. Merritt, Daniel A. Effron, and Benoît Monin, "Moral Self-Licensing: When Being Good Frees Us to Be Bad," *Social and Personality Psychology Compass* 4(5) (2010), pp. 344–357.

138. Ayelet Fishbach and Ravi Dhar, "Goals as Excuses or Guides: The Liberating Effect of Perceived Goal Progress on Choice," *Journal of Consumer Research* 32(3) (December 2005), pp. 370–377.

139. Jennifer Jordan, Elizabeth Mullen, and J. Keith Murnighan, "Striving for the Moral Self: The Effects of Recalling Past Moral Actions on Future Moral Behavior," *Personality and Social Psychology Bulletin* 37(5) (2011), pp. 701–713.

140. Martin S. Hagger, Chantelle Wood, Chris Stiff, and Nikos L. D. Chatzisarantis, "Ego Depletion and the Strength Model of Self-Control: A Meta-analysis," *Psychological Bulletin* 136(40) (2010), pp. 495–525. Although this effect has been found in many studies, there are some recent attempts to replicate these results that call them into question.

141. Kelly McGonigal, *The Willpower Instinct* (New York: Avery, 2012), p. 87.

142. Janet Swim et al., *Psychology and Global Climate Change: Addressing a Multifaceted Phenomenon and Set of Challenges*, a report by the American Psychological Association's Task Force on the Interface between Psychology and Global Climate Change (Washington, DC: American Psychological Association, 2009), p. 94.

CHAPTER 7

1. See, for example, Bill McKibben, "Global Warming's Terrifying New Math," *Rolling Stone*, July 19, 2012, http://www.rollingstone.com/politics/news/global-warmings-terrifying-new-math-20120719; Johan Rockstrom and Mattias Klum, *Big World, Small Planet: Abundance within Planetary Boundaries* (New Haven: Yale University Press, 2015).

2. Theodore Seuss Geisel (Dr. Seuss), *The Lorax* (New York: Random House, 1971).

Aarts, Henk, and Ap Dijksterhuis. 2003. "The Silence of the Library: Environment, Situational Norm, and Social Behavior." *Journal of Personality and Social Psychology* 84(1): 18–28.

Aarts, Henk, Bas Verplanken, and Ad van Knippenberg. 1997. "Habit and Information Use in Travel Mode Choices." *Acta Psychologica* 96(1): 1–14.

Abelson, Robert P. 1981. "Psychological Status of the Script Concept." *American Psychologist* 36(7): 715–729.

Adriaanse, Marieke A., Gabriele Oettingen, Peter M. Gollwitzer, Erin P. Hennes, Denise T. D. De Ridder, and John B. F. De Wit. 2010. "When Planning Is Not Enough: Fighting Unhealthy Snacking Habits by Mental Contrasting with Implementation Intentions (MCII)." *European Journal of Social Psychology* 40(7): 1277–1293.

Ajzen, Icek. 1985. *From Intentions to Actions: A Theory of Planned Behavior.* Berlin: Springer.

Ajzen, Icek. 1991. "The Theory of Planned Behavior." *Organizational Behavior and Human Decision Processes* 50(2): 179–211.

Ajzen, Icek, and Martin Fishbein. 1997. "Attitude-Behavior Relations: A Theoretical Analysis and Review of Empirical Research." *Psychological Bulletin* 84(5): 888–918.

Aklin, Michaël, and Johannes Urpelainen. 2014. "Perceptions of Scientific Dissent Undermine Public Support for Environmental Policy." *Environmental Science and Policy* 38: 173–177.

Alcott, Blake. 2005. "Jevons' Paradox." *Ecological Economics* 54: 9–21.

Amabile, Teresa M. 1996. *Creativity in Context.* Boulder: Westview Press.

Ambec, Stefan, Mark A. Cohen, Stewart Elgie, and Paul Lanoie. 2013. "The Porter Hypothesis at 20: Can Environmental Regulation Enhance Innovation and Competitiveness?" *Review of Environmental Economics and Policy* 7(1): 2–22.

Andreasen, Alan R. 1984. "Life Status Changes and Changes in Consumer Preferences and Satisfaction." *Journal of Consumer Research* 11(3): 784–794.

Ariely, Dan, Uri Gneezy, George Loewenstein, and Nina Mazar. 2009. "Large Stakes and Big Mistakes." *Review of Economic Studies* 76(2): 451–469.

Aronson, Joshua, Hart Blanton, and Joel Cooper. 1995. "From Dissonance to Disidentification: Selectivity in the Self-Affirmation Process." *Journal of Personality and Social Psychology* 68(6): 986–996.

Assardourian, Erik, and Christopher Flavin. 2004. *State of the World 2004: A Worldwatch Institute Report on Progress toward a Sustainable Society. Special Focus: The Consumer Society.* New York: Norton.

Athay, Michael, and John M. Darley. 1981. "Toward an Interaction-Centered Theory of Personality." In Nancy Cantor and John F. Kihlstrom, eds., *Personality, Cognition, and Social Interaction,* 281–308. New York: Routledge.

Atkin, Emily. 2014. "The Canadian Government Doesn't Let Its Meteorologists Talk about Climate Change." *Climate Progress,* May 28.

Axelrod, Robert, and William D. Hamilton. 1981. "The Evolution of Cooperation." *Science* 211 (March): 1390–1396.

Baldé, C. P., F. Wang, F., R. Kuehr, and J. Huisman. 2015. *The Global E-Waste Monitor – 2014.* Bonn: United Nations University IAS—SCYCLE.

Bamberg, Sebastian. 2000. "The Promotion of New Behavior by Forming an Implementation Intention: Results of a Field Experiment in the Domain of Travel Mode Choice." *Journal of Applied Social Psychology* 30(9): 1903–1922.

Bamberg, Sebastian, and Peter Schmidt. 2001. "Theory-Driven Subgroup-Specific Evaluation of an Intervention to Reduce Private Car Use." *Journal of Applied Social Psychology* 31(6): 1300–1329.

Barg, Stephan. 1996. "Eliminating Perverse Subsidies: What's the Problem?" In OECD, *Subsidies and Environment: Exploring the Linkages,* 23–42. Paris: OECD.

Bargh, John A., and Tanya L. Chartrand. 1999. "The Unbearable Automaticity of Being." *American Psychologist* 54(7): 462–479.

Barkin, J. Samuel. 2006. "Discounting the Discount Rate: Ecocentrism and Environmental Economics." *Global Environmental Politics* 6(4) (November): 56–72.

Baron, Jonathan, and Ilana Ritov. 1994. "Reference Points and Omission Bias." *Organizational Behavior and Human Decision Processes* 59: 475–498.

Barr, Stewart, and Andrew Gilg. 2006. "Sustainable Lifestyles: Framing Environmental Action in and around the Home." *Geoforum* 37(6): 906–920.

Barr, Stewart, Andrew W. Gilg, and Nicholas Ford. 2005. "The Household Energy Gap: Examining the Divide between Habitual- and Purchase-Related Conservation Behaviours." *Energy Policy* 33(11): 1425–1444.

Beach, Lee Roy, and Terence R. Mitchell. 1978. "A Contingency Model for the Selection of Decision Strategies." *Academy of Management Review* 3(3): 439–449.

Bearden, William O., and Michael J. Etzel. 1982. "Reference Group Influence on Product and Brand Purchase Decisions." *Journal of Consumer Research* 9 (September): 183–94.

Becker, Lawrence J. 1978. "Joint Effect of Feedback and Goal Setting on Performance: A Field Study of Residential Energy Conservation." *Journal of Applied Psychology* 63(4): 428–433.

Belk, Russell W. 1988. "Possessions and the Extended Self." *Journal of Consumer Research* 15(2): 139–168.

Bem, Daryl J. 1972. "Self-Perception Theory." In Leonard Berkowitz, ed., *Advances in Experimental Social Psychology,* vol. 6, 1–62. New York: Academic Press.

Ben-Bassat, Avi, and Momi Dahan. 2012. "Social Identity and Voting Behavior." *Public Choice* 151(1–2): 193–214.

Benartzi, Shlomo, and Richard H. Thaler. 2007. "Heuristics and Biases in Retirement Savings Behavior." *Journal of Economic Perspectives* 21(3): 81–104.

Bennhold, Katri. 2013. "The Ministry of Nudges." *New York Times*, December 8, B1, B4.

Berkman, Michael B., and Eric Plutzer. 2009. "Scientific Expertise and the Culture War: Public Opinion and the Teaching of Evolution in the American States." *Perspectives on Politics* 7(3): 485–499.

Best, Henning, and Thorsten Kneip. 2011. "The Impact of Attitudes and Behavioral Costs on Environmental Behavior: A Natural Experiment on Household Waste Recycling." *Social Science Research* 40(3): 917–930.

Bhattacharjee, Amit, Jonah Berger, and Geeta Menon, 2014. "When Identity Marketing Backfires: Consumer Agency in Identity Expression." *Journal of Consumer Research* 2(4) (August): 294–309.

Biel, Anders, and John Thøgersen. 2007. "Activation of Social Norms in Social Dilemmas: A Review of the Evidence and Reflections on the Implications for Environmental Behaviour." *Journal of Economic Psychology* 28(1): 93–112.

Black, J. Stanley, Paul C. Stern, and Julie T. Elworth. 1985. "Personal and Contextual Influences on Household Energy Adaptations." *Journal of Applied Psychology* 70(1): 3–21.

Bleich, Sara N., Julia A. Wolfson, and Marian P. Jarlenski. 2015. "Calorie Changes in Chain Restaurant Menu Items: Implications for Obesity and Evaluations of Menu Labeling." *American Journal of Preventive Medicine* 48(1): 70–75.

Boldero, Jennifer. 1995. "The Prediction of Household Recycling of Newspapers: The Role of Attitudes, Intentions, and Situational Factors." *Journal of Applied Social Psychology* 25(5): 440–462.

Boone, Christophe, Carolyn H. Declerck, and Sigrid Suetens. 2008. "Subtle Social Cues, Explicit Incentives and Cooperation in Social Dilemmas." *Evolution and Human Behavior* 29(3): 179–188.

Bougherara, Douadia, Gilles Grolleau, and Luc Thiébaut. 2005. "Can Labelling Policies Do More Harm Than Good? An Analysis Applied to Environmental Labelling Schemes." *European Journal of Law and Economics* 19(1): 5–16.

Bouton, Mark E. 2002. "Context, Ambiguity, and Unlearning: Sources of Relapse after Behavioral Extinction." *Biological Psychiatry* 52(10): 976–986.

Bradford, Alina. 2015. "Deforestation: Facts, Causes and Effects." *Live Science*, March 4.

Bradsher, Keith. 2002. *High and Mighty: SUVs—the World's Most Dangerous Vehicles and How They Got That* Way. New York: Public Affairs.

Bratanova, Boyka, Steve Loughnan, and Birgitta Gatersleben. 2012. "The Moral Circle as a Common Motivational Cause of Cross-Situational Pro-environmentalism." *European Journal of Social Psychology* 42(5): 539–545.

Brook, Amara. 2011. "Ecological Footprint Feedback: Motivating or Discouraging?" *Social Influence* 6(2): 113–128.

Brown, Christina L., and Aradhna Krishna. 2004. "The Skeptical Shopper: A Metacognitive Account for the Effects of Default Options on Choice." *Journal of Consumer Research*, 31(3) (December): 529–539.

Brunnermeier, Smita B., and Mark A. Cohen. 2003. "Determinants of Environmental Innovation in U.S. Manufacturing Industries." *Journal of Environmental Economics and Management* 45(2): 278–293.

Bullock, Graham. 2010. "The Poor Man's Strategy? Information-Based Environmental Governance in Hard Times." Paper presented at the American Political Science Association Annual Meeting.

Carroll, Gabriel D., James J. Choi, David Laibson, Brigitte C. Madrian, and Andrew Metrick. 2009. "Optimal Defaults and Active Decisions." *Quarterly Journal of Economics* 124(4): 1639–1674.

Carrus, Giuseppe, Paola Passafaro, and Mirilia Bonnes. 2008. "Emotions, Habits and Rational Choices in Ecological Behaviours: The Case of Recycling and Use of Public Transportation." *Journal of Environmental Psychology* 28(1): 51–62.

Chandra, Ambarish, Sumeet Gulati, and Milind Kandlikar. 2010. "Green Drivers or Free Riders? An Analysis of Tax Rebates for Hybrid Vehicles." *Journal of Environmental Economics and Management* 60: 78–93.

Chawla, Louise, and Debra Flanders Cushing. 2007. "Education for Strategic Environmental Behavior." *Environmental Education Research* 13(4): 437–452.

Cheung, Shu Fai, Darius K.-S. Chan, and Zoe S.-Y. Wong. 1999. "Reexamining the Theory of Planned Behavior in Understanding Wastepaper Recycling." *Environment and Behavior* 31(5): 587–612.

Choi, James J., David Laibson, Brigitte C. Madrian, and Andrew Metrick. 2002. "Defined Contribution Pensions: Plan Rules, Participant Choices, and the Path of Least Resistance." In *Tax Policy and the Economy*, vol. 16, 67–114. Cambridge, MA: MIT Press.

Chung, Shan-Shan, and Monica Miu-Yin Leung. 2007. "The Value-Action Gap in Waste Recycling: The Case of Undergraduates in Hong Kong." *Environmental Management* 40(4): 603–612.

Cialdini, Robert B. 2003. "Crafting Normative Messages to Protect the Environment." *Current Directions in Psychological Science* 12(4): 105–109.

Cialdini, Robert B., Raymond R. Reno, and Carl A. Kallgren. 1990. "A Focus Theory of Normative Conduct: Recycling the Concept of Norms to Reduce Littering in Public Places." *Journal of Personality and Social Psychology* 58(6): 1015–1026.

Cialdini, Robert B., and Melanie R. Trost. 1998. "Social Influence: Social Norms, Conformity and Compliance." In Daniel T. Gilbert, Susan T. Fiske, and Gardner Ed Lindzey, eds., *The Handbook of Social Psychology*, 4th ed., vol. 2, 151–192. New York: McGraw-Hill.

Clapp, Jennifer. 2001. *Toxic Exports: The Transfer of Hazardous Wastes from Rich to Poor Countries*. Ithaca, NY: Cornell University Press.

Clapp, Jennifer. 2012. "The Rising Tide against Plastic Waste: Unpacking the Industry Attempts to Influence the Debate." In Stephanie Foote and Elizabeth Mazzolini, eds., *Histories of the Dustheap*, 199–225. Cambridge, MA: MIT Press.

Clayton, Susan. 2003. "Environmental Identity: A Conceptual and Operational Definition." In Susan Clayton and Susan Opotow, eds., *Identity and the Natural Environment: The Psychological Significance of Nature*, 45–65. Cambridge, MA: MIT Press.

CNW Marketing. 2007. "Dust to Dust: The Energy Cost of New Vehicles from Concept to Disposal." This report is no longer available on the web.

Coase, Ronald H. 1960. "The Problem of Social Cost." *Journal of Law and Economics* 3 (October): 1–44.

Cohen, Anna-Lisa, Ute C. Bayer, Alexander Jaudas, and Peter M. Gollwitzer. 2008. "Self-Regulatory Strategy and Executive Control: Implementation Intentions Modulate Task Switching and Simon Task Performance." *Psychological Research* 72(1): 12–26.

Cohen, Michael R. 1973. "Environmental Information versus Environmental Attitudes." *Journal of Environmental Education* 5(2): 5–8.

Cohn & Wolfe, Lander Associates, Penn, Schoen & Berland. 2011. "Green Brands Survey."

Coleman, James S. 1988. "Free Riders and Zealots: The Role of Social Networks." *Sociological Theory* 6(1): 52–57.

CONE Communications / ECHO. 2013. "Global CSR Study." Website.

Connolly, Barbara. 1999. "Asymmetrical Rivalry in Common Pool Resources and European Responses to Acid Rain." In J. Samuel Barkin and George E. Shambaugh, eds., *Anarchy and the Environment*, 130. Albany: SUNY Press.

Cornelissen, Gert, Mario Pandelaere, Luk Warlop, and Siegfried Dewitte. 2008. "Positive Cueing: Promoting Sustainable Consumer Behavior by Cueing Common Environmental Behaviors as Environmental." *International Journal of Research in Marketing* 25(1): 46–55.

Cox, Stan. 2010. *Losing Our Cool: Uncomfortable Truths about Our Air-Conditioned World*. New York: New Press.

Craig, C. Samuel, and John M. McCann. 1978. "Assessing Communication Effects on Energy Conservation." *Journal of Consumer Research* 5(2): 82–88.

Crozier, Michel. 1964. *The Bureaucratic Phenomenon: An Examination of Bureaucracy in Modern Organizations and Its Cultural Setting in France*. Chicago: University of Chicago Press.

Cunningham, William A., Kristopher J. Preacher, and Mahzarin R. Banaji. 2001. "Implicit Attitude Measures: Consistency, Stability, and Convergent Validity." *Psychological Science* 12(2): 163–170.

Cyert, Richard M., and James G. March. 1963. *A Behavioral Theory of the Firm*. Englewood Cliffs, NJ: Prentice Hall.

Dahl, Melissa. 2014. "Think It'll Take 21 Days to Make Your Resolution a Habit? Try Tripling That." *Today*, January 1.

Danner, Unna N., Henk Aarts, and Nanne K. Vries. 2008. "Habit vs. Intention in the Prediction of Future Behaviour: The Role of Frequency, Context Stability and Mental Accessibility of Past Behaviour." *British Journal of Social Psychology* 47(2): 245–265.

Darby, Sarah. 2001. "Making It Obvious: Designing Feedback into Energy Consumption." In Paolo Bertoldi, Andrea Ricciardi, and Aníbal T. de Almeida, eds., *Energy Efficiency in Household Appliances and Lighting*, 685–696. Berlin: Springer.

Darby, Sarah. 2008. "Energy Feedback in Buildings: Improving the Infrastructure for Demand Reduction." *Building Research and Information* 36(5): 499–508.

Dauvergne, Peter, and Jane Lister. 2013. *Eco-Business: A Big-Brand Takeover of Sustainability*. Cambridge, MA: MIT Press.

Dean, Jeremy. 2013. *Making Habits, Breaking Habits: Why We Do Things, Why We Don't, and How to Make Any Change Stick*. Boston: Da Capo.

Deci, Edward L. 1972. "The Effects of Contingent and Noncontingent Rewards and Controls on Intrinsic Motivation." *Organizational Behavior and Human Performance* 8(2): 217–229.

Deci, Edward L., Richard Koestner, and Richard M. Ryan. 2001 "Extrinsic Rewards and Intrinsic Motivation in Education: Reconsidered Once Again." *Review of Educational Research* 71(1), pp. 1–27.

Deci, Edward L., and Richard M. Ryan. 1985. *Intrinsic Motivation and Self-Determination in Human Behavior*. New York: Plenum Press.

Deci, Edward L., Richard M. Ryan, and Richard Koestner. 1999. "A Meta-analytic Review of Experiments Examining the Effects of Extrinsic Rewards on Intrinsic Motivation." *Psychological Bulletin* 125(6): 627–688.

De Groot, Judith I. M., and Geertje Schuitema. 2012. "How to Make the Unpopular Popular? Policy Characteristics, Social Norms and the Acceptability of Environmental Policies." *Environmental Science and Policy* 19–20: 100–107.

DeJoy, David M. 1989. "The Optimism Bias and Traffic Accident Risk Perception." *Accident Analysis and Prevention* 21(4): 333–340.

DeSombre, Elizabeth R. 2000. "The Experience of the Montreal Protocol: Particularly Remarkable and Remarkably Particular." *UCLA Journal of Environmental Law and Policy* 19: 49–81.

DeSombre, Elizabeth R. 2008. "Globalization, Competition and Convergence: Shipping and the Race to the Middle." *Global Governance* 14(2) (April–June): 179–198.

DeSombre, Elizabeth R., and J. Samuel Barkin. 2011. *Fish*. Cambridge, MA: Polity Press.

Dettmann-Easler, Detra, and James L. Pease. 1999. "Evaluating the Effectiveness of Residential Environmental Education Programs in Fostering Positive Attitudes toward Wildlife." *Journal of Environmental Education* 31(1): 33–39.

Devine-Wright, Patrick. 2009. "Rethinking NIMBYism: The Role of Place Attachment and Place Identity in Explaining Place-Protective Action." *Journal of Community and Applied Social Psychology* 19(6): 426–441.

Dietz, Thomas, Amy Fitzgerald, and Rachael Shwom. 2005. "Environmental Values." *Annual Review of Environment and Resources* 30(1): 335–372.

Docan, Tony N. 2006. "Positive and Negative Incentives in the Classroom: An Analysis of Grading Systems and Student Motivation." *Journal of Scholarship of Teaching and Learning* 6(2) (October): 21–40.

Doll, Jörg, and Icek Ajzen. 1992. "Accessibility and Stability of Predictors in the Theory of Planned Behavior." *Journal of Personality and Social Psychology* 63(5): 754–765.

Dono, Joanne, Janine Webb, and Ben Richardson. 2010. "The Relationship between Environmental Activism, Pro-environmental Behaviour and Social Identity." *Journal of Environmental Psychology* 30(2): 178–186.

Drexler, Alejandro, Greg Fischer, and Antoinette Schoar. 2014. "Keeping It Simple: Financial Literacy and Rules of Thumb." *American Economic Journal: Applied Economics* 6(2): 1–31.

Duffy, Sean, and Michelle Verges. 2009. "It Matters a Hole Lot: Perceptual Affordances of Waste Containers Influence Recycling Compliance." *Environment and Behavior* 41(5): 741–749.

Duhigg, Charles. 2012. *The Power of Habit: Why We Do What We Do in Life and Business.* New York: Random House: 19.

Dunlap, Riley E., and Peter J. Jacques. 2013. "Climate Change Denial Books and Conservative Think Tanks: Exploring the Connection." *American Behavioral Scientist* 57(6): 699–731.

Dunlap, Riley E., and Aaron M. McCright. 2008. "Social Movement Identity: Validating a Measure of Identification with the Environmental Movement." *Social Science Quarterly* 89(5): 1045–1065.

Edwards, Kari, and Edward E. Smith. 1996. "A Disconfirmation Bias in the Evaluation of Arguments." *Journal of Personality and Social Psychology* 71(1): 5–24.

Elliot, Andrew J., and Patricia G. Devine. 1994. "On the Motivational Nature of Cognitive Dissonance: Dissonance as Psychological Discomfort." *Journal of Personality and Social Psychology* 67(3): 382–394.

Elster, Jon. 1989. "Social Norms and Economic Theory." *Journal of Economic Perspectives* 3(4): 99–117.

Engber, Daniel. 2013. "A Nickels Isn't Worth a Cent: Why the Bottle Deposit Should Be Much, Much Higher." *Slate*, August 27. Available at http://www.slate.com/articles/health_and_science/science/2013/08/bottle_deposit_should_keep_up_with_inflation_time_to_raise_fee_from_a_nickel.html.

Environment Committee, House of Commons. 1991. *Eco-labeling: Eighth Report of the House of Commons.* London: HMSO.

Erikson, Erik H. 1994. *Identity: Youth and Crisis.* New York: Norton.

Eriksson, Louise, Jörgen Garvill, and Annika M. Nordlund. 2008. "Interrupting Habitual Car Use: The Importance of Car Habit Strength and Moral Motivation for Personal Car Use Reduction." *Transportation Research Part F: Traffic Psychology and Behaviour* 11(1): 10–23.

Farmer, Charles M., and JoAnn K. Wells. 2010. "Effect of Enhanced Seat Belt Reminders on Driver Fatality Risk." *Journal of Safety Research* 41(1): 53–57.

Farmer, Charles M., and Allan F. Williams. 2005. "Effect on Fatality Risk of Changing from Secondary to Primary Seat Belt Enforcement." *Journal of Safety Research* 36(2): 189–194.

Fazio, Russell H., and Carol J. Williams. 1986. "Attitude Accessibility as a Moderator of the Attitude-Perception and Attitude-Behavior Relations: An Investigation of the 1984 Presidential Election." *Journal of Personality and Social Psychology* 51(3): 505–514.

Fazio, Russell H., and Mark P. Zanna. 1981. "Direct Experience and Attitude-Behavior Consistency." *Advances in Experimental Social Psychology* 14: 161–202.

Fehr, Ernst, and Armin Falk. 2002. "Psychological Foundations of Incentives." *European Economic Review* 46: 687–724.

Feinberg, Matthew, and Robb Willer. 2011. "Apocalypse Soon? Dire Messages Reduce Belief in Global Warming by Contradicting Just-World Beliefs." *Psychological Science* 22(1): 34–38.

Feldman, Martha S., and Brian T. Pentland. 2003. "Reconceptualizing Organizational Routines as a Source of Flexibility and Change." *Administrative Science Quarterly* 48(1): 94–118.

Fhanér, Gunilla, and Monica Hane. 1979. "Seat Belts: Opinion Effects of Law-Induced Use." *Journal of Applied Psychology* 64(2): 205–212.

Fielding, Kelly S., Deborah J. Terry, Barbara M. Masser, and Michael A. Hogg. 2008. "Integrating Social Identity Theory and the Theory of Planned Behaviour to Explain Decisions to Engage in Sustainable Agricultural Practices." *British Journal of Social Psychology* 47(1): 23–48.

Finger, Matthias. 1994. "From Knowledge to Action? Exploring the Relationships between Environmental Experiences, Learning, and Behavior." *Journal of Social Issues* 50(3) (1994), pp. 141–160.

Finkel, Steven, Edward N. Muller, and Karl-Dieter Opp. "Personal Influence, Collective Rationality, and Mass Political Action." *American Political Science Review* 83(3) (September): 885–903.

Fischbacher, Urs, Simon Gächter, and Ernst Fehr. 2001. "Are People Conditionally Cooperative? Evidence from a Public Goods Experiment." *Economics Letters* 71(3): 397–404.

Fishbach, Ayelet, and Ravi Dhar. 2005. "Goals as Excuses or Guides: The Liberating Effect of Perceived Goal Progress on Choice." *Journal of Consumer Research* 32(3) (December): 370–377.

Fishbein, Martin. 1967. "A Consideration of Beliefs, and Their Role in Attitude Measurement." In Fishbein, ed., *Readings in Attitude Theory and Measurement*, 257–266. New York: Wiley.

Fishbein, Martin, and Icek Ajzen. 1975. *Belief, Attitude, Intention and Behavior: An Introduction to Theory and Research*. Reading, MA: Addison-Wesley.

Fisher, Ann, Gary H. McClelland, and William D. Schulze. 1988. "Measures of Willingness to Pay versus Willingness to Accept: Evidence, Explanations, and Potential Reconciliation." In George L. Peterson, Beverly L. Driver, and Robin Gregory, eds., *Amenity Resource Valuation: Integrating Economics with Other Disciplines*, 127–134. State College, PA: Venture.

Flynn, James, Paul Slovic, and Chris K. Mertz. 1994. "Gender, Race, and Perception of Environmental Health Risks." *Risk Analysis* 14(6): 1101–1108.

Forehand, Mark R., Rohit Deshpandé, and Americus Reed II. 2002. "Identity Salience and the Influence of Differential Activation of the Social Self-Schema on Advertising Response." *Journal of Applied Psychology* 87(6): 1086–1099.

Frank, Robert H., Thomas Gilovich, and Dennis T. Regan. 1993. "Does Studying Economics Inhibit Cooperation?" *Journal of Economic Perspectives* 7(2) (Spring): 159–171.

Franzen, Axel, and Dominikus Vogl. 2013. "Two Decades of Measuring Environmental Attitudes: A Comparative Analysis of 33 Countries." *Global Environmental Change* 23(5): 1001–1008.

Frey, Bruno S. 1997. "On the Relationship Between Intrinsic and Extrinsic Work Motivation." *International Journal of Industrial Organization* 15(4) (July): 427–439.

Fuji, Satoshi, and Ryuichi Kitamura. 2003. "What Does a One-Month Free Bus Ticket Do to Habitual Drivers?" *Transportation* 30: 81–95.

Fuji, Satoshi. 2006. "Environmental Concern, Attitude toward Frugality, and Ease of Behavior as Determinants of Pro-environmental Behavior Intentions." *Journal of Environmental Psychology* 26(4): 262–268.

Gabel, H. Landis, and Bernard Sinclair-Desgagné. 1997. "The Firm, Its Routines, and the Environment." INSEAD Working Paper 97/05/EPS. Fontainbleau.

Gallagher, Kelly Sims, and Erich Muehlegger. 2011. "Giving Green to Get Green? Incentives and Consumer Adoption of Hybrid Vehicle Technology." *Journal of Environmental Economics and Management* 61: 1–15.

Gallastegui, Ibon Galarraga. 2002. "The Use of Eco-Labels: A Review of the Literature." *European Environment* 12(6): 316–331.

Gao, Leilei, S. Christian Wheeler, and Baba Shiv. 2009. "The 'Shaken Self': Product Choices as a Means of Restoring Self-View Confidence." *Journal of Consumer Research* 36(1): 29–38.

Gardiner, Stephen M. "The Global Warming Tragedy and the Dangerous Illusion of the Kyoto Protocol." *Ethics and International Affairs* 18(1) (2004), 23–39.

Gardner, Benjamin, Gert-Jan de Bruijn, and Phillippa Lally. 2011. "A Systematic Review and Meta-analysis of Applications of the Self-Report Habit Index to Nutrition and Physical Activity Behaviour." *Annals of Behavioral Medicine* 42(2): 174–187.

Gardner, Benjamin, Gert-Jan de Bruijn, and Phillippa Lally. 2012. "Habit, Identity, and Repetitive Action: A Prospective Study of Binge-Drinking in UK Students." *British Journal of Health Psychology* 17(3): 565–581.

Gardner, Gerald T., and Paul C. Stern. 2002. *Environmental Problems and Human Behavior*. 2nd ed. Boston: Pearson Custom Publishing.

Gärling, Tommy, Satoshi Fujii, and Ole Boe. 2001. "Empirical Tests of a Model of Determinants of Script-Based Driving Choice." *Transportation Research Part F: Traffic Psychology and Behaviour* 4(2): 89–102.

Gately, Dermot. 1980. "Individual Discount Rates and the Purchase and Utilization of Energy-Using Durables: Comment." *Bell Journal of Economics* 11(1) (Spring): 373–374.

Geisel, Theodore Seuss (Dr. Seuss). 1971. *The Lorax*. New York: Random House.

Gersick, Connie J. G., and J. Richard Hackman. 1990. "Habitual Routines in Task-Performing Groups." *Organizational Behavior and Human Decision Processes* 47(1): 65–97.

Gillingham, Kenneth, and James Sweeney. 2010. "Market Failure and the Structure of Externalities." In Boaz Moselle, Jorge Padilla, and Richard Schmalensee, eds., *Harnessing Renewable Energy in Electric Power Systems*, 69–91. Washington, DC: Earthscan.

Gilovich, Thomas. 1987. "Secondhand Information and Social Judgment." *Journal of Experimental Social Psychology* 23.1: 59–74.

Ginges, Jeremy, and Scott Atranm. 2009. "Noninstrumental Reasoning over Sacred Values: An Indonesian Case Study." *Psychology of Learning and Motivation* 50: 193–206.

Givens, Jennifer E., and Andrew K. Jorgenson. 2013. "Individual Environmental Concern in the World Polity: A Multilevel Analysis." *Social Science Research* 42(2): 418–431.

Glasman, Laura R., and Dolores Albarracín. 2006. "Forming Attitudes That Predict Future Behavior: A Meta-analysis of the Attitude-Behavior Relation." *Psychological Bulletin* 132(5): 778–822.

Gleick, Peter. 2007. "Hummer versus Prius: 'Dust to Dust' Report Misleads the Media and Public with Bad Science." Pacific Institute, Oakland, CA.

Glucksberg, Sam. 1962. "The Influence of Strength of Drive on Functional Fixedness and Perceptual Recognition." *Journal of Experimental Psychology* 63: 36–41.

Gneezy, Uri, and Aldo Rustichini. 2000. "A Fine Is a Price." *Journal of Legal Studies* 29 (January): 1–17.

Goldstein, Noah J., Robert B. Cialdini, and Vladas Griskevicius. 2008. "A Room with a Viewpoint: Using Social Norms to Motivate Environmental Conservation in Hotels." *Journal of Consumer Research* 35(3): 472–482.

Goleman, Daniel. 1994. "Hidden Rules Often Distort Ideas of Risk." *New York Times*, February 1, C1.

Green, Andrew. 2006. "You Can't Pay Them Enough: Subsidies, Environmental Law, and Social Norms." *Harvard Environmental Law Review* 30: 407–440.

Gregory, Gary D., and Michael Di Leo. 2003. "Repeated Behavior and Environmental Psychology: The Role of Personal Involvement and Habit Formation in Explaining Water Consumption." *Journal of Applied Social Psychology* 33(6): 1261–1296.

Gregory, Robin, Sarah Lichtenstein, and Donald MacGregor. 1993. "The Role of Past States in Determining Reference Points for Policy Decisions." *Organizational Behavior and Human Decision Processes* 55(2): 195–206.

Griffin, Dale, and Amos Tversky. 1992. "The Weighing of Evidence and the Determinants of Confidence." *Cognitive Psychology* 24: 411.

Grønhøj, Alice, and John Thøgersen. 2012. "Action Speaks Louder Than Words: The Effect of Personal Attitudes and Family Norms on Adolescents' Pro-environmental Behaviour." *Journal of Economic Psychology* 33(1): 292–302.

Guagnano, Gregory A., Paul C. Stern, and Thomas Dietz. 1995. "Influences on Attitude-Behavior Relationships: A Natural Experiment with Curbside Recycling." *Environment and Behavior* 27(5): 699–718.

Gürek, Özgur, Bernd Irlenbusch, and Betting Rockenbach. 2000. "Motivating Teammates: The Leader's Choice between Positive and Negative Incentives." *Journal of Economic Psychology* 30: 591–607.

Hagger, Martin S., Chantelle Wood, Chris Stiff, and Nikos L. D. Chatzisarantis. 2012. "Ego Depletion and the Strength Model of Self-Control: A Meta-analysis." *Psychological Bulletin* 136(40): 495–525.

Halvorsen, Bente. 2008. "Effects of Norms and Opportunity Cost of Time on Household Recycling." *Land Economics* 84(3) (August): 501–516.

Hanisch, Carola. 2000. "Is Extended Producer Responsibility Effective?" *Environmental Science and Technology* 34(7): 170A–175A.

Hansla, André, Amelie Gamble, Asgeir Juliusson, and Tommy Gärling. 2008. "The Relationships between Awareness of Consequences, Environmental Concern, and Value Orientations." *Journal of Environmental Psychology* 28(1): 1–9.

Hardin, Garrett. 1968. "The Tragedy of the Commons." *Science* 162 (December 13): 1243–1248.

Hardin, Russel. 1982. *Collective Action.* Baltimore: Johns Hopkins University Press.

Hargreaves, Tom, Michael Nye, and Jacquelin Burgess. 2010. "Making Energy Visible: A Qualitative Field Study of How Householders Interact with Feedback from Smart Energy Monitors." *Energy Policy* 38(10): 6111–6119.

Harish, Alon. 2012. "New Law in North Carolina Bans Latest Scientific Predictions of Sea-Level Rise." *ABC News*, August 2.

Hauenstein, Heidi, and Laura Schewel. 2007. "Checking Dust to Dust's Assumptions about the Prius and the Hummer." Rocky Mountain Institute, Boulder.

Hausman, Jerry A. 1979. "Individual Discount Rates and the Purchase and Utilization of Energy-Using Durables." *Bell Journal of Economics* 10(1) (Spring): 33–54.

Heberlein, Thomas A. 2012. "Navigating Environmental Attitudes." *Conservation Biology* 26(4): 583–585.

Heberlein, Thomas A. 2012. *Navigating Environmental Attitudes.* Oxford: Oxford University Press.

Heberlein, Thomas A., and J. Stanley Black. 1967. "Attitudinal Specificity and the Prediction of Behavior in a Field Setting." *Journal of Personality and Social Psychology* 33(4): 474–479.

Heberlein, Thomas A., and G. Keith Warriner. 1983. "The Influence of Price and Attitude on Shifting Residential Electricity Consumption from On- to Off-Peak Periods." *Journal of Economic Psychology* 4(1): 107–130.

Hedlin, Simon. 2015. "Is Guilt a Good Motivator for Pro-social Behaviour?" *Angle Journal.* 9 October.

Higgens, Paul A. T. 2005. "Exercise-Based Transportation Reduces Oil Dependence, Carbon Emissions and Obesity." *Environmental Conservation* 32(3): 197–202.

Hines, Jody M., Harold R. Hungerford, and Audrey N. Tomera. 1987. "Analysis and Synthesis of Research on Responsible Environmental Behavior: A Meta-analysis." *Journal of Environmental Education* 18(2): 1–8.

Hoornweg, Daniel, and Perinaz Bhada-Tata. 2015. "What a Waste: A Global Review of Solid Waste Management." Urban Development Series Knowledge Papers No 15. World Bank, March.

Hornik, Jacob, Joseph Cherian, Michelle Madansky, and Chem Narayana. 1995. "Determinants of Recycling Behavior: A Synthesis of Research Results." *Journal of Socio-economics* 24(1): 105–127.

Humes, Edward. 2011. *Force of Nature: The Unlikely Story of Wal-Mart's Green Revolution.* New York: HarperCollins.

Hutton, R. Bruce. 1982. "Advertising and the Department of Energy's Campaign for Energy Conservation." *Journal of Advertising* 11(2): 27–39.

Intergovernmental Panel on Climate Change. 2014. *Climate Change 2014: Mitigation of Climate Change.* Contribution of Working Group III to the Fifth Assessment Report of the Intergovernmental Panel on Climate Change. New York: Cambridge University Press.

Intergovernmental Panel on Climate Change. 2014. "Climate Change 2014: Synthesis Report, Summary for Policy Makers." In *Fifth Assessment Report.* Geneva: IPCC.

Irwin, Julie R., and Jonathan Baron. 2001. "Response Mode Effects and Moral Values." *Organizational Behavior and Human Decision Processes* 84(2): 177–197.

Issenberg, Sasha. 2012. *The Victory Lab: The Secret Science of Winning Campaigns.* New York: Crown Publishers.

Jacobs, Tom. 2011. "Environmental Footprints May Produce Backlash." *Miller-McCune,* May 2.

Jacoby, Jacob. 1984. "Perspectives on Information Overload." *Journal of Consumer Research* 10(4): 432–435.

Jacques, Peter. 2006. "The Rearguard of Modernity: Environmental Skepticism as a Struggle of Citizenship." *Global Environmental Politics* 6(1): 76–101.

Jacques, Peter J., Riley E. Dunlap, and Mark Freeman. 2008. "The Organisation of Denial: Conservative Think Tanks and Environmental Scepticism." *Environmental Politics* 17(3): 349–385.

Jaffe, Adam B., Richard G. Newell, and Robert N. Stavins. 2002. "Environmental Policy and Technological Change." *Environmental and Resource Economics* 22: 41–69.

Jaffe, Adam B., Steven R. Peterson, Paul R. Portney, and Robert N. Stavins. 1995. "Environmental Regulation and the Competitiveness of U.S. Manufacturing: What Does the Evidence Tell Us?" *Journal of Economic Literature* 33(1): 132–163.

Jamieson, Dale. 1996. "Scientific Uncertainty and the Political Process." *Annals of the American Academy of Political and Social Sciences* 545 (May): 35–43.

Jamieson, David W., and Mark P. Zanna. 1989. "Need for Structure in Attitude Formation and Expression." In Anthony R. Pratkanis, Steven J. Breckler, and Anthony G. Greenwald, eds. *Attitude Structure and Function*, 383–406. New York: Psychology Press.

Janis, Irving L., and Leon Mann. 1997. *Decision Making: A Psychological Analysis of Conflict, Choice, and Commitment.* New York: Free Press.

Jevons, William Stanley. 1865. *The Coal Question: An Inquiry Concerning the Progress of the Nation, and the Possible Exhaustion of Our Coal-Mines.* New York: Augustus Kelly.

Ji, Mindy F., and Wendy Wood. 2007. "Purchase and Consumption Habits: Not Necessarily What You Intend." *Journal of Consumer Psychology* 17(4): 261–276.

Jobe, Margaret M. 1999. "The Power of Information: The Example of the US Toxics Release Inventory." *Journal of Government Information* 26(3): 287–295.

Johnson, Eric J., and Daniel G. Goldstein. 2004. "Defaults and Donation Decisions." *Transplantation* 78(12) (December 27): 1713–1716.

Johnson, Eric J., and Daniel G. Goldstein. 2003. "Do Defaults Save Lives?" *Science* 302 (November 21): 1338–1339.

Johnson, Eric J., Steven Bellman, and Gerald L. Lohse. 2003. "Cognitive Lock-In and the Power Law of Practice." *Journal of Marketing* 67: 62–75.

Johnson, Eric J., John Hershey, Jacqueline Meszaros, and Howard Kunreuther. 1993. "Framing, Probability Distortions, and Insurance Decisions." *Journal of Risk and Uncertainty* 7: 35–51.

Johnson, Eric J., John Hershey, Jacqueline Meszaros, and Howard Kunreuther. 1993. *Framing, Probability Distortions, and Insurance Decisions.* Dordrecht: Springer.

Joireman, Jeffrey A., Terell P. Lasane, Jennifer Bennett, Diana Richards, and Salma Solaimani. 2001. "Integrating Social Value Orientation and the Consideration of Future Consequences within the Extended Norm Activation Model of Proenvironmental Behaviour." *British Journal of Social Psychology* 40(1): 133–155.

Joireman, Jeffrey A., Paul A. M. van Lange, and Mark van Vugt. 2004. "Who Cares about the Environmental Impact of Cars? Those with an Eye toward the Future." *Environment and Behavior* 36(2): 187–206.

Jordan, Jennifer, Elizabeth Mullen, and J. Keith Murnighan. 2011. "Striving for the Moral Self: The Effects of Recalling Past Moral Actions on Future Moral Behavior." *Personality and Social Psychology Bulletin* 37(5): 701–713.

Kahan, Dan M., Donald Braman, John Gastil, Paul Slovic, and C. K. Mertz. 2007. "Culture and Identity-Protective Cognition: Explaining the White-Male Effect in Risk Perception." *Journal of Empirical Legal Studies* 4(3): 465–505.

Kahneman, Daniel, Jack L. Knetsch, and Richard H. Thaler. 1990. "Experimental Tests of the Endowment Effect and the Coase Theorem." *Journal of Political Economy* 98(6) (December): 1325–1348.

Kahneman, Daniel, Jack L. Knetsch, and Richard H. Thaler. 1999. "The Endowment Effect, Loss Aversion, and Status Quo Bias." *Journal of Economic Perspectives* 5(1) (Winter): 193–206.

Kahneman, Daniel, and Amos Tversky. 1979. "Prospect Theory: An Analysis of Decision under Risk." *Econometrica: Journal of the Econometric Society* 47: 263–292.

Kaplan, Matt. 2011. "Why Dire Climate Warnings Boost Skepticism." *Nature News*, January 4.

Karkkainen, Bradley C. 2000. "Information as Environmental Regulation: TRI and Performance Benchmarking, Precursor to a New Paradigm." *Georgetown Law Journal* 89: 257–370.

Karmarkar, Uma R., and Bryan Bollinger. 2015. "BYOB: How Bringing Your Own Shopping Bags Leads to Treating Yourself and the Environment." *Journal of Marketing* 79(4): 1–15.

Kates, Robert W. 1962. "Hazard and Choice Perception in Flood Plain Management." Research Paper 78, Department of Geography, University of Chicago.

Kempton, Willett, and Dorothy C. Holland, "Identity and Sustained Environmental Practice." In Susan Clayton and Susan Opotow, eds., *Identity and the Natural Environment: The Psychological Significance of Nature*, 317–341. Cambridge, MA: MIT Press.

Kerr, Norbert L. 1995. "Norms in Social Dilemmas." In David A. Schroeder, ed., *Social Dilemmas: Perspectives on Individuals and Groups* (Westport, CT: Greenwood Publishing Group): 31–48.

Khan, Uzma, and Ravi Dhar. 2006. "Licensing Effect in Consumer Choice." *Journal of Marketing Research* 43(2): 259–266.

Khanna, Madhu, Wilma Rose H. Quimio, and Dora Bojilova. 1998. "Toxics Release Information: A Policy Tool for Environmental Protection." *Journal of Environmental Economics and Management* 36(3): 243–266.

Klandermans, Bert. 1988. "Union Action and the Free-Rider Dilemma." In L. Kriesberg and B. Misztal, eds., *Research in Social Movements, Conflict and Change*, vol. 10, *Social Movements as a Factor of Change in the Contemporary World*, 7–92. Greenwich, CT: JAI Press.

Klöckner, Christian A., Ellen Matthies, and Marcel Hunecke. 2003. "Problems of Operationalizing Habits and Integrating Habits in Normative Decision-Making Models." *Journal of Applied Social Psychology* 33(2): 396–417.

Knetsch, Jack L., and John A. Sinden. 1984. "Willingness to Pay and Compensation Demanded: Experimental Evidence of an Unexpected Disparity in Measures of Value." *Quarterly Journal of Economics* 99(3): 507–521.

Koch, Sigmund. 1956. "Behavior as 'Intrinsically' Regulated: Work Notes towards a Pre-theory of Phenomena Called 'Motivational.'" In *Nebraska Symposium on Motivation*, vol. 4. Lincoln: University of Nebraska Press.

Konar, Shameek, and Mark A. Cohen. 1997. "Information as Regulation: The Effect of Community Right to Know Laws on Toxic Emissions." *Journal of Environmental Economics and Management* 32(1): 109–124.

Kühl, Aline, et al. 2009. "The Role of Saiga Poaching in Rural Communities: Linkages between Attitudes, Socio-economic Circumstances and Behaviour." *Biological Conservation* 142(7): 1442–1449.

Kunda, Ziva. 1990. "The Case for Motivated Reasoning." *Psychological Bulletin* 108(3): 480–498.

Kurkalova, Lyubov, Catherine Kling, and Jinhua Zhao. 2006. "Green Subsidies in Agriculture: Estimating the Adoption Costs of Conservation Tillage from Observed Behavior." *Canadian Journal of Agricultural Economics* 54: 247–267.

Lacasse, Katherine. 2014. "The Importance of Being Green: The Influence of Green Behaviors on Americans' Political Attitudes toward Climate Change." *Environment and Behavior* 47(7): 1–28.

Lacetera, Nicola, and Mario Macias. 2008. "Motivating Altruism: A Field Study." Institute for the Study of Labor Discussion Paper No. 3770. October 28.

Laffont, Jean-Jacques, and Jean Tirole. 1988. "The Dynamics of Incentive Contracts." *Econometrica* 56(5) (September): 1153–1175.

Lawrance, Emily C. 1991. "Poverty and the Rate of Time Preference: Evidence from Panel Data." *Journal of Political Economy* 99(1) (February): 54–77.

Lazarus, Richard Stanley, and Susan Folkman. 1984. *Stress, Appraisal, and Coping.* New York: Springer.

LeBoeuf, Robyn A., Eldar Shafir, and Julia Belyavsky Bayuk. 2010. "The Conflicting Choices of Alternating Selves." *Organizational Behavior and Human Decision Processes* 111(1): 48–61.

Lee, Lichang, Jane Allyn Piliavin, and Vaughn R. A. Call. 1999. "Giving Time, Money, and Blood: Similarities and Differences." *Social Psychology Quarterly* 62(3): 276–290.

Lehman, Darrin R., and Shelley E. Taylor. 1987. "Date with an Earthquake: Coping with a Probable, Unpredictable Disaster." *Personality and Social Psychology Bulletin* 13(4): 546–555.

Leire, Charlotte, and Åke Thidell. 2005. "Product-Related Environmental Information to Guide Consumer Purchases—a Review and Analysis of Research on Perceptions, Understanding and Use among Nordic Consumers." *Journal of Cleaner Production* 13(10): 1061–1070.

Lepper, Mark, David Greene, and Robert Nisbett. 1973. "Undermining Children's Intrinsic Interest with Extrinsic Rewards: A Test of the 'Overjustification' Hypothesis." *Journal of Personality and Social Psychology* 28(1): 129–137.

Lerner, Melvin J. 1980. *The Belief in a Just World: A Fundamental Delusion.* New York: Plenum Press.

Leventhal, Howard. 1970. "Findings and Theory in the Study of Fear Communications." *Advances in Experimental Social Psychology* 5: 119–186.

Leventhal, Howard, Robert Singer, and Susan Jones. 1965. "Effects of Fear and Specificity of Recommendation upon Attitudes and Behavior." *Journal of Personality and Social Psychology* 2(1): 20–29.

Leventhal, Howard, Jean C. Watts, and Francia Pagano. 1967. "Effects of Fear and Instructions on How to Cope with Danger." *Journal of Personality and Social Psychology* 6(3): 313–321.

Levitt, Lynn, and Gloria Leventhal. 1986. "Little Reduction: How Effective Is the New York State Bottle Bill?" *Environment and Behavior* 18: 467–479.

Liberman, Akiva, and Shelly Chaiken. 1992. "Defensive Processing of Personally Relevant Health Messages." *Personality and Social Psychology Bulletin* 18(6): 669–679.

Lichtenstein, Sarah, Paul Slovic, Baruch Fischhoff, Mark Layman, and Barbara Combs. 1978. "Judged Frequency of Lethal Events." *Journal of Experimental Psychology: Human Learning and Memory* 4(6): 551–578.

Lipson, Charles. 1984. "International Cooperation in Economic and Security Affairs." *World Politics* 37: 1–23.

Lizza, Ryan. 2016. "Ted Cruz's Iowa Mailers Are More Fraudulent Than Everyone Thinks." *New Yorker*, January 31.

Locke, Edwin A., Norman Cartledge, and Jeffrey Koeppel. 1968. "Motivational Effects of Knowledge of Results: A Goal-Setting Phenomenon?" *Psychological Bulletin* 70(6): 474–485.

Lovins, Amory B. 2011. "On the Rebound: A Letter in Response to David Owen's Article." *New Yorker*, January 17.

Ludwig, Timothy D., Timothy W. Gray, and Allison Rowell. 1998. "Increasing Recycling in Academic Buildings: A Systematic Replication." *Journal of Applied Behavior Analysis* 31(4) (Winter): 683–686.

Machlup, Fritz. 1946. "Marginal Analysis and Empirical Research." *American Economic Review* 36: 519–554.

Madrian, Brigitte C., and Dennis F. Shea. 2001. "The Power of Suggestion: Inertia in 401(i) Participation and Savings Behavior." *Quarterly Journal of Economics* 116(4) (November): 1149–1187.

Maio, Gregory R., James M. Olson, Mark M. Bernard, and Michelle A. Luke. 2003. "Ideologies, Values, Attitudes, and Behavior." In John Delamater, ed., *Handbook of Social Psychology*, 283–308. New York: Kluwer Academic / Plenum Publishers.

Makhijani, Arjun, and Kevin R. Gurney. 1995. *Mending the Ozone Hole*. Cambridge, MA: MIT Press.

Malone, Thomas W., and Kevin Crowston. 1994. "The Interdisciplinary Study of Coordination." *ACM Computing Surveys (CSUR)* 26(1): 87–119.

Management Information Services. 2011. "60 Years of Energy Incentives: Analysis of Federal Expenditures for Energy Development." Paper prepared for the Nuclear Energy Institute in Washington, DC, October.

Maniates, Michael F. 2001. "Individualization: Plant a Tree, Buy a Bike, Save the World?" *Global Environmental Politics* 1(3) (August): 31–52.

Mannetti, Lucia, Antonio Pierro, and Stefano Livi. 2004. "Recycling: Planned and Self-Expressive Behaviour." *Journal of Environmental Psychology* 24(2): 227–236.

Marwell, Gerald, and Ruth E. Ames. 1979. "Experiments on the Provision of Public Goods I: Resources, Interests, Group Size, and the Free-Rider Problem." *American Journal of Sociology* 84(6) (May): 1335–1360.

Marwell, Gerald, and Ruth E. Ames. 1981. "Economists Free Ride, Does Anyone Else? Experiments on the Provision of Public Goods, IV." *Journal of Public Economics* 15(3) (June): 295–310.

Marwell, Gerald, and Pamela Oliver. 1933. *The Critical Mass in Collective Action: A Micro-Social Theory.* Cambridge: Cambridge University Press.

Mas, Alexandre. 2014. "Does Transparency Lead to Pay Compression?" National Bureau of Economic Research Paper No. w20558. Available online at https://www.princeton. edu/~amas/papers/transparency.pdf.

Mathur, Anil, George P. Moschis, and Euehun Lee. 2008. "A Longitudinal Study of the Effects of Life Status Changes on Changes in Consumer Preferences." *Journal of the Academy of Marketing Science* 36(2): 234–246.

Mazar, Nina, and Chen-Bo Zhong. 2010. "Do Green Products Make Us Better People?" *Psychological Science* 21(4): 494–498.

McCalley, L. T., and Cees J. H. Midden. 2002. "Energy Conservation through Product-Integrated Feedback: The Roles of Goal-Setting and Social Orientation." *Journal of Economic Psychology* 23(5): 589–603.

McCarthy, Tom. 2015. "Florida Banned State Workers from Using 'Climate Change'— Report." *The Guardian*, March 8.

McCright, Aaron M., and Riley E. Dunlap. 2011. "Cool Dudes: The Denial of Climate Change among Conservative White Males in the United States." *Global Environmental Change* 21(4): 1163–1172.

McCright, Aaron M., and Riley E. Dunlap. 2011. "The Politicization of Climate Change and Polarization in the American Public's Views of Global Warming, 2001–2010." *Sociological Quarterly* 52(2): 155–194.

McDonnell, Tim. 2015. "Another State Agency Just Banned the Words 'Climate Change.'" *Mother Jones*, April 8.

McGonigal, Kelly. 2012. *The Willpower Instinct.* New York: Avery.

McKenzie, Craig R. M., Michael J. Liersch, and Stacey R. Finkelstein. 2006. "Recommendations Implicit in Policy Defaults." *Psychological Science* 17: 414–420.

McKenzie-Mohr, Doug. 2000. "Promoting Sustainable Behavior: An Introduction to Community-Based Social Marketing." *Journal of Social Issues* 56(3): 543–554.

McKenzie-Mohr, Doug. 2011. *Fostering Sustainable Behavior: An Introduction to Community-Based Social Marketing.* Gabriola Island, BC: New Society Publishers.

McKibben, Bill. 2012. "Global Warming's Terrifying New Math." *Rolling Stone*, July 19.

Mellström, Carl, and Magnus Johannesson. 2008. "Crowding Out in Blood Donation: Was Titmuss Right?" *Journal of the European Economic Association* 6(4) (June): 845–863.

Merritt, Anna C., Daniel A. Effron, and Benoît Monin. 2012. "Moral Self-Licensing: When Being Good Frees Us to Be Bad." *Social and Personality Psychology Compass* 4(5): 344–357.

Michele, Reilly. 2010. "Eat Lower—and Better—on the Food Chain." *AgMag* blog, October 25.

Miller, Claire Cain. 2016. "What We Can Do to Close the Pay Gap." *New York Times* (Business), January 17, 6.

Minson, Julia A., and Benoît Monin. 2012. "Do-Gooder Derogation: Disparaging Morally Motivated Minorities to Defuse Anticipated Reproach." *Social Psychological and Personality Science* 3(2): 200–207.

Mittal, Banwari. 1988. "Achieving Higher Seat Belt Usage: The Role of Habit in Bridging the Attitude-Behavior Gap." *Journal of Applied Social Psychology* 18(12): 993–1016.

Monin, Benoît, and Dale T. Miller. 2001. "Moral Credentials and the Expression of Prejudice." *Journal of Personality and Social Psychology* 81(1): 33–43.

Morris, Julian. 1997. *Green Goods? Consumers, Product Labels and the Environment.* London: IEA Environment Unit.

Moser, Susanne C., and Lisa Dilling. 2004. "Making Climate Hot." *Environment: Science and Policy for Sustainable Development* 46(10): 32–46.

MSNBC News Services. 2005. "Is Wal-mart Going Green?" NBCNews.com, October 25.

Murtagh, Niamh, Birgitta Gatersleben, and David Uzzell. 2012. "Self-Identity Threat and Resistance to Change: Evidence from Regular Travel Behaviour." *Journal of Environmental Psychology* 32(4): 318–326.

Naderi, Iman, and David Strutton. 2013. "I Support Sustainability but Only When Doing So Reflects Fabulously on Me: Can Green Narcissists Be Cultivated?" *Journal of Macromarketing* 35(1): 1–14.

Naderi, Iman, and David Strutton. 2014. "Can Normal Narcissism Be Managed to Promote Green Product Purchases? Investigating a Counterintuitive Proposition." *Journal of Applied Social Psychology* 44(5): 375–391.

Nelder, Chris. 2011. "Reframing the Transportation Debate." *SmartPlanet*, October 19.

Nelson, Richard R., and Sidney G. Winter. 1982. *An Evolutionary Theory of Economic Change.* Cambridge, MA: Belknap Press of Harvard University Press.

Newcomb, Theodore Mead, Kathryn E. Koenig, Richard Flacks, and Donald P. Warwick. 1967. *Persistence and Change: Bennington College and Its Students after 25 Years.* New York: Wiley.

Nolan, Jessica M., P. Wesley Schultz, Robert B. Cialdini, Noah J. Goldstein, and Vladas Griskevicius. 2008. "Normative Social Influence Is Underdetected." *Personality and Social Psychology Bulletin* 34(7): 913–923.

Norman, Paul. 2011. "The Theory of Planned Behavior and Binge Drinking among Undergraduate Students: Assessing the Impact of Habit Strength." *Addictive Behaviors* 36: 502–507.

Nyborg, Karine, and Mari Rege. 2003. "On Social Norms: The Evolution of Considerate Smoking Behavior." *Journal of Economic Behavior and Organization* 52(3): 323–340.

Nyhan, Brendan, and Jason Reifler. 2010. "When Corrections Fail: The Persistence of Political Misperceptions." *Political Behavior* 32(2): 303–330.

Nyhan, Brendan, Jason Reifler, Sean Richey, and Gary L. Freed. 2014. "Effective Messages in Vaccine Promotion: A Randomized Trial." *Pediatrics* 133(4) (March 3), peds. 2013-2365.

Nyhan, Brendan, Jason Reifler, and Peter A. Ubel. 2013. "The Hazards of Correcting Myths about Health Care Reform." *Medical Care* 51(2): 127–132.

Oliver, Pamela. 1980. "Rewards and Punishments as Selective Incentives for Collective Action: Theoretical Investigations." *American Journal of Sociology* 85(6) (May): 1356–1375.

Oliver, Pamela. 1984. "'If You Don't Do It, Nobody Else Will': Active and Token Contributors to Local Collective Action." *American Sociological Review* 49(5) (October): 601–610.

Olson, Mancur. 1971. *The Logic of Collective Action*. Cambridge, MA: Harvard University Press.

O'Neill, Saffron, and Sophie Nicholson-Cole. 2009. "Fear Won't Do It: Promoting Positive Engagement with Climate Change through Visual and Iconic Representations." *Science Communication* 30(3): 355–379.

Oreskes, Naomi, and Erik M. Conway. 2010. *Merchants of Doubt: How a Handful of Scientists Obscured the Truth on Issues from Tobacco Smoke to Global Warming*. New York: Bloomsbury Publishing.

Organization for Economic Cooperation and Development. 1997. "Eco-Labeling: Actual Effects of Selected Programme." OECD/GD(97)/105, Paris.

Oskamp, Stuart, et al. 1991. "Factors Influencing Household Recycling Behavior." *Environment and Behavior* 23(4): 494–519.

Ostria, Marcelo. 2013. "How U.S. Agricultural Subsidies Harm the Environment, Taxpayers, and the Poor." Issue Briefs—Energy and Natural Resources No. 126, National Center for Policy Analysis, August 7.

Ostrom, Elinor. 1990. *Governing the Commons: The Evolution of Institutions for Collective Action*. Cambridge: Cambridge University Press.

Ostrom, Elinor. 2000. "Collective Action and the Evolution of Social Norms." *Journal of Economic Perspectives* 14(3) (Summer): 137–158.

Ouellette, Judith A., and Wendy Wood. 1998. "Habit and Intention in Everyday Life: The Multiple Processes by Which Past Behavior Predicts Future Behavior." *Psychological Bulletin* 124(1): 54–74.

Outen, Ronald B. 1999. "Designing Information Rules to Encourage Better Environmental Performance." Paper presented at the conference "Environmental Policies in the New Millennium: Incentive-Based Approaches."

Owen, David. 2010. "The Efficiency Dilemma." *New Yorker*, December, 78–85.

Oye, Kenneth A., and James H. Maxwell. 1995. "Self-Interest and Environmental Management." In Robert O. Keohane and Elinor Ostrom, eds., *Local Commons and Global Interdependence*, 191–221. London: Sage Publications.

Page, Benjamin I., Robert Y. Shapiro, and Glenn R. Dempsey. 1987. "What Moves Public Opinion?" *American Political Science Review* 81(1): 23–43.

Pardini, Anton U., and Richard D. Katzev. 1983. "The Effect of Strength of Commitment on Newspaper Recycling." *Journal of Environmental Systems* 13(3): 245–254.

Park, C. Whan, Sung Youl Jun, and Deborah J. MacInnis. 2000. "Choosing What I Want versus Rejecting What I Do Not Want: An Application of Decision Framing to Product Option Choice Decisions." *Journal of Marketing Research* 37(2): 187–202.

Pichert, Daniel, and Konstantinos V. Katsikopoulos. 2008. "Green Defaults: Information Presentation and Pro-environmental Behaviour." *Journal of Environmental Psychology* 28: 63–73.

Pieters, Jan H. M. 1999. "Subsidies and the Environment: What Subsidies and Tax Incentives Affect Production Decisions to the Detriment of the Environment." In Kai Schlegelmilch, ed., *Green Budget Reform in Europe* 259–265. Berlin: Springer.

Pink, Daniel H. 2009. *Drive: The Surprising Truth about What Motivates Us.* New York: Riverhead Books.

Polanyi, Michael. 1967. *The Tacit Dimension.* Garden City, NY: Anchor Books.

Pollan, Michael. 2009. *Food Rules: An Eater's Manual.* New York: Penguin Group.

Pooley, Julie Ann, and Moira O'Connor. 2000. "Environmental Education and Attitudes: Emotions and Beliefs Are What Is Needed." *Environment and Behavior* 32(5): 711–723.

Porter, Michael E. "America's Green Strategy." *Scientific American* 264(4) (April 1991): 168.

Porter, Michael E., and Claas van der Linde. 1995. "Green and Competitive: Ending the Stalemate." *Harvard Business Review* Reprint No. 95507.

Porter, Michael E., and Claas van der Linde. 1995. "Toward a New Conception of the Environment-Competitiveness Relationship." *Journal of Economic Perspectives* 9(4): 97–118.

Posner, Richard A. "The Problematics of Moral and Legal Theory." *Harvard Law Review* (1998): 1637–1717.

Rabalais, Nancy N., R. Eugene Turner, and William J. Wiseman Jr. 2002. "Gulf of Mexico Hypoxia, a.k.a. 'The Dead Zone.'" *Annual Review of Ecology and Systematics* 33: 235–263.

Rauscher, Michael. 2003. "Tall Smokestacks and Transfrontier Pollution: A Tale for Orestia and Trebeisia." In Rüdiger Pethig and Michael Rauscher, *Challenges to the World Economy*, 356–366. Berlin: Springer.

Reed, Americus. 2004. "Activating the Self-Importance of Consumer Selves: Exploring Identity Salience Effects on Judgments." *Journal of Consumer Research* 31(2): 286–95.

Reed, Americus, Mark R. Forehand, Stefano Puntoni, and Luk Warlop. 2012. "Identity-Based Consumer Behavior." *International Journal of Research in Marketing*, 29(4): 310–21.

Reid, Dennis H., Paul D. Luyben, Robert J. Rawers, and Jon S. Bailey. 1976. "Newspaper Recycling Behavior: The Effects of Prompting and Proximity of Containers." *Environment and Behavior* 8(3): 471–482.

Reimer, Torsten, Anne-Louise Bornstein, and Klaus Opwis. 2012. "Positive and Negative Transfer Effects in Groups." In Tilmann Betsch and Susanne Haberstroh, eds., *The Routines of Decision Making*, 175–192. New York: Psychology Press.

Reiter, Douglas K., Mark W. Brunson, and Robert H. Schmidt. 1999. "Public Attitudes toward Wildlife Damage Management and Policy." *Wildlife Society Bulletin* 27(3): 746–758.

Reno, Raymond R., Robert B. Cialdini, and Carl A. Kallgren. 1993. "The Transsituational Influence of Social Norms." *Journal of Personality and Social Psychology* 64(1): 104–112.

Reschovsky, James D., and Sarah E. Stone. 1994. "Market Incentives to Encourage Household Waste Recycling: Paying for What You Throw Away." *Journal of Policy Analysis and Management* 13(1) (Winter): 120–139.

Resource Conservation Alliance and Government Purchasing Project. "Focus on Government Purchasing." Using Less Wood: Quick Facts Series.

Rippetoe, Patricia A., and Ronald W. Rogers. 1987. "Effects of Components of Protection-Motivation Theory on Adaptive and Maladaptive Coping with a Health Threat." *Journal of Personality and Social Psychology* 52(3): 596–604.

Rockstrom, Johan, and Mattias Klum, 2015. *Big World, Small Planet: Abundance within Planetary Boundaries*. New Haven: Yale University Press.

Rogers, Ronald W., and C. Ronald Mewborn. 1976. "Fear Appeals and Attitude Change: Effects of a Threat's Noxiousness, Probability of Occurrence, and the Efficacy of Coping Responses." *Journal of Personality and Social Psychology* 34(1): 54–61.

Rohan, Meg J. 2000. "A Rose by Any Name? The Values Construct." *Personality and Social Psychology Review* 4(3): 255–277.

Rosenfeld, Jake, and Patrick Denice. 2015. "The Power of Transparency: Evidence from a British Workplace Survey." *American Sociological Review* 80(5): 1045–1068.

Ross, Michael, Cathy McFarland, Michael Conway, and Mark P. Zanna. 1983. "Reciprocal Relation between Attitudes and Behavior Recall: Committing People to Newly Formed Attitudes." *Journal of Personality and Social Psychology* 45(2): 257–267.

Ruiter, Robert A. C., Charles Abraham, and Gerjo Kok. 2001. "Scary Warnings and Rational Precautions: A Review of the Psychology of Fear Appeals." *Psychology and Health* 16(6): 613–630.

Sachdeva, Sonya, Rumen Iliev, and Douglas L. Medin. 2009. "Sinning Saints and Saintly Sinners: The Paradox of Moral Self-Regulation." *Psychological Science* 20(4): 523–528.

Sagoff, Mark. 1992. "At the Shrine of Our Lady of Fatima, or Why Political Questions Are Not All Economic." In W. Michael Hoffman and Jennifer Mills Moore, eds., *Business Ethics: Readings and Cases in Corporate Morality*, 2nd ed., 494–503. New York: McGraw-Hill.

Samuelson, Robert. 2013. "Why (Sigh!) Farm Subsidies Survive." *Real Clear Politics*, June 13.

Samuelson, William, and Richard Zeckhauser. 1988. "Status Quo Bias in Decision Making." *Journal of Risk and Uncertainty* 1: 7–59.

Salancik, Gerald R., and Mary Conway. 1975. "Attitude Inferences from Salient and Relevant Cognitive Content about Behavior." *Journal of Personality and Social Psychology* 32(5): 829–840.

Sandel, Michael J. 1997. "It's Immoral to Buy the Right to Pollute." *New York Times*, December 15, A29.

Sarokin, David, and Warren Muir. 1985. "Too Little Toxic Waste Data." *New York Times*, October 7, A31.

Schultz, P. Wesley. 2002. "Knowledge, Information, and Household Recycling: Examining the Knowledge-Deficit Model of Behavior Change." In Thomas Dietz and Paul C. Stern, eds., *New Tools for Environmental Protection: Education, Information, and Voluntary Measures*, 67–82. Washington, DC: National Academy Press.

Schultz, P. Wesley, Valdiney V. Gouveia, Linda D. Cameron, Geetika Tankha, Peter Schmuck, and Marek Franěk. 2005. "Values and Their Relationship to Environmental Concern and Conservation Behavior." *Journal of Cross-Cultural Psychology* 36(4): 457–475.

Schultz, P. Wesley, Jessica M. Nolan, Robert B. Cialdini, Noah J. Goldstein, and Vladas Griskevicius. 2007. "The Constructive, Destructive, and Reconstructive Power of Social Norms." *Psychological Science* 18(5): 429–434.

Schultz, P. Wesley, and Lynnette C. Zelezny. 1998. "Values and Proenvironmental Behavior: A Five-Country Survey." *Journal of Cross-Cultural Psychology* 29(4): 540–558.

Sellen, Abigail J., and Richard H. R. Harper. 2002. *The Myth of the Paperless Office.* Cambridge, MA: MIT Press.

Shavelson, Richard J., and Roger Bolus. 1982. "Self-Concept: The Interplay of Theory and Methods." *Journal of Educational Psychology* 74(1): 3–17.

Sheeran, Paschal. 2002. "Intention—Behavior Relations: A Conceptual and Empirical Review." *European Review of Social Psychology* 12(1): 1–36.

Sher, Shlomi, and Craig R. M. McKenzie. 2006. "Information Leakage from Logically Equivalent Frames." *Cognition* 101(3): 467–494.

Simmons, Deborah, and Ron Widmar. 1990. "Motivations and Barriers to Recycling: Toward a Strategy for Public Education." *Journal of Environmental Education* 22(1): 13–18.

Simon, Herbert A. 1959. "Theories of Decision-Making in Economics and Behavioral Science." *American Economic Review* 49(3): 253–283.

Simon, Herbert A. 1997. *Models of Bounded Rationality: Empirically Grounded Economic Reason.* Vol. 3. Cambridge, MA: MIT Press.

Slovic, Paul, Baruch Fischhoff, and Sarah Lichtenstein. 1978. "Accident Probabilities and Seat Belt Usage: A Psychological Perspective." *Accident Analysis and Prevention* 10: 281–285.

Slovic, Paul, Baruch Fischhoff, and Sarah Lichtenstein. 1979. "Rating the Risks." *Environment* 21(3): 14–39.

Slovic, Paul, Baruch Fischhoff, and Sarah Lichtenstein. 1985. "Characterizing Perceived Risk." In Robert W. Kates, Christoph Hohenemser, and Jeanne X. Kasperson, eds. *Perilous Progress: Managing the Hazards of Technology*, 91–125. Boulder: Westview Press.

Slovic, Paul, Baruch Fischhoff, Sarah Lichtenstein, Bernard Corrigan, and Barbara Combs. 1977. "Preference for Insuring against Probable Small Losses: Insurance Implications." *Journal of Risk and Insurance* 44(2): 237–258.

Small, Kenneth A., and Kurt van Dender. 2007. "If Cars Were More Efficient, Would We Use Less Fuel?" *Access* 31 (Fall): 8–13.

Smil, Vaclav. 2002. "Worldwide Transformation of Diets, Burdens of Meat Production and Opportunities for Novel Food Proteins." *Enzyme and Microbial Technology* 30: 305–311.

Smil, Vaclav. 2003. *Energy at the Crossroads: Global Perspectives and Uncertainties.* Cambridge, MA: MIT Press.

Smith, Zachary A. 1995. *The Environmental Policy Paradox.* 2nd ed. Englewood Cliffs, NJ: Prentice Hall.

Sorrell, Steve. 2009. "Jevons' Paradox Revisited: The Evidence for Backfire from Improved Energy Efficiency." *Energy Policy* 37: 1456–1469.

Sparks, Paul, and Richard Shepherd. 1992. "Self-Identity and the Theory of Planned Behavior: Assessing the Role of Identification with 'Green Consumerism.'" *Social Psychology Quarterly* 55(4): 388–399.

Spector, Dina. 2012. "18 Facts about Walmart That Will Blow Your Mind." *Business Insider*, November 15.

Steel, Brent S. 1996. "Thinking Globally and Acting Locally? Environmental Attitudes, Behavior and Activism." *Journal of Environmental Management* 47(1): 27–36.

Steele, Jennifer R., and Nalini Ambady. 2006. "'Math is Hard!': The Effect of Gender Priming on Women's Attitudes." *Journal of Experimental Social Psychology* 42(4): 428–436.

Steinberg, Paul F. 2015. *Who Rules the Earth? How Social Rules Shape Our Planet and Our Lives.* Oxford: Oxford University Press.

Sterman, John D. 1989. "Modeling Managerial Behavior: Misperceptions of Feedback in a Dynamic Decision Making Experiment." *Management Science* 35(3): 321–339.

Sterman, John D. 2000. *Business Dynamics: Systems Thinking and Modeling for a Complex World.* Boston: Irwin/McGraw-Hill.

Stern, Paul C. 1986. "What Economics Doesn't Say about Energy Use." *Journal of Policy Analysis and Management* 5(2) (Winter): 200–227.

Stern, Paul C. 1999. "Information, Incentives, and Proenvironmental Consumer Behavior." *Journal of Consumer Policy* 22: 461–478.

Stern, Paul C. 2000. "Toward a Coherent Theory of Environmentally Significant Behavior." *Journal of Social Issues* 56(3): 407–424.

Stern, Paul C. 2002. "Changing Behavior in Households and Communities: What Have We Learned?" In Thomas Dietz and Paul C. Stern, eds., *New Tools for Environmental Protection: Education, Information, and Voluntary Measures*, 201–211. Washington, DC: National Academy Press.

Stern, Paul C., Thomas Dietz, Troy D. Abel, Gregory A. Guagnano, and Linda Kalof. 1999. "A Value-Belief-Norm Theory of Support for Social Movements: The Case of Environmentalism." *Human Ecology Review* 6(2): 81–97.

Stern, Paul C., Linda Kalof, Thomas Dietz, and Gregory A. Guagnano. 1995. "Values, Beliefs, and Proenvironmental Action: Attitude Formation toward Emergent Attitude Objects." *Journal of Applied Social Psychology* 25(18): 1611–1636.

Stets, Jan E., and Chris F. Biga. 2003. "Bringing Identity Theory into Environmental Sociology." *Sociological Theory* 21(4) (November 12): 398–423.

Stillwell, Victoria. "The Value of Redirection." *Positively: The Future of Dog Training.* https://positively.com/victorias-blog/the-value-of-redirection/.

Stradling, Stephen. 2002. "Persuading People out of Their Cars." Inaugural Lecture, Napier University, March 27.

Sutter, Matthia, Stefan Haigner, and Martin Kocher. 2008. "Choosing the Carrot or the Stick: Endogenous Institutional Choice in Social Dilemma Situations." Working Papers in Economics and Statistics No. 2008-07, University of Innsbruck.

Suvorov, Anton. 2003. "Addiction to Rewards." Toulouse School of Economics, November. Available online at http://www.nes.ru/public-presentations/suvorov_js-08-12-03.pdf.

Swim, Janet, et al. 2009. *Psychology and Global Climate Change: Addressing a Multi-faceted Phenomenon and Set of Challenges.* A Report by the American Psychological Association's Task Force on the Interface between Psychology and Global Climate Change. Washington, DC: American Psychological Association.

Taber, Charles S., and Milton Lodge. 2006. "Motivated Skepticism in the Evaluation of Political Beliefs." *American Journal of Political Science* 50(3): 755–769.

Tanner, Carmen, and Sybille Wölfing Kast. 2003. "Promoting Sustainable Consumption: Determinants of Green Purchases by Swiss Consumers." *Psychology and Marketing* 20(10): 883–902.

Tetlock, Philip E., Orie V. Kristel, S. Beth Elson, Melanie C. Green, and Jennifer S. Lerner. 2000. "The Psychology of the Unthinkable: Taboo Trade-offs, Forbidden Base Rates, and Heretical Counterfactuals." *Journal of Personality and Social Psychology* 78(5): 853–870.

Thaler, Richard H. 1980. "Toward a Positive Theory of Consumer Choice." *Journal of Economic Behavior and Organization* 1(1): 39–60.

Thaler, Richard H., and Cass R. Sunstein. 2003. "Libertarian Paternalism." *American Economic Review* 93(2): 175–179.

Thøgersen, John. 2002. "Promoting 'Green' Consumer Behavior with Eco-Labels." In Thomas Dietz and Paul C. Stern, eds., *New Tools for Environmental Protection: Education, Information, and Voluntary Measures*, 83–104. Washington, DC: National Academy Press.

Thøgersen, John, and Folke Ölander. 2006. "To What Degree Are Environmentally Beneficial Choices Reflective of a General Conservation Stance?" *Environment and Behavior* 38(4): 550–569.

Thoits, Peggy A., and Lauren K. Virshup. 1997. "Me's and We's: Forms and Functions of Social Identities." In Richard D. Ashmore and Lee Jussim, eds., *Self and Identity: Fundamental Issues*, 106–136. Oxford: Oxford University Press.

Thompson, Joseph W., Shirley Tyson, Paula Card-Higginson, Richard F. Jacobs, J. Gary Wheeler, Pippa Simpson, James E. Bost, Kevin W. Ryan, and Daniel A. Salmon. 2007. "Impact of Addition of Philosophical Exemptions on Childhood Immunization Rates." *American Journal of Preventive Medicine* 32(3): 194–201.

Tierney, John. 2000. "A Tale of Two Fisheries." *New York Times Magazine*, August 27.

Tierney, John. 2008. "How Virtuous Is Ed Begley Jr.?" *TierneyLab* blog, *The New York Times* 25 February.

Tietenberg, Tom. 2000. *Environmental and Natural Resource Economics*. 5th ed. Boston: Addison-Wesley.

Titmuss, Richard M. 1970. *The Gift Relationship: From Human Blood to Social Policy*. London: Allen and Unwin.

Tittle, Charles R., and Richard J. Hill. 1967. "Attitude Measurement and Prediction of Behavior: An Evaluation of Conditions and Measurement Techniques." *Sociometry* 30(2) (June): 199–213.

Tversky, Amos, and Daniel Kahneman. 1973. "Availability: A Heuristic for Judging Frequency and Probability." *Cognitive Psychology* 5(2): 207–232.

Tversky, Amos, and Daniel Kahneman. 1974. "Judgment under Uncertainty: Heuristics and Biases." *Science* 185(4157): 1124–1131.

Uhlaner, Carole Jean. 1989. "'Relational Goods' and Participation: Incorporating Sociability into a Theory of Rational Action." *Public Choice* 62(3): 253–285.

Ulrich, Karl T. 2006. "The Environmental Paradox of Bicycling." Working Paper, Department of Operations and Information Management, Wharton School, July.

UPS. 2013. "Big Data = Wins for the Environment." UPS website.

US General Accounting Office. 1991. "Toxic Chemicals: EPA's Toxics Release Inventory Is Useful but Can Be Improved." GAO/RCED-91-121, Washington, DC.

van der Werff, Ellen, Linda Steg, and Kees Keizer. 2013. "It Is a Moral Issue: The Relationship between Environmental Self-Identity, Obligation-Based Intrinsic

Motivation and Pro-environmental Behaviour." *Global Environmental Change* 23(5): 1258–1265.

van der Werff, Ellen, Linda Steg, and Kees Keizer. 2013. "The Value of Environmental Self-Identity: The Relationship between Biospheric Values, Environmental Self-Identity and Environmental Preferences, Intentions and Behaviour." *Journal of Environmental Psychology* 34: 55–63.

van Raaij, W. Fred, and Theo M. M. Verhallen. 1983. "Patterns of Residential Energy Behavior." *Journal of Economic Psychology* 4(1): 85–106.

Vasi, I. B., and M. Macy. 2003. "The Mobilizer's Dilemma: Crisis, Empowerment and Collective Action." *Social Forces* 81(3): 979–998.

Vaughn, Kelly. 2012. "Jevons Paradox: The Debate That Just Won't Die." *RMI Outlet*, Rocky Mountain Institute, March 20.

Verplanken, Bas, and Henk Aarts. 1999. "Habit, Attitude, and Planned Behaviour: Is Habit an Empty Construct or an Interesting Case of Goal-Directed Automaticity?" *European Review of Social Psychology* 10(1): 101–134.

Verplanken, Bas, Henk Aarts, and Ad van Knippenberg. 1997. "Habit, Information Acquisition, and the Process of Making Travel Mode Choices." *European Journal of Social Psychology* 27(5): 539–560.

Verplanken, Bas, Henk Aarts, Ad Knippenberg, and Carina Knippenberg. 1994. "Attitude versus General Habit: Antecedents of Travel Mode Choice." *Journal of Applied Social Psychology* 24(4): 285–300.

Verplanken Bas, and Rob W. Holland. 2002. "Motivated Decision Making: Effects of Activation and Self-Centrality of Values on Choices and Behavior." *Journal of Personality and Social Psychology* 82(3): 434–447.

Verplanken, Bas, Ian Walker, Adrian Davis, and Michaela Jurasek. 2008. "Context Change and Travel Mode Choice: Combining the Habit Discontinuity and Self-Activation Hypotheses." *Journal of Environmental Psychology* 28(2): 121–127.

Verplanken, Bas, and Wendy Wood. 2006. "Interventions to Break and Create Consumer Habits." *Journal of Public Policy and Marketing* 25(1): 90–103.

Vorkinn, Marit, and Hanne Riese. 2001. "Environmental Concern in a Local Context: The Significance of Place Attachment." *Environment and Behavior* 33(2): 249–263.

Wade-Benzoni, Kimberly A., Min Li, Leigh L. Thompson, and Max H. Bazerman. 2007. "The Malleability of Environmentalism." *Analyses of Social Issues and Public Policy* 7(1): 163–189.

Wagner, Marcus. 2003. *The Porter Hypothesis Revisited: A Literature Review of Theoretical Models and Empirical Tests.* Leuneburg: Center for Sustainability Management.

Wallace, Harry M., and Roy F. Baumeister. 2002. "The Performance of Narcissists Rises and Falls with Perceived Opportunity for Glory." *Journal of Personality and Social Psychology* 82(5): 819–834.

Walmart. "Environmental Sustainability—Truck Fleet." Walmart website.

Weinstein, Neil D. 1984. "Why It Won't Happen to Me: Perceptions of Risk Factors and Susceptibility." *Health Psychology* 3(5): 431–457.

Whitmarsh, Lorraine, and Saffron O'Neill. 2010. "Green Identity, Green Living? The Role of Pro-environmental Self-Identity in Determining Consistency across Diverse Pro-environmental Behaviours." *Journal of Environmental Psychology* 30(3): 305–314.

Wicker, Allan W. 1969. "Attitudes versus Actions: The Relationship of Verbal and Overt Behavioral Responses to Attitude Objects." *Journal of Social Issues* 25(4): 41–78.

Wilhite, Harold, and Rich Ling. 1995. "Measured Energy Savings from a More Informative Energy Bill." *Energy and Buildings* 22(2): 145–155.

Wilson, Timothy D., Christopher E. Houston, Kathryn M. Etling, and Nancy Brekke. 1996. "A New Look at Anchoring Effects: Basic Anchoring and Its Antecedents." *Journal of Experimental Psychology: General* 125(4): 387–402.

Witte, Kim. 1992. "Putting the Fear Back into Fear Appeals: The Extended Parallel Process Model." *Communications Monographs* 59(4): 329–349.

Witte, Kim, and Mike Allen. 2000. "A Meta-analysis of Fear Appeals: Implications for Effective Public Health Campaigns." *Health Education and Behavior* 27(5): 591–615.

Wittenbraker, John, Brenda Lynn Gibbs, and Lynn R. Kahle. 1983. "Seat Belt Attitudes, Habits, and Behaviors: An Adaptive Amendment to the Fishbein Model." *Journal of Applied Social Psychology* 13(5): 406–421.

Wood, Wendy, Jeffrey M. Quinn, and Deborah A. Kashy. 2002. "Habits in Everyday Life: Thought, Emotion, and Action." *Journal of Personality and Social Psychology* 83(6): 1281–1297.

Wood, Wendy, Leona Tam, and Melissa Guerrero Witt. 2005. "Changing Circumstances, Disrupting Habits." *Journal of Personality and Social Psychology* 88(6): 918–933.

World Bank. 1999. *Curbing the Epidemic: Governments and the Economics of Tobacco Control.* Washington DC: World Bank.

Wu, Xiaoping, Shuai Deng, Xiaohong Du, and Jing Ma. 2014. "Green-Wave Traffic Theory Optimization and Analysis." *World Journal of Engineering and Technology* 2(3): 14–19.

Yin, Henry H., and Barbara J. Knowlton. 2006. "The Role of the Basal Ganglia in Habit Formation." *Nature Reviews Neuroscience* 7(6): 464–476.

York, Richard. 2006. "Ecological Paradoxes: William Stanley Jevons and the Paperless Office." *Human Ecology Review* 13(2): 143–147.

Zaccaro, Stephen J., Virginia Blair, Christopher Peterson, and Michelle Zazanis. 1995. "Collective Efficacy." In J. E. Maddux, ed., *Self-Efficacy, Adaptation, and Adjustment*, 305–328. New York: Plenum Press.

Zajonc, Robert Boleslaw. 1965. "Social Facilitation." *Science* 149(3681): 269–274.

Zanna, Mark P., and John K. Rempel. 1988. "Attitudes: A New Look at an Old Concept." In Daniel Bar-Tal and Arie W. Kruglanski, eds., *The Social Psychology of Knowledge*, 315–334. New York: Cambridge University Press.

Printed in the USA/Agawam, MA
February 6, 2019

696924.060